BATTLES

OF THE

CIVIL WAR

1861 ~ 1865

BATTLES
OF THE
CIVIL WAR
1861 ~ 1865

FROM FORT SUMTER TO PETERSBURG

KEVIN J. DOUGHERTY   MARTIN J. DOUGHERTY   PARKER HILLS   CHRIS McNAB   MICHAEL F. PAVKOVIC

METRO BOOKS
New York

METRO BOOKS
New York

An Imprint of Sterling Publishing Co., Inc.
1166 Avenue of the Americas
New York, NY 10036

ISBN 978-1-4351-3272-6

For information about custom editions, special sales, and premium and corporate purchases, please contact Sterling Special Sales at 800-805-5489 or specialsales@sterlingpublishing.com.

Manufactured in China

6 8 10 9 7 5

www.sterlingpublishing.com

Project Editor: Michael Spilling
Picture Research: Terry Forshaw
Design: Jerry Williams
Illustrations: Julian Baker

PICTURE CREDITS

All maps produced by JB Illustrations © Amber Books
Unless credited below all illustrations are © Amber Books

Amber Books: 18, 20, 24(b), 25, 28, 38, 40, 47, 57(t), 62(t), 69, 76, 89, 95(b),
   100(t), 101, 105, 112, 121, 179(b), 206(b)
Art-Tech/John Batchelor: 26(b), 30, 73(t), 90(t), 128(t), 186(t), 191, 192(t)
Art-Tech/De Agostini: 199(t)
Art-Tech/MARS: 63, 114, 118, 138, 149, 161, 171
Cody Images: 48, 62(b), 70, 77, 82, 124, 141, 154, 187, 188, 190
Corbis: 20/21, 92, 128(b), 130, 196/197
Defence Visual Information Center: 9, 11, 43, 60, 66, 86, 91, 122, 139(b),
   157, 163(b), 216(t), 217

Mary Evans Picture Library: 26(t), 125
Getty Images: 52, 78/79
Library of Congress: 6, 10, 14, 15, 17, 24(t), 27, 34, 36, 37, 46(b),
   49, 50, 53(t),
   56, 57(b), 67(t), 72, 73(b), 80, 83, 87, 90(b), 94, 95(t), 100(b),
   102, 104, 108(b),
   109, 110, 111, 115, 120, 129, 131, 132, 139(t), 140, 142, 144,
   145, 148(b), 150,
   152, 155, 163(t), 164, 166, 170(both), 172, 174, 175, 180,
   186(b), 192(b), 193,
   198, 199(b), 200, 202/203, 206(t), 207, 208, 210/211, 214,
   216(b)
Don Troiani, Military and Historical Image Bank: 13, 31, 40/41, 59,
   68, 88/89, 98/99, 135, 151,
   162, 167, 182/183, 214/215

CONTENTS

INTRODUCTION

FROM 1861 TO 1865, THE CIVIL WAR RAVAGED THE UNITED STATES. IT WAS A WAR SOME HAVE CALLED 'THE SECOND AMERICAN REVOLUTION', AND INDEED THERE WAS MUCH THAT WAS REVOLUTIONARY ABOUT IT. NEW WEAPONS MADE THE WAR MORE LETHAL. NEW ATTITUDES CHANGED THE WAR'S IMPACT ON CIVILIANS. NEW OBJECTIVES TRANSFORMED THE WAR'S PURPOSE. NEW TECHNOLOGY MADE TRANSPORTATION AND COMMUNICATIONS ELEMENTS OF BATTLEFIELD STRATEGY AS NEVER BEFORE. NEW ARMIES WERE LARGER THAN ANY THAT AMERICA HAD PREVIOUSLY EXPERIENCED. THE END RESULT WAS A TOTAL WAR IN WHICH THE UNION AND THE CONFEDERACY FOUGHT FOR THEIR VERY SURVIVAL.

In the early years of the war, the Federal cavalry was no match for its Confederate counterpart. Confederate cavalryman Major-General JEB 'Jeb' Stuart (1833–64) would be especially active, riding all the way around George B McClellan's (1826–85) army on the Virginia Peninsula.

Although a variety of factors triggered the Civil War, slavery, and more specifically the expansion of slavery, was the principal cause. By the mid-nineteenth century, slavery had become the South's bedrock institution. Its impact had grown beyond providing the labour force for the South's agricultural economy. Slavery had become the basic assumption by which white Southerners defined relations between the white and black races, and the slaveholding planter class had come to dominate politics in the South.

The North also benefited from slavery thanks to the economic synergy of the triangular trade between Europe, Africa and the Americas. Nonetheless, the Northern economy was based more on industry than agriculture, and slavery never took root in the North. Instead, many Northerners

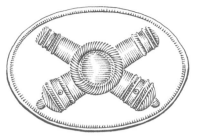
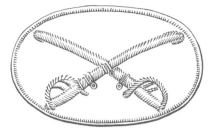

turned against slavery and a vocal minority became ardent abolitionists.

The result was that sectional differences resulting from slavery came to dominate American politics. The balance of power between slave and free states was a tenuous one and all national political decisions reflected its importance. For example, whenever a territory applied for statehood, its status as a free or slave state had to be considered. In this way the Missouri Compromise of 1820 allowed Maine to enter the Union as a free state, and Missouri to enter as a slave state in order to maintain the balance. However, the compromise specified that no other slave states from the unorganized Louisiana Purchase territory would be allowed north of Missouri's southern boundary.

Another crisis was avoided in 1832 over a protective tariff that increased the price of imported manufactured goods. Many Southerners felt this legislation unfairly benefited the North, and South Carolina's rice industry found it especially objectionable. In response to the tariff, South Carolina declared that a state had the right to void any act of Congress that the state considered illegal. This 'Nullification Crisis' highlighted the growing sectional economical differences, while also giving voice to the political concept of states' rights. President Andrew Jackson (1767–1845) sent naval vessels to Charleston as a Federal show of force, while elder statesman Henry Clay (1777–1852) ultimately crafted a compromise tariff to resolve the crisis. Nonetheless, South Carolina's position as a flashpoint in challenging the Federal government was established.

In 1846, the United States went to war with Mexico, an act that would, seemingly, be devoid of slavery implications, but many Northerners saw the war as an attempt by

the South to gain more territory for slavery. Indeed, Congressman David Wilmot (1814–68) of Pennsylvania introduced a resolution that would have prevented any land gained in the war from becoming slave territory. This 'Wilmot Proviso' failed, but it served to demonstrate the role slavery had come to play in national politics.

Another compromise was needed in 1850 when territories gained from Mexico prepared to enter the Union. California was admitted as a free state and it was decided that slavery in New Mexico and Utah would be decided by popular sovereignty. In addition, the slave trade was prohibited in the District of Columbia and a more stringent fugitive slave law was passed that required all US citizens to assist in the return of runaway slaves. The Compromise of 1850, partly Clay's work once again, was yet another attempt to meet the competing demands of the free and slave states.

The Kansas–Nebraska Act of 1854 declared that the slavery issue in Kansas and Nebraska would be decided by popular sovereignty. Because this act specifically repealed the Missouri Compromise of 1820, it drew the ire of many abolitionists. Zealots like John Brown (1800–59) made the territory 'Bleeding Kansas' as they fought to sway attitudes.

With this experience under his belt, Brown went east to Harpers Ferry, Virginia, where he raided an arsenal in an attempt to lead an armed slave revolt. Forces commanded by Lieutenant-Colonel Robert E Lee (1807–70) crushed the revolt, but it highlighted a deep-seated Southern fear of slave rebellion and resulted in a crackdown on slave behaviour throughout the South.

SECESSION
While all these incidents helped exacerbate sectional differences, the event that actually

Cap badges of the Union military: infantry, artillery and cavalry. Civil War soldiers depicted their branches by wearing unique insignia. The Corps of Engineers was considered the elite branch. During the war, Federal Brigadier-General Philip Kearny (1815–62) also introduced the practice of designated unit affiliation by a distinctive patch.

led to secession was the election of President Abraham Lincoln (1809–65) on 6 November 1860. Many Southerners interpreted Lincoln's election as sounding the death knell for their way of life and on 20 December, South Carolina voted to secede. The Deep South states of Mississippi, Alabama, Louisiana, Georgia, Florida and Texas followed.

As the Southern states seceded, they usually took with them the Federal garrisons within their borders. One notable exception was Fort Sumter, South Carolina, where a brave band of soldiers led by Major Robert Anderson (1805–71) refused to surrender. Fort Sumter became the epicentre of the growing sectional crisis. The Confederate government could no more tolerate this presence of 'foreign' military on its soil than the Federal government could legitimize secession by abandoning the fort. A tense standoff continued for several weeks. Then, on 12 April 1861, Confederate artillery under the command of General PGT Beauregard (1818–93) began bombarding Fort Sumter. Anderson, isolated and running low on provisions, had little choice but to surrender on 14 April.

In the aftermath of this attack on the US flag, President Lincoln called for 75,000 three-month volunteers to suppress the rebellion. This action forced the states of the upper South to decide between two alternatives: fight against their brother Southerners or leave the Union. Virginia, Arkansas, North Carolina and Tennessee all chose the latter course, bringing to 11 the total number of states that had seceded.

Of critical importance to both sides were the border states of Missouri, Kentucky and Maryland. These were slave states with strong connections to the South. Although

Opposite: Though having only a very limited military background, Abraham Lincoln proved to be a highly effective wartime president. In many cases he grasped broad strategic concepts before his generals did.

there was considerable pro-Confederacy sentiment in these states, they stopped short of secession. They would become a battleground, especially early in war, as the North sought to secure them for the Union, and the South sought to win them over to the Confederacy. Of critical importance was Maryland because of its proximity to Washington DC, the Federal capital.

THE SIDES COMPARED

As both the North and the South prepared for war, the North enjoyed a remarkable advantage in almost every measurable statistic. The North had a population of 20 million compared to 9 million in the South, of whom only 5.5 million were white. The North had over 110,000 manufacturing establishments while the South had just 18,000. The North had 35,400km (22,000 miles) of railroad to the South's 13,680 (8500). Even in agriculture the North outperformed the South, holding 75 per cent of the nation's farm acreage, producing 60 per cent of its livestock, 67 per cent of its corn and 81 per cent of its wheat. In sum, the North controlled 75 per cent of the nation's total wealth. Militarily, the North had 16,000 men in its army and 90 warships in its navy. In establishing itself as a nation, the fledgling Confederacy would be starting from scratch in many areas.

Nonetheless, the Confederacy had several key advantages. Most notable was what it would take to win the war. The South merely had to defend itself long enough to make the North grow tired of fighting. The North, on the other hand, had the more difficult task of going on the offensive and wresting back the Southern territory. The Confederacy also had high hopes for foreign intervention based on the assumption that European demand for cotton would not tolerate interruption. Finally, the South had the benefit of interior lines: the military principle that a force able to exploit its central position relative to the enemy has the advantage.

Enlisted soldiers in the Civil War wore straight, 'stove pipe' trousers that were cut fairly full. Creasing was not practised and trousers were pressed round, if at all. US Army issue trousers were made of sky blue kersey, and Confederate soldiers wore grey or butternut.

INTRODUCTION

The Civil War was the first great railroad war. Railroads were used to move troops and equipment and became critical in keeping supplies flowing to armies in the field.

Both sides formulated their strategies amid these advantages and disadvantages. The initial plan for the Federals was the Anaconda Plan, developed by the aging Mexican War (1846–48) hero, Lieutenant-General Winfield Scott (1786–1866). Scott's plan was to raise a huge army, blockade the Confederate coast with the superior Federal Navy, secure the Mississippi River, thereby cutting the South in two, and then wait. It was a well-thought-out plan that, ultimately, would reflect much of how the Federals fought the war; but in 1861, it was rejected as taking too long. Most Northerners expected a quick end to the war and President Lincoln knew that time was on the Confederacy's side. Thus, Scott's Anaconda Plan was rejected in favour of an immediate offensive against the Confederate capital of Richmond.

The South soon realized that it could not defend its entire vast frontier, although President Jefferson Davis (1808–89) was under huge political pressure from state governors to do so. Instead, Davis adopted an 'offensive-defensive' strategy by which the Confederacy would allow a Federal thrust to develop, determine its main axis of advance and then, at the advantageous moment, concentrate and counterattack to cut it off. The strategy was recognition of the North's resource advantage.

LEADERSHIP

On paper, Jefferson Davis looked much better suited than Abraham Lincoln to the role of wartime president. Davis had graduated from West Point, been a hero in the Mexican War and been an outstanding Secretary of War. Lincoln, on the other hand, had no military experience, save as a captain in the militia during the Black Hawk War. There, Lincoln joked, he had only fought mosquitoes.

In fact, Lincoln proved to be an excellent commander-in-chief, grasping the changing nature of war and its broad strategic implications before many of his generals. His was willing to push his presidential powers and suppress some civil liberties, such as suspending habeas corpus and censoring newspapers, to meet the emergencies of war. Most importantly, Lincoln understood that the policy of conciliation was not going to work. Lincoln knew that the South would have to be forced, rather than coaxed, back into the Union. Nonetheless, Lincoln would have to cycle through the likes of Irvin McDowell (1818–85), George B McClellan, John Pope (1822–92), McClellan again, Ambrose Burnside (1824–81), Joseph Hooker (1814–79) and George G Meade (1815–72) before finally finding in Ulysses S Grant (1822–85) a commanding general who shared his strategic vision.

What Grant brought to the Federal high command was a grand strategy that would press the Confederacy from all sides. Additionally, Grant understood that the tremendous manpower and resource advantage enjoyed by the Federals would allow him to continue to engage the Confederates, even if he suffered high casualties in the process.

Opposite: Jefferson Davis had impressive military experience as a graduate of West Point, a hero in the Mexican War of 1846–48 and an outstanding Secretary of War. As President of the Confederacy he would face many challenges in trying to build a new nation in time of war.

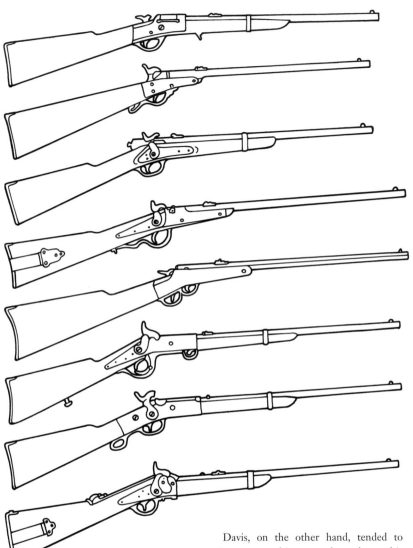

Used primarily by cavalry on both sides, the carbine came into its own in the Civil War. Above is a selection of single-shot carbines. From the top: the Warner, the Maynard, the Palmer, the Gallager, the Wesson, the Burnside, the Perry Navy carbine and the Merrill.

War had learned their trade as junior officers during the Mexican War. Among those Mexican War veterans who led the Confederate armies were Lee, Thomas 'Stonewall' Jackson (1824–63), Joseph E Johnston (1807–91), James Longstreet (1821–1904), Braxton Bragg (1817–76), AP Hill (1825–65) and Beauregard. Grant, McClellan, Pope, Winfield Scott Hancock (1824–86), Hooker, Meade and George H Thomas (1816–70) had seen Mexican War service for the Federals. Because of this the Mexican War has been called 'a dress rehearsal for the Civil War', although certainly not all its lessons were transferable to the latter conflict.

Another important proving ground for the Civil War generalship was West Point. In one list of 60 major Civil War battles, West Point graduates commanded on both sides in 55 of them. In the remaining five battles, a West Point graduate commanded on one of the two sides. At West Point, these officers were exposed to the military theories of Antoine-Henri Jomini (1779–1869) and his geometrical approach to war, which emphasized interior lines. The end result, according to one observer, was that 'many a Civil War general went into battle with a sword in one hand and Jomini's *Summary of the Art of War* in the other'.

A major challenge for the Civil War officer was the unprecedented size of the armies. In the Mexican War, Winfield Scott's entire army had totalled fewer than 13,000 men. Such a number would hardly make a respectable corps in the Civil War. McClellan, for example, had 104,300 men available at the beginning of the Seven Days' Battles.

Lee led some 70,000 men into Pennsylvania for his Gettysburg Campaign. At the Wilderness, Grant attacked Lee with more than 100,000. These enormous armies would stretch Civil War command and control to the utmost, especially given the limited means of communications and the fact that many of the soldiers were independent-thinking and relatively inexperienced volunteers.

WEAPONS AND TACTICS
In 1853, the US Army had adopted the rifled infantry musket. By this time, a

Davis, on the other hand, tended to micromanage his generals and use his military expertise to immerse himself in details at the expense of greater strategic considerations. Furthermore, the strong individual sentiment and resistance to centralized government among most Southerners prevented Davis from exercising expanded wartime powers as Lincoln did. Davis was fortunate in quickly finding a trusted military commander in Lee, but, unlike Grant on the Union side, Lee was reluctant to exert his authority beyond his own theatre of operations. Moreover, the Confederacy's finite pool of manpower made Confederate casualties irreplaceable and limited Lee's options.

In many cases the men who led the Federal and Confederate forces in the Civil

French Army captain named Claude E Minie (1804–79) had developed a way to load a rifled musket as easily as a smoothbore. The 'Minie ball' was a cylindro-conoidal bullet that was slightly smaller in diameter than the barrel and, thus, could be easily dropped down the barrel. One end, however, was hollow, so, when the rifle was fired, expanding gas widened the sides of the hollow end, causing the bullet to grip the rifling and create the spinning effect needed for accuracy. To take advantage of this technology, the United States adapted the Model 1855 Springfield rifle to take .58 calibre Minie ammunition. The difference was significant. The smoothbore musket had a range of 91–182m (100–200 yards). The new rifle was effective from 366–549m (400–600 yards).

However, this change in technology was not accompanied by a drastic change in tactics. Civil War formations remained fixed

in the Napoleonic style, with men standing shoulder to shoulder, and small intervals between units. The lines were maintained rigidly parallel to allow for a massed or uniform volley at the halt, and to maximize the shock effect. Commanders knew such a formation presented a vulnerable target, but they felt that an attack coming in successive waves would eventually overwhelm the defenders and carry the field.

In actuality, this increased range combined with the tactic of fighting behind heavy breastworks greatly increased the power of the defence. Frontal attacks such as Fredericksburg, Pickett's Charge and Kennesaw proved deadly to the attackers. To avoid attacking into the teeth of the enemy's defences, many Civil War generals began using turning movements and envelopments to strike the less-protected flanks. The battles of Second Manassas and Chancellorsville are excellent examples.

Union Colonel Strong Vincent steadies the 16th Michigan as they defend Little Roundtop at the Battle of Gettysburg, 2 July 1863.

INTRODUCTION

The Confederacy faced a serious disadvantage in terms of available manpower. The North had a population of 20 million compared to just 9 million in the South. Of that 9 million, only 5.5 million were white.

One result of this increased power of the defence was that battles took longer to fight and the ability to achieve a decisive result became increasingly elusive. Lee's ability to disengage after his defeat at Gettysburg is a good example.

Other important technological advances that had an impact on the Civil War were the telegraph and the railroad. The telegraph allowed both operational and strategic communications. Operators could hook insulated wire into existing trunk lines to reach into the civilian telegraph network and extend communications from the battlefield to the rear areas. For example, during the Peninsula Campaign, Thaddeus Sobieski Constantine Lowe (1831–1913) would ascend above the battlefield in a balloon and telegraph his observations to eagerly awaiting Federal commanders. The telegraph also allowed the administrations and War Departments in Washington and Richmond to communicate directly with their commanders in the field.

The Civil War was the 'first great

railroad war'. The Jominian influence of interior lines made railroads an attractive means of moving troops rapidly across great distances. Although the geography appeared to give the Confederacy an advantage in interior lines, the superior Federal rail system often proved an effective counter. The rail movement of 25,000 Federal soldiers, travelling 1931km (1200 miles) from Virginia to the Chattanooga front, in late 1863 is a good example.

THE BATTLES

The history of the Civil War contains many interesting facets. Entire volumes cover its economic, diplomatic, social and other aspects. The focus of this particular study is military engagement as seen through the 20 most important battles of the war.

According to the Civil War Sites Advisory Commission there were 10,500 armed conflicts in the Civil War, ranging from major battles to minor skirmishes. Of these, the commission identified 384 or 3.7 per cent of the total as having military significance. Obviously whittling this list down to the 20 most important is no easy task. The battles selected for this book were ones that markedly contributed to how the war was fought or how it turned out. Therefore some famous battles such as Fredericksburg did not make the list because they did not alter the overall strategic situation and some decisive Federal victories such as Fort Fisher were omitted because they occurred so late that the war's outcome was already inevitable.

Also conspicuously absent is Sherman's March to the Sea and subsequent Carolinas Campaign. While this campaign was among the most important in the war, the weak Confederate resistance and Sherman's tactic of avoiding Confederate armies resulted in few pitched battles that were on a scale with others covered in this book. The campaign, however, is mentioned in the discussion of Kennesaw and the Atlanta Campaign which made the March to the Sea possible. A brief explanation of why the particular battles were selected for this book follows.

1861

The opening battle of Fort Sumter ensured that the sectional differences would not be settled peacefully. First Manassas showed both sides that the war was going to be a long one. It was also a demonstration of the important part that railroads would play in the war.

1862

Fort Donelson was the first major Federal victory, reversing a string of debacles and opening up the way to Nashville. The Shenandoah Valley Campaign included several battles, but Kernstown is highlighted here because it was after this defeat that Federal forces were first withheld from joining Major-General George McClellan on the Virginia Peninsula. The Valley Campaign is also an excellent example of the adroit use of Jomini's concept of interior lines. Shiloh ensured Federal control of western and middle Tennessee. New Orleans cost the South its largest city and part of the Mississippi River. The Peninsula Campaign comprised several battles, to include the Seven Days' Battles, but Gaines' Mill is highlighted here because it was this defeat that led McClellan to announce his plan to withdraw. The Peninsula Campaign is also important because it marked General Robert E Lee's assumption of command of the Army of Northern Virginia.

Second Manassas was the Confederate victory that facilitated the invasion of Maryland. Antietam was the Federal victory that repulsed that invasion and gave

Between the Potomac and the Rio Grande, the Confederate coast stretched across 5711km (3549 miles) of shoreline with 189 harbour and river openings. Many coastal battles would occur at places like Fort Sumter and New Orleans.

President Lincoln the victory he needed to announce the Emancipation Proclamation. The Emancipation Proclamation expanded the Federal objective of the war beyond merely restoring the Union to include, also, the ending of slavery. As such, it changed the very nature of the war. Corinth ended the Confederate hopes of major operations in Tennessee and allowed Major-General Ulysses S Grant to concentrate on Vicksburg. The Federal victory at Perryville halted the Confederate drive into Kentucky, an important border state.

1863

Chancellorsville encouraged Lee to launch his second invasion into Northern territory, but it also cost him his trusted subordinate Lieutenant-General 'Stonewall' Jackson. The Vicksburg Campaign gave the Federals control of the Mississippi River and split the Confederacy in two. It included many battles, but Champion Hill is highlighted here because it was this defeat that forced Lieutenant-General John Pemberton (1814–81) to withdraw to Vicksburg, where Grant subjected him to a siege. Gettysburg thwarted Lee's second invasion of the North and also cost Lee enough men to preclude future offensives. Chattanooga and Chickamauga opened the Deep South to Federal invasion.

1864

The Wilderness and Spotsylvania Courthouse showed that Grant, unlike his predecessors, would not retreat, but instead would continue to apply the relentless pressure that would ultimately lead to Federal victory. The Atlanta Campaign ensured Lincoln's re-election, which meant there would be no peaceful settlement to the war. It included many battles, but Kennesaw is highlighted here because it was the only instance in which Major-General William Tecumseh Sherman (1820–91) deviated from his pattern of flank manoeuvres and engaged in a costly frontal attack. Mobile Bay represented the loss of the South's last

The first black soldiers went into battle in 1863. By the end of the war, 10 percent of the Federal Army, a total of 180,000 men, would be black soldiers.

major port on the Gulf of Mexico and, along with Atlanta, helped ensure that Lincoln would be re-elected. While Sherman was embarking on his March to the Sea after the Atlanta Campaign, Confederate Lieutenant General John Bell Hood launched a desperate move into Tennessee to attempt to cut off Sherman from the north. The Federal victories at Franklin and Nashville virtually eliminated Hood's Army of Tennessee and left Lee's Army of Northern Virginia as the Confederacy's only substantial military force.

1865

Finally, the siege of Petersburg, culminating in the Federal victory at Five Forks, ended Lee's opportunity for manoeuvre and thus sealed the fate of the Army of Northern Virginia and, with it, the Confederacy. Of course, Civil War historians and buffs may be able to make a case for replacing one battle from our list with another, but, given our criteria, we are fairly confident this list represents the 20 most militarily significant battles in the war.

BEYOND THE CIVIL WAR

The Federal victory in the Civil War resulted in the continuance of the United States as a politically united nation with strengthened federal authority. As such it was the pivotal experience in American history. That is not to say, however, that with the surrender at Appomattox everything took care of itself. The legacy of the Civil War continues in the United States today, and some of the conflict's issues remain unresolved.

With the end of the Civil War, the United States faced the difficult task of re-establishing a nation that had been disrupted by four years of civil strife. Lincoln had envisioned a quick restoration, establishing civilian governments in the former Confederate states as quickly as practicable. However, after Lincoln's assassination, the Radical Republicans in Congress, who had long been pressing Lincoln for a stricter prosecution of the war, dismissed Lincoln's plan. The new president, Andrew Johnson (1808–75), tried to implement a plan that was in many ways slightly harsher than Lincoln's but, in so doing, Johnson was attacked fiercely by the Radical Republicans. The end result was Congressional control of Reconstruction, the process by which the defeated Confederate states would progress to re-entering the Union.

Reconstruction was a tumultuous period in American history that saw the military occupation of the ex-Confederacy, the impeachment of President Johnson, the sometimes painful transition of the slaves to freemen, the influx of carpetbaggers who often exploited the new political situation in the South and the rise of the Ku Klux Klan as an organization of white Southerners dedicated to maintaining the old social order. Reconstruction finally ended with the Compromise of 1877, in which contested voter returns in South Carolina, Florida and Louisiana were resolved in favour of Rutherford B Hayes (1822–93). Hayes became President of the United States and in exchange he promised to withdraw all remaining Federal troops from the South, ending Reconstruction and permitting white Southerners to reassert control. With this transfer of power the Southern states began to pass Jim Crow laws and other policies that reversed the gains made by black people.

In spite of the imperfections of Reconstruction, the Civil War resulted in the emancipation of some 3.5 million slaves within the Confederacy, and the Thirteenth Amendment (1865) ultimately ended slavery in the United States. To be sure, the end of slavery did not equate to immediate equality among the races in the United States. It remained for the slow and steady progress of the civil rights movement, a movement that continues today, to bring about genuine change.

Even now, more than 140 years after Appomattox, signs of the Civil War still permeate the American landscape. Confederate memorials grace many Southern towns. Controversies over the Confederate battle flag excite various emotions. Civil War re-enactors establish camps and refight battles. Many US Army posts are named after Civil War generals. Both documentaries and dramas about the Civil War win awards. Battlefield parks such as Gettysburg draw millions of visitors each year, while preservationists and developers battle over the relative merits of urban sprawl.

Clearly, the Civil War is indelibly etched in the American consciousness. Even this book is a small part of preserving its memory.

Ships land supplies in a Federal river port on the eastern seaboard. The Union Army had a massive advantage in men and materiel over their Confederate counterparts, and it is this that influenced the outcome of the war more than any other factor.

FORT SUMTER
APRIL 1861

THE BATTLE OF FORT SUMTER IN APRIL 1861 WAS SMALL IN SCALE BUT EPIC IN IMPORT. THE ISOLATED FORT OFF THE SOUTH CAROLINA COASTLINE BECAME THE FOCUS OF GROWING ANTAGONISM BETWEEN THE FEDERAL NORTH AND THE SECESSIONIST SOUTH. THE RESULTING TWO-DAY ACTION SAW THE FIRST SHOTS FIRED IN WHAT WOULD BECOME THE AMERICAN CIVIL WAR.

WHY DID IT HAPPEN?

WHO A small Union garrison occupied Fort Sumter. Sumter was effectively besieged, then bombarded, by surrounding Confederate batteries.

WHAT The battle was an artillery duel, the Confederates deploying nearly 50 heavy-calibre guns and mortars. Union troops had 60 guns, but not all could be used and many had limited range and ammunition.

WHERE The waters of Charleston harbour, between Morris Island and James Island to the south, and Sullivan's Island to the north.

WHEN April 1861.

WHY South Carolina's secessionist government sought to take possession of the forts within the state, while the US government declared them Federal property.

OUTCOME A 36-hour Confederate bombardment forced the Union garrison to surrender Fort Sumter. The action began the American Civil War.

By early 1861, the United States was in a state of political and social crisis. Antagonism between the US Federal government and the Southern states over issues such as slavery and states' rights reached a crescendo with the election of President Abraham Lincoln (1809–65) in November 1860 (he was sworn in on 4 March 1861). Lincoln, a constitutionalist, argued that any secession from the Union was illegal, although defiance quickly stirred in several rebel states. By the end of January 1861 seven states had declared secession, and together formed the Confederate States of America on 4 February, with its own president, Jefferson Davis (1808–89), elected on 9 February.

One of the early actions of the breakaway states was to take over Federal forts and bases within their territories, well aware that the new South needed to make preparations for possible hostilities. However, Federal garrisons remained in place at many locations – potential power kegs in the pressure cooker of secession. The tension was particularly high in South Carolina, the first state to secede, around the harbour at Charleston.

The approach to the harbour was a broad waterway framed by two landmasses that formed entrance waters of roughly 2.4km (1.5 miles) across. At the southern end of the gap was Morris Island, which drove a long rocky promontory out into the bay

In 1860 President James Buchanan (1791–1868) struggled to cope with the growing political crisis. It was made worse by the men of the Covode Committee (pictured right), who investigated the president for possible impeachment.

known as Cummings Point. To the west of Morris Island, further inland, was James Island. (Morris and James islands are here described as separate features, but they effectively formed one river-slashed landmass running into Charleston harbour.) On the other side of the bay was Sullivan's Island and mainland Mount Pleasant. The city of Charleston lay protected by these northern and southern arms of the South Carolina coastline, at the confluence of the Cooper and Ashley rivers.

The whole approach to Charleston was framed with fortifications and coastal guns. On Morris Island were batteries on Cummings Point and, moving south, Fort Wagner and Fort Shaw. Fort Johnson sat on the northernmost tip of James Island, while Sullivan's Island guarded the northern entrance to the harbour with Fort Moultrie and a floating battery off the west tip of the island, an iron-coated raft containing two 43-pounder and two 32-pounder guns. Other batteries were found along the edge of Mount Pleasant, and another fort, Castle Pinkney, sat well back on an island at the mouth of the Cooper River.

There remained one other fort in the area – Fort Sumter. Fort Sumter sat on an island of its own between Morris Island and Sullivan's Island, dominating the entrance to Charleston harbour and sitting on its own specially constructed sand bar. The fort was a solid five-sided structure, built after the war of 1812. At its longest point it was 57.9m (190ft) in length, and it was capable of taking up to 135 guns of various calibres (although it never reached this complement of weaponry). The fortress walls were 1.5m (5ft) thick. Sumter was a powerful emplacement, the centrepiece of the Charleston defences, with control over all shipping wanting to enter the harbour waters. It was this fort that would spark the American Civil War.

ANTAGONISM

With South Carolina's official secession declared on 20 December 1860, there remained the issue of ownership of all the harbour fortresses and batteries. These were considered as Federal possessions by the US government, but the state governor, Francis W Pickens (1805–69), argued that all property within state borders should become state-owned. While Fort Sumter was not occupied, Fort Moultrie was held by a small US Army force of two companies of the First US Artillery, commanded by Major Robert Anderson (1805–71). Anderson was a talented and well-connected officer. He had graduated from West Point in 1825 and had served with distinction in the Second Seminole War (1835–42) and the Mexican War (1846–48); during the former conflict he served on General Winfield Scott's (1786–1866) staff. He was appointed to the command of the First US Artillery on 5 October 1857. Because Anderson was competent while also loyal to the Union (despite his having been

SOUTH CAROLINA HARBOUR GUARD

This South Carolina harbour guardsman wears a uniform typical of the early Confederacy. He has a grey-blue jacket and trousers, the former having a simple soft collar. Head wear is the traditional grey-blue kepi. A brown leather shoulder strap and belt hold equipment, and this soldier also has a simple cloth knapsack worn over his right shoulder. The soldier's rifle is a percussion-cap type, which gave improved ignition performance over earlier flintlock weapons. In this early stage of the war, Confederate uniforms could come from multiple, usually local, sources. It wasn't until 1862 that the Confederate government started to take central responsibility for military clothing.

LOCATION

The forts along the eastern seaboard had a critical importance during the Civil War. Whoever controlled the coast would have greater logistical control, and therefore could dominate the coastal cities in the east.

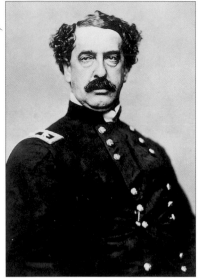

Major-General Abner Doubleday (1819–93) was second-in-command to Robert Anderson at Fort Sumter (he was at the time a captain). He rose to fame by personally aiming the cannon that fired the first Union shot from Sumter.

THE OPPOSED FORCES

FEDERAL
A small garrison of US Army troops confined in Fort Sumter.

CONFEDERATE
Various South Carolina militia units and artillery batteries, gathered around Charleston harbour.

born in Louisville, Kentucky), he was soon appointed to the Charleston command. With secession declared, the status of his Federal troops was uncertain, hence three commissioners from the South Carolina Convention – Robert W Barnwell (1801–82), James H Adams (1812–61) and James L Orr (1822–73) – were sent to Washington DC to negotiate for the non-violent transfer of Moultrie to the state. The conditions of the negotiations were that no side should engage the other while talks were taking place, nor should the disposition of forces at the harbour change.

On 26 December 1860, Anderson broke these conditions. In a secret night-time manoeuvre, he transferred his troops over to Fort Sumter and took up positions. Anderson's manoeuvre may have been politically inflammatory, but it made some military sense. Fort Moultrie was a powerful fortress, but its gun defences were designed to deliver fire out to sea. Against a land attack – the likeliest assault route should South Carolina decide to take the fort by force – it was badly configured. (During subsequent negotiations Anderson stated that he specifically feared a landing of state troops on the sand hills north of the fort.) Fort Sumter gave Anderson 360-degree protection from assault.

The state authorities soon dispatched representation to Anderson. A cordial meeting between Anderson and Colonel Johnston Pettigrew (1828–63) of the First South Carolina Rifles on 27 December saw no resolution – Anderson reasserted his right to command over all the harbour defences, despite Pettigrew emphasizing that if the situation was not resolved, then violence would be the likely outcome. Anderson also said that he knew of no conditional arrangements between South Carolina and Washington DC, and that he had to make his own decisions in the absence of guidance from the Federal government. Pettigrew returned from the meeting without satisfaction. Anderson, meanwhile, hoisted the Union flag over the fort and initiated intensive efforts to prepare its defences for action.

Despite the increase in tension, Governor Pickens and his authorities were hesitant about the use of force, as was the

Confederate government headed by Jefferson Davis. Nevertheless, on 9 January 1861, the US steamer *The Star of the West* attempted a resupply run to Fort Sumter, but was met with fire from the batteries along Morris Island plus some shots from Fort Moultrie. The ship was not damaged, but it was forced to turn about. Anderson declared the action unjustifiable, adding that if an apology was not forthcoming, he might turn his own guns on Charleston's shipping. Although a truce of sorts was

declared, both sides expedited their preparations for war.

OPENING SHOTS

By the beginning of March 1861, Fort Sumter was effectively under siege, and its supplies were beginning to run low. Its position was also looking increasingly vulnerable. All surrounding forts had been occupied by Confederate troops, and had been deliberately up-gunned. At Fort Moultrie, for example, the artillery commander Lieutenant-Colonel RS Ripley (1823–87) positioned a total of 26 artillery pieces, ranging from 24-pounders through to 25cm (10in) mortars, to fire on Fort Sumter if necessary. At Cummings Point were six 25cm (10in) mortars and six direct-fire guns. Fort Johnson contained four mortars and a 24-pounder gun. Add in the capability of the floating and other batteries, and in total there would be more than 40 guns of various different calibres capable of firing on Fort Sumter by the time hostilities broke out in April. (A Union estimate of the Confederate artillery firing on Fort Sumter during the action was 30 guns and 17 mortars.) Furthermore, 500 troops from various state militias were made ready to form assault parties.

A vivid depiction of the Confederate bombardment of Fort Sumter. The Confederate batteries were able to deliver almost 360-degree direct or indirect fire, using a mix of solid shot and explosive-filled shells.

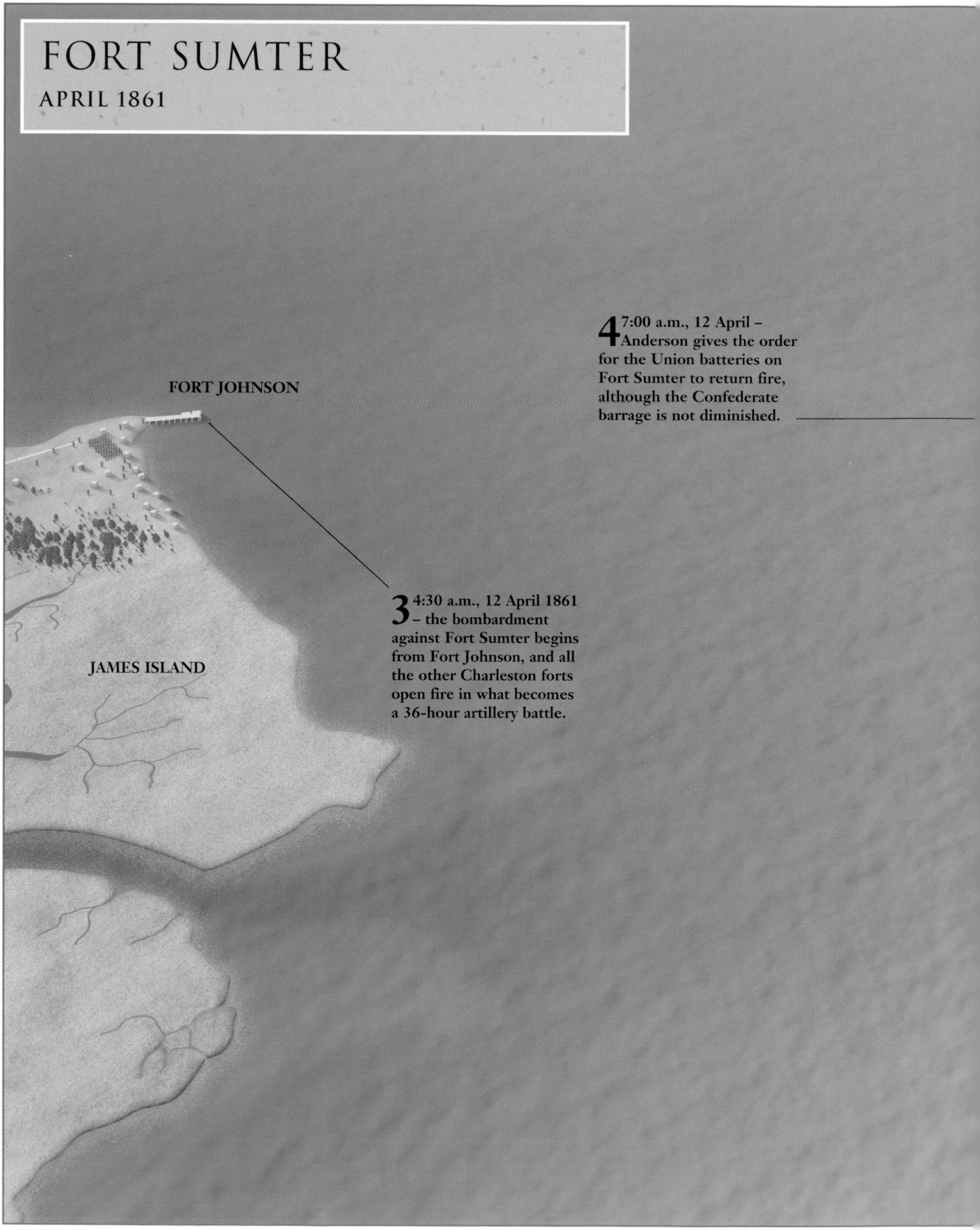

FORT SUMTER
APRIL 1861

4 7:00 a.m., 12 April – Anderson gives the order for the Union batteries on Fort Sumter to return fire, although the Confederate barrage is not diminished.

FORT JOHNSON

3 4:30 a.m., 12 April 1861 – the bombardment against Fort Sumter begins from Fort Johnson, and all the other Charleston forts open fire in what becomes a 36-hour artillery battle.

JAMES ISLAND

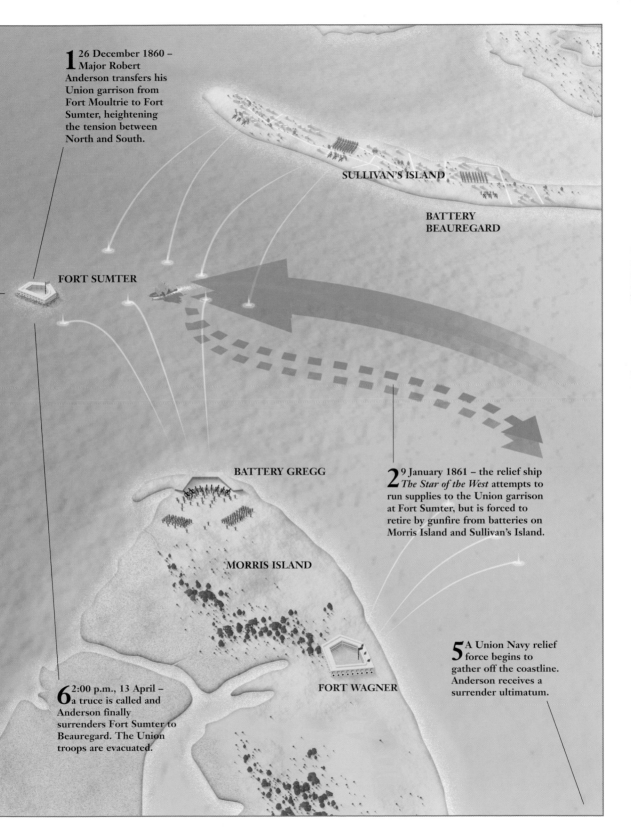

1 26 December 1860 – Major Robert Anderson transfers his Union garrison from Fort Moultrie to Fort Sumter, heightening the tension between North and South.

SULLIVAN'S ISLAND

BATTERY BEAUREGARD

FORT SUMTER

BATTERY GREGG

2 9 January 1861 – the relief ship *The Star of the West* attempts to run supplies to the Union garrison at Fort Sumter, but is forced to retire by gunfire from batteries on Morris Island and Sullivan's Island.

MORRIS ISLAND

5 A Union Navy relief force begins to gather off the coastline. Anderson receives a surrender ultimatum.

FORT WAGNER

6 2:00 p.m., 13 April – a truce is called and Anderson finally surrenders Fort Sumter to Beauregard. The Union troops are evacuated.

The rebel troops surrounding Fort Sumter also received a new overall commander. On 27 February, PGT Beauregard (1818–93), who would become one of the great commanders of the Civil War, was appointed a brigadier-general in the new Confederate Army. On 1 March, he took command over all the forces around Charleston. With supreme irony, Anderson had actually been Beauregard's artillery instructor at West Point, and Beauregard had also served as Anderson's assistant. Such a relationship ensured a high degree of civility and respect between the two men, but preparations for war continued.

Left: A photograph of Fort Sumter taken after the battle clearly shows the 1.5m (5ft) thick walls that were the fort's greatest defence. The wheeled gun that sits at the top would have a limited range for the inter-fort engagement.

Below: A depiction of the action on board the Confederate floating battery in Charleston harbour. The battery had four heavy artillery pieces.

Beauregard made sure that all troops were well trained, particularly in the use of artillery. On Fort Sumter, meanwhile, supplies were running critically short.

Events took a new turn on 4 April. Lincoln was becoming increasingly concerned about the fate of the Fort Sumter garrison, and ordered a naval relief expedition to be dispatched. His note to Pickens informed the governor that 'an attempt will be made to supply Fort Sumter with provisions only, and that if such attempt be not resisted, no effort to throw in men, arms, or ammunition will be made without further notice, [except] in case of an attack on the fort.'

A violent debate amongst the Southern governments now followed, but the decision was made to bombard and take Fort Sumter before the relief fleet could replenish it. Beauregard received his instructions about Fort Sumter from the Secretary of War: 'You will at once demand its evacuation, and if this is refused proceed, in such a manner you may determine, to reduce it.'

On 11 April, Beauregard issued an instruction to Anderson saying that the Union troops had to abandon the fort or it would be taken by force. Anderson's response was brief and to the point:

'General: I have the honor to acknowledge the receipt of your communication demanding the evacuation of this fort, and to say, in reply thereto, that it is a demand with which I regret that my sense of honor, and of my obligations to my government, prevent my compliance. Thanking you for the fair, manly and courteous terms proposed, and for the high compliment paid me, I am, General, very respectfully, your obedient servant, ROBERT ANDERSON, Major, First Artillery, Commanding.'

Subsequent communications did not ease the gathering tension, particularly as the US relief force was already gathering for its run in to Fort Sumter. Then, at 3:20 a.m. on 12

Robert Anderson. Despite the loss of Fort Sumter, Anderson was feted as a hero in the North. He was promoted to brigadier-general, but retired from the Army in 1863 because of ill health.

The 1861 battle was far from the end of Fort Sumter's travails. Between 1863 and 1865 the fort was under regular, intense Union bombardment. Here Union Parrott guns prepare to fire upon the much abused fort at the end of 1863.

April, Beauregard told Anderson that in one hour's time the first shots would be fired.

He was true to his word. At 4:30 a.m. a mortar was fired from Fort Johnson, whereupon a 36-hour bombardment of the fort began. The fire was incredibly intense – Fort Moultrie alone fired 2490 projectiles into the fort structure. In terms of defence, Anderson was faced with a problem. His firepower within Fort Sumter was not inconsiderable. Captain JG Foster (1823–74) of the Corps of Engineers, US Army, who served in Fort Sumter, listed the fort's defences as follows:

'Barbette tier: *Right flank, one 10-inch columbiad, four 8-inch columbiads, four 42-pounders. Right face, none. Left face, three 8-inch sea-coast howitzers, one 32-pounder. Left flank, one 10-inch columbiad, two 8-inch columbiads, two 42-pounders. Gorge, one 8-inch sea-coast howitzer, two 32-pounders, six 24-pounders. Total in barbette, 27 guns.*

Casemate tier: *Right flank, one 42-pounder, four 32-pounders. Right face, three 42-pounders. Left face, ten 32-pounders. Left flank, five 32-pounders. Gorge, two 32-pounders. Total in casemate, 21 guns. Total available in both tiers, 48 guns.*

Besides the above, there were arranged on the parade, to serve mortars, one 10-inch columbiad to throw shells into Charleston and four 8-inch columbiads to throw shells into the batteries on Cummings Point.'

Despite such a contingent of firepower, Foster admits that the casemate guns were the only ones used. The guns on the uppermost level were too exposed to enemy fire, while those below often had

The Coehorn mortar was named after its inventor, the Dutch officer Baron van Coehorn (1641–1704). It had a relatively fixed trajectory and a calibre ranging from 114mm (4.5in) to more than 250mm (10in). Such mortars were used in the Charleston batteries.

insufficient elevation to fire over the walls. Nonetheless, Anderson did order fire to commence at 7:00 a.m., but it had little effect in lessening the onslaught. The many small-calibre guns did not have the range or penetration to do serious damage to the enemy fort structures. Once the Fort Sumter garrison began firing, another problem facing Anderson's men (of whom 16 were musicians, not frontline troops) was a rapid depletion of ammunition – the garrison had only 700 rounds to begin with. By the middle of 12 April, only six guns were still able to fire.

Within Fort Sumter, by contrast, the Confederate fire delivered steady destruction. The main barracks caught fire

---

Preparations for the Union flag-raising over Fort Sumter on 14 April 1865. Robert Anderson himself performed the flag-raising, having come out of retirement two months earlier.

three times and the fires had to be extinguished by hand. Foster noted that: 'The direction of the enemy's shells being from the northeast, north, southwest, and southeast, sought every part of the work, and the fuses being well graduated, exploded in most instances just within the line of parapet.' Numerous Union guns were put out of action, and the tiered walls collapsed at many points. The fort's main gates were also blown open.

SURRENDER

As day broke on 13 April, the last rice supplies were served to the Union troops – a small amount of pork was the only food left. More significantly, hot shot had ignited an uncontrollable fire around the fort's magazine. Only 50 barrels of powder were saved before the magazine had to be sealed with earth and ominously left to burn. Fire also spread to the barracks, pushing the defenders out to the fort's walls. Loose

barrels of powder and explosive munitions began to detonate in the heat. It was clear to Anderson that Fort Sumter's resistance was unsustainable. At 2:00 p.m. on 13 April, a truce was finally agreed and the firing stopped. Negotiations for surrender of the fort were undertaken, the Union troops agreeing to make a transfer at 2:30 p.m. on 14 April. The US ships off the coast would take the men back north. Ironically, although the destruction within Fort Sumter was intense, the only fatality incurred was when Union troops, by agreement with Beauregard, fired a salute to the US flag, during which a gun and a pile of cartridges exploded.

Fort Sumter became a Confederate possession on 14 April, but few imagined the conflict the battle would begin. Lincoln called for a volunteer force to retake the forts. Lincoln did indeed take back Sumter, but that day did not come until 14 April 1865, after four years of bloody war.

FIRST MANASSAS
21 JULY 1861

BY THE END OF 1860, THE UNITED STATES FACED A CRISIS THAT THREATENED TO DISMEMBER THE UNION. IN DECEMBER OF THAT YEAR, SOUTH CAROLINA WAS THE FIRST STATE TO SECEDE AND WAS SOON JOINED BY OTHERS WHO TOGETHER FORMED THE CONFEDERACY. BY APRIL 1861, THE ONLY RECOURSE WAS THE USE OF FORCE. THE FIRST SALVO WAS FIRED BY THE CONFEDERATES AS THEY BOMBARDED FORT SUMTER AT CHARLESTON ON 12–13 APRIL. THE WAR HAD BEGUN.

WHY DID IT HAPPEN?

WHO The Union Army of Northeastern Virginia (35,000) under Brigadier-General Irvin McDowell (1818–85) attacked the Confederate Army of the Potomac (22,000) under Brigadier-General PGT Beauregard (1818–93), later reinforced by some 12,000 troops under Brigadier-General Joseph E Johnston (1807–91).

WHAT McDowell's forces launched a series of attacks against the Confederates defending the Bull Run stream.

WHERE Along the Bull Run stream north of Manassas Junction, some 40km (25 miles) southwest of Washington DC.

WHEN 21 July 1861.

WHY The Union forces executed a number of poorly coordinated attacks. While enjoying initial success, the Union army was ultimately thrown back in confusion.

OUTCOME The Union troops were routed back to Washington and ceased to exist as a viable fighting force.

As a result of the bombardment of Fort Sumter, President Abraham Lincoln (1809–65), who had only been in office for a month, faced a war for which the Union was ill-prepared. The US Army at the time numbered only 16,000 men, its main purpose to serve as a constabulary force, in particular against the various Native American tribes along the western frontier. As a result, the great majority of the US regulars were deployed west of the Mississippi River. The remaining troops were used to guard the various government installations in the east, including arsenals

Joe Johnston was a West Point graduate who had served in the US Army prior to the war. He had reached the position of Quartermaster-General before the war's outbreak, but, hailing from Virginia, he joined the forces of the Confederacy.

and coastal fortifications, such as Fort Sumter; or they were deployed in small outposts along the border with Canada. Given these duties, most Army regiments rarely served together as units but were instead parcelled out as company-sized garrisons, so the troops were not prepared for the kind of large-scale manoeuvres that would be necessary for the imminent hostilities. To exacerbate matters, some 1200 of these troops stationed in Texas were unable to extricate themselves from Confederate territory before hostilities commenced, and were made prisoners of war.

Like their troops, the officer corps of the US Army was ill-prepared for the looming hostilities. The senior officers were an aged group led by Brevet Lieutenant-General Winfield Scott (1786–1866). Scott was a veteran of both the War of 1812 and the Mexican War (1846–48) but, by 1861, at the age of 75, he was so old and infirm that he could neither ride a horse nor command an army in the field, even though he was the only Union officer who had any experience

of commanding large bodies of troops in battle. The other senior officers were mostly in their mid-60s. Two of the three general officers of the line were over 70, and the third was 60.

In the case of the junior- and field-grade officers, the men were perhaps better prepared physically for the war, but they too had a problem to overcome, namely a lack of experience in fighting large-scale conventional war. Most of these officers had never commanded more than a company-sized garrison in action on account of the Army's role at that time and the way in which it was deployed. When the Civil War began, these officers had only theoretical knowledge of how larger units such as battalions or regiments functioned, based primarily on their drill manuals, and knew virtually nothing at all about higher military formations such as brigades and divisions.

Since the Army regulars were too few and ill-prepared for the war that now faced the Union, President Lincoln was forced to rely on other sources of military manpower.

The First Battle of Manassas took place in the 161km (100-mile) corridor between the two capitals, Richmond and Washington. This area was the central theatre of the entire war, where many of the best-known battles of the conflict took place.

NEW YORK STATE MILITIA

One of the more famous units of the Civil War was the 'Fighting' 69th New York State Militia which fought as part of William T Sherman's (1820–91) brigade at the First Battle of Manassas under Colonel Michael Corcoran (1827–63). The regiment was composed of Irish immigrants and was one of the first units of 90-day volunteers to enlist for the war. The regiment was sent to defend Washington and spent much of its time in garrison drilling under the watchful eyes of its officers and was soon recognized as a competently trained unit. After sweeping over Matthews Hill, the 69th was hotly engaged in a firefight with the Louisiana Tigers, a Zouave regiment, and after two volleys drove the Tigers back. After this, the 69th re-formed and repeatedly attacked Confederate positions on Henry House Hill, having discarded their knapsacks, some even charging in bare-chested, but were repulsed. After four attacks, Sherman's brigade was forced to retreat and the 69th helped cover the retreat, even forming a square against pursuing cavalry.

This Model 1841 field piece could fire a 2.7kg (6lb) round more than 1550m (1700 yards). It was used extensively during the Mexican War (1846–48), but by the time of the Civil War it was considered obsolete. Nevertheless, Confederate batteries made extensive use of the six-pounder at Manassas.

In theory, there was a large militia that could be called up to support the Army in such a crisis, but the militia had not been closely regulated in recent years.

As a result, many of the militia rolls were hopelessly out of date and many militia units did not perform any form of regular muster or drill. Although there were some quality militia units, these were divided between the Union and the Confederacy. Nonetheless, on 15 April, Lincoln issued a call for 75,000 militiamen from those states still loyal to the Union, and his request was not only met but exceeded. These troops were to be enrolled for a period of three months as required under the various Militia Acts. It quickly became clear that this force would not be adequate for the task at hand, so Lincoln unilaterally decided to approve the addition of some 20,000 troops (10 regiments) to the US Army. Additionally, he called on the states to provide more than 40,000 volunteers whose regiments would be enlisted for three years.

The Confederacy faced similar problems. It had no regular troops at its disposal, and although the Confederate Congress did approve the creation of a standing army, it never really materialized.

There was, however, a cadre of experienced officers, as some 20 per cent of the 1100 officers of the US Army resigned their commissions and took up arms for the Confederacy. President Jefferson Davis (1808–89), like Lincoln, was therefore forced to rely on militiamen and volunteers. In March 1861, Davis was authorized to call up

the state militias for a period of 60 days and to enlist an additional 100,000 volunteers for the cause.

THE CAMPAIGN

In the months following the outbreak of hostilities, both sides hurriedly collected, trained, and deployed their forces. Given that a mere 161km (100 miles) separated the two capitals of Washington and Richmond, this area in between would clearly become an important theatre of operations. Federal troops gathered in Washington and soon crossed the Potomac River in order to occupy Alexandria, Virginia. At the same time, troops began the task of erecting a significant complex of fortifications to defend the city and to protect the troops organizing and training there.

As the Union forces mustered, it became necessary to appoint a commander since Winfield Scott was incapable of taking the field himself. Scott had a couple of candidates from the Army's senior leadership in mind, but political pressure from a member of President Lincoln's cabinet forced him to appoint a younger officer, Brevet Major Irvin McDowell, to command the troops who would form the Union's main field force. McDowell, a 42-year-old who had graduated from West Point, was therefore promoted to brigadier-general and given command of the Army of Northeastern Virginia numbering more than 35,000 men. A smaller force of 18,000 troops was placed under the command of Major-General Robert Patterson (1792–

1881), a 69-year-old veteran who had served with Scott in Mexico and been one of Scott's choices for McDowell's command. Patterson had previously been given command of Union troops but had not shown himself to be an energetic leader.

At the same time, the Confederates formed their forces in the theatre. The main force was to be commanded by 43-year-old Brigadier-General PGT Beauregard, a classmate of McDowell's who had led the attack on Fort Sumter. Beauregard commanded 22,000 men stationed around Manassas Junction, an important rail point that also sat astride two important roads that led from Washington and Richmond. There was a second large concentration of 11,000 Confederate troops at Harpers Ferry to the northwest under Brigadier-General Joseph E Johnston.

By June, the Union forces were under both political and military pressure to prepare an offensive strategy. Many Northern leaders assumed the rebellion would collapse if the Union Army could seek and win a single, decisive battle. The Northern press began to echo these sentiments with stories that began with the mantra 'Forward to Richmond'. Moreover, although Scott understood that Union troops were still forming and training, there was a serious danger associated with delaying the attack, namely that many of the militia units who formed a significant portion of the Union Army were nearing the end of their enlistments, and if action were not imminent, these troops would simply go home. As a result, by the end of June, Scott asked McDowell and his staff to prepare a campaign plan to move against the Confederate troops located south of Washington DC.

McDowell's plan centred on his army advancing in three prongs against Beauregard at Manassas, while Patterson and his troops moved on Harpers Ferry, pinning Johnston and his forces and preventing the two Confederate armies

THE OPPOSED FORCES

FEDERAL
Five divisions (mostly militia and short-term volunteers)
Total: 35,000

CONFEDERATE
Two armies made up of
11 brigades
Total: 34,000

During the Civil War, both Union and Confederate armies possessed units of Zouaves who wore uniforms based upon those of France's North African units which had fought in the Crimean War (1854–56). Their bright uniforms and exotic look made them a popular motif for militia units. Here Zouaves are shown fighting off a cavalry attack, a relatively rare occurrence during the conflict.

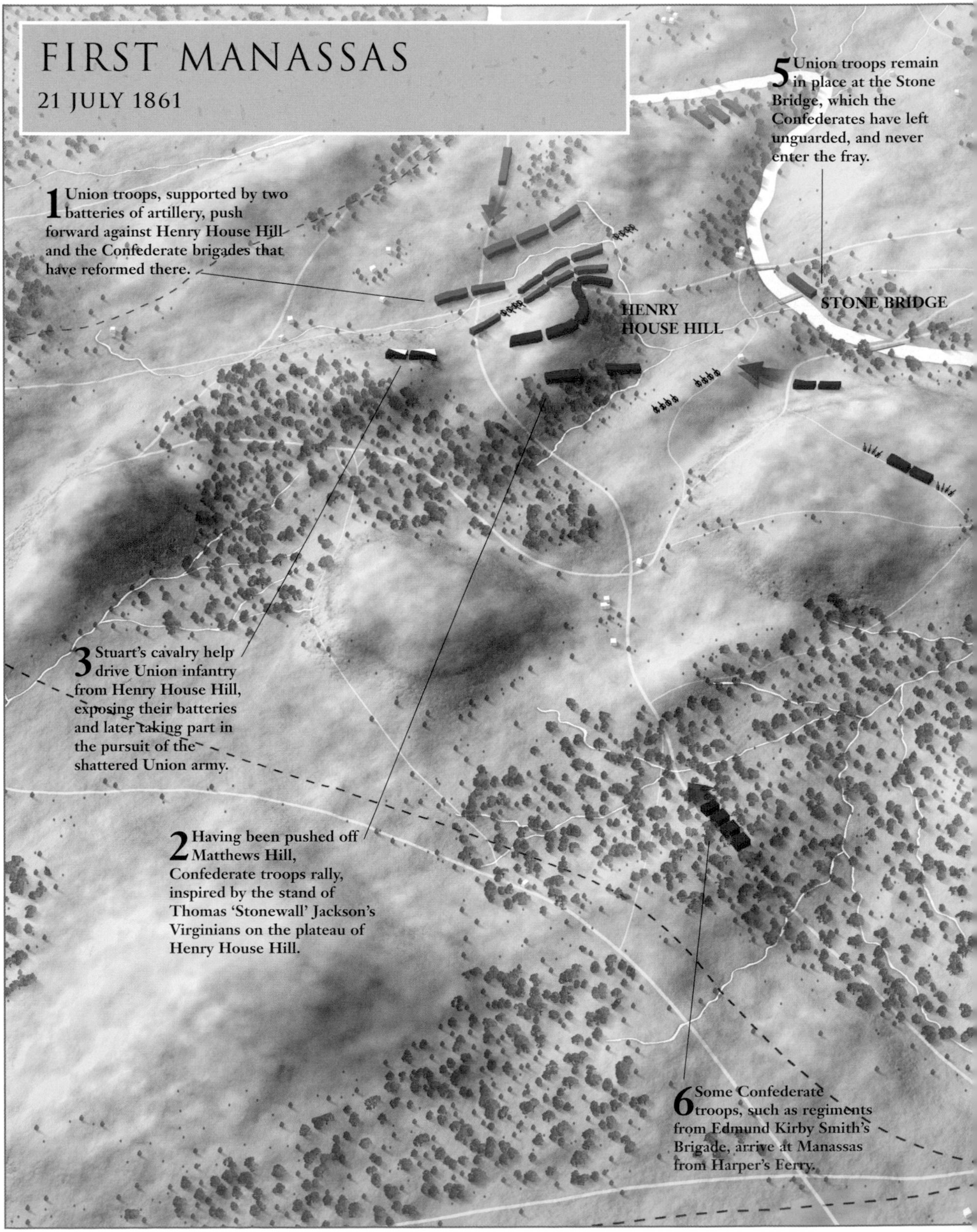

FIRST MANASSAS
21 JULY 1861

1 Union troops, supported by two batteries of artillery, push forward against Henry House Hill and the Confederate brigades that have reformed there.

5 Union troops remain in place at the Stone Bridge, which the Confederates have left unguarded, and never enter the fray.

STONE BRIDGE

HENRY HOUSE HILL

3 Stuart's cavalry help drive Union infantry from Henry House Hill, exposing their batteries and later taking part in the pursuit of the shattered Union army.

2 Having been pushed off Matthews Hill, Confederate troops rally, inspired by the stand of Thomas 'Stonewall' Jackson's Virginians on the plateau of Henry House Hill.

6 Some Confederate troops, such as regiments from Edmund Kirby Smith's Brigade, arrive at Manassas from Harper's Ferry.

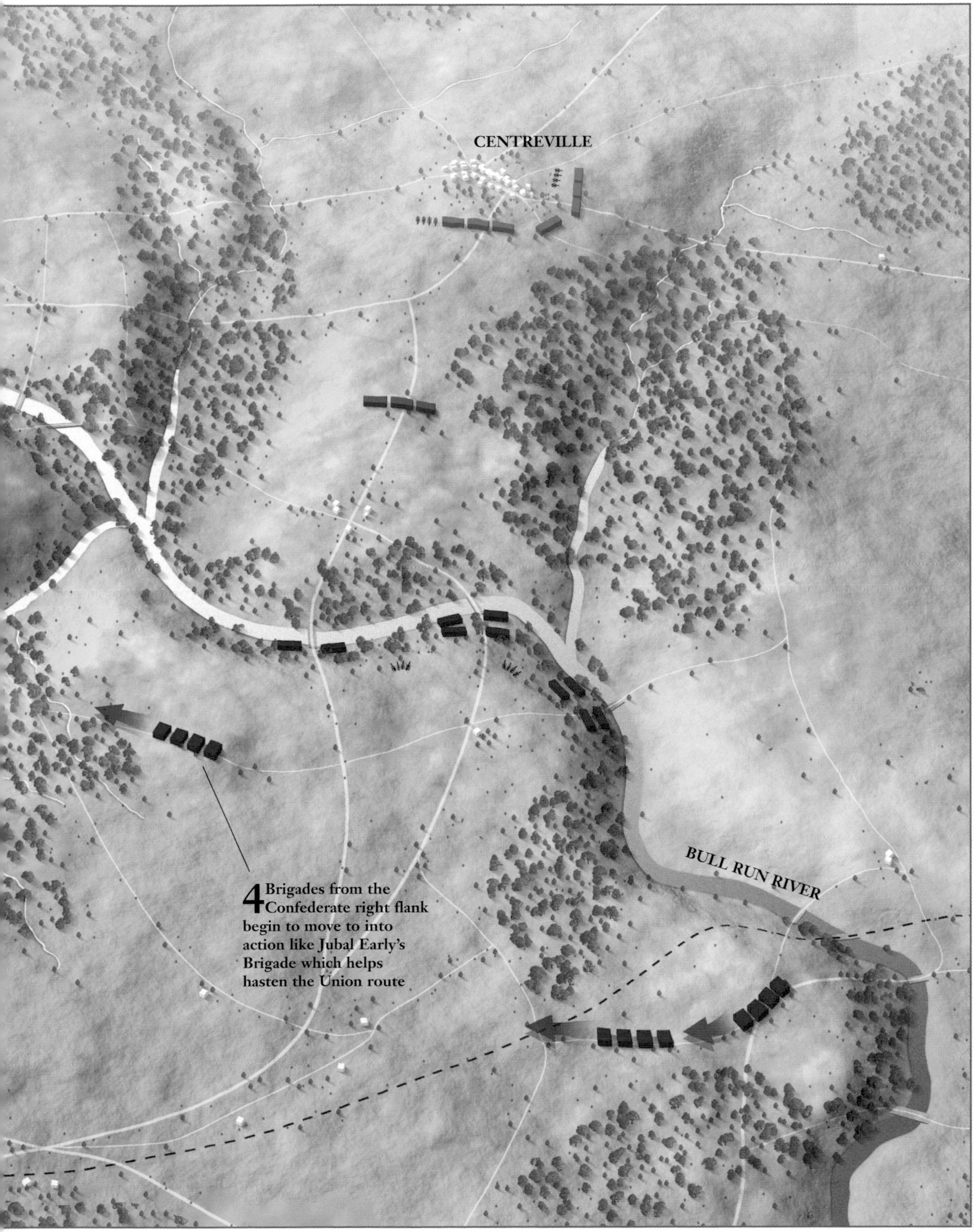

CENTREVILLE

BULL RUN RIVER

4 Brigades from the Confederate right flank begin to move to into action like Jubal Early's Brigade which helps hasten the Union route

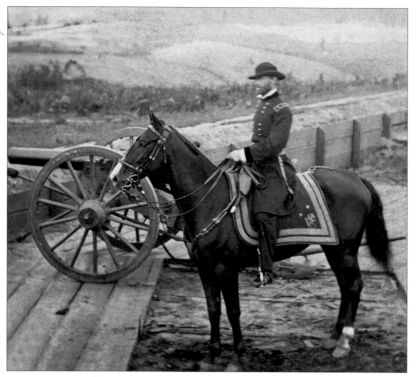

William T Sherman on his horse 'Duke' outside Atlanta in 1864. At the First Battle of Manassas, Sherman commanded the Third Brigade of Tyler's division which launched an attack against the Confederate flank, driving them from Matthews Hill. Although Sherman was wounded, he was one of the few Union officers to distinguish himself.

a halt at Fairfax Courthouse at noon to rest his troops and to restore communications with one of his divisions.

McDowell's slow advance and the delay at Fairfax Courthouse gave Beauregard time to redeploy and request reinforcement. Initially, Beauregard had deployed his forces on both sides of the Bull Run stream, but now he was able to pull all of his forces south of the stream and place them to cover key crossing points. Moreover, on 17 July, he was able to contact the government in Richmond, informing President Davis of this major Union offensive. Davis responded by ordering a few scattered units to join Beauregard, and ordered Joe Johnston to quit his position at Winchester and use the railroad to move his army to Manassas in support.

DISPOSITION OF FORCES

McDowell decided on a new plan of attack now that his forces were concentrated. This plan was to use one of his divisions, the First, to pin the main force of Confederates deployed along the Bull Run stream, while the remainder of his forces made a flanking manoeuvre to the east, turning the enemy's right flank. On 18 July, McDowell ordered the First Division under the command of Brigadier-General Daniel Tyler (1797–1882) to Centreville in preparation for the attack. Tyler was to occupy the town but avoid engaging the enemy.

McDowell, meanwhile, reconnoitred the roads and terrain in preparation for his flanking manoeuvre. From the beginning, things went wrong. McDowell discovered that neither the roads nor the terrain would allow him easily to turn the Confederate right, so he ordered the remaining divisions to follow Tyler to Centreville. As it happens, Tyler exceeded his orders and dispatched a brigade beyond Centreville to seize Blackburn's Ford, where Brigadier-General James Longstreet's (1821–1904) Virginians and Colonel Jubal Early's (1816–94) brigade soon engaged them. The Union troops were pushed back, causing considerable dismay among the other troops of Tyler's division.

Confused and frustrated, McDowell spent the next two days reorganizing his forces and drawing up another battle plan.

from joining forces. Scott approved the plan and ordered McDowell to move on 8 July, while Patterson was to move against Johnston on 2 July. But things did not go according to plan. It took McDowell until 16 July to get his inexperienced troops organized, supplied and on the move. In the meantime, Patterson crossed the Potomac, but advanced in such a way that Johnston, who had withdrawn to Winchester, was still able to support Beauregard.

On 16 July, McDowell's army was on the move. It was organized into five divisions – four of these divisions (the First, Second, Third and Fifth) advanced towards Manassas Junction, while the remaining division (the Fourth), consisting of eight regiments of volunteers and militia primarily from New Jersey, was left in Arlington as a reserve. The march was a difficult one for the green Union troops, who were unaccustomed to marching long distances loaded with their equipment and supplies. Many soldiers fell out of the column, often stopping to pick berries along the side of the road, forcing McDowell to halt his columns in order to allow stragglers to rejoin the ranks. The next day, he called

He decided to use Tyler's First Division, less the brigade that had been engaged on 18 July, for an advance against the Confederate forces along the Bull Run, focusing on the troops that held Stone Bridge. This was not to be the main attack, but rather a feint to hold the enemy's attention.

The main attack was to be a large flank march by Colonel David Hunter's (1802–86) Second Division and Colonel Samuel P Heintzelman's (1805–80) Third Division. They were to march to the northwest and appear on the Confederate left, crossing the Bull Run at Sudley Springs Ford and Poplar Ford.

Having crossed the Bull Run stream, they would then have been in a position to roll up the enemy's positions. The Fifth Division under Colonel Dixon Stansbury Miles (1804–62) was to serve as the attacking forces' reserve. McDowell's plan was sound but required a level of coordination more appropriate to the well-trained, disciplined troops of a Frederick the Great or a Napoleon, not the green troops under his command.

While McDowell was planning, Beauregard began receiving his much-needed reinforcements. On 18 July, Johnston began marching his troops, screened by Colonel JEB 'Jeb' Stuart's (1833–64) cavalry regiment, to Piedmont, where they would embark on trains and then proceed to Manassas Junction. Unfortunately, a lack of railroad capacity meant that these troops would arrive over the course of three days. On 19 July, Brigadier-General Thomas Jackson (1824–63) and his five regiments of Virginians arrived, along with two regiments from Georgia under Brigadier-General Francis Bartow (1816–61). On the following day, three regiments from Brigadier-General Barnard Elliott Bee's (1824–61) brigade arrived along with Brigadier-General Johnston. Also on 19 July, Jeb Stuart's cavalry and the Confederate artillery arrived, after having

STUART'S CAVALRY

JEB Stuart earned the reputation as one of the most dashing cavalry commanders of the Civil War. But despite this reputation, gone were the days of the massed cavalry charges of the Napoleonic era. The reasons behind this were the relatively low ratio of cavalry serving in Civil War armies and the growing lethality of infantry firearms and artillery. The Manassas campaign shows how Stuart would use his cavalry throughout the war. He commanded all of the Confederate horsemen. These troopers screened the movement of General Johnston's troops as they disengaged in the Shenandoah Valley and moved to Manassas. During the battle itself, they made a charge on Henry House Hill to drive away Union infantry, thus exposing two Union batteries. After the battle, some of Stuart's cavalry were involved in pursuing the fleeing Union forces. The massing of Confederate cavalry under Stuart would allow him to make his famous raids later in the war, although his detachment sometimes worked against the Confederacy such as at the Battle of Gettysburg where he was effectively out of the battle.

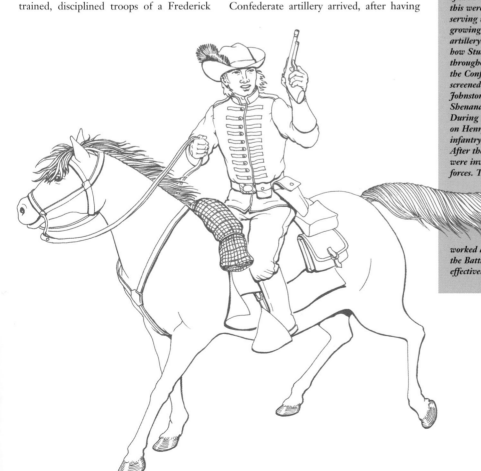

marched from Winchester. A fourth brigade under Brigadier-General Edmund Kirby Smith (1824–93) would not arrive until the afternoon of 21 July, after battle had already been joined. Most of the reinforcements were initially posted on the Confederate right, where McDowell had intended to launch his earlier flanking attack.

THE BATTLE

In order for McDowell's plan to work, Tyler needed to begin moving his troops well before dawn, since his troops needed to move forward before the other divisions could move down the road for their flank march. Tyler was to have started at 2:30 a.m., but, perhaps overly cautious as a result of the affair at Blackburn's Ford, he moved more slowly, not getting under way until after 3:30 a.m. and not reaching his position near the Stone Bridge until nearly 6:00 a.m. This resulted in delaying the movements of Hunter's and Heintzelman's divisions.

As Tyler's troops reached the Stone Bridge, they skirmished with a small Confederate force under the command of Colonel Nathan George Evans (1824–68). Evans was suspicious that this large Union force did not press the attack when he learned from some of his troops posted as

pickets, and from an officer stationed in the Signal Corps tower at Manassas Junction, that a large force of Union troops was moving to his left and preparing to cross the Bull Run at Sudley Springs Ford. Evans acted with initiative and, leaving a small force at the Stone Bridge, moved the majority of his troops, a regiment of South Carolinians and a battalion from Louisiana, to meet the new threat. Fortunately for Evans, the Union troops did not cross at 7:00 a.m. as planned, but nearly two hours later as a result of the delay from earlier that morning. Evans occupied a small hill, Matthews Hill, and vigorously engaged the Union troops of Hunter's division in a lengthy firefight, while the latter formed their battle lines. In the course of this engagement, Hunter, who had joined a regiment of Rhode Islanders, was wounded.

This allowed Beauregard, who saw how the Union attack was developing, to send reinforcements to the Confederate left, including the troops of Bee and Bartow, although they became more heavily engaged than was planned. These troops fought a desperate action for much of the morning, but the weight of numbers that favoured the Union forces began to tell and by midday the Confederates were compelled to retreat.

Fortunately, the Union forces did not press the attack, which allowed Jackson's troops, supported by artillery and, later, other units to occupy a new defensive position on Henry House Hill. This allowed the remnants of the troops from Matthews Hill to regroup. It was at this point that Bee, trying to rally his troops, pointed at the Virginians and told his men 'There stands Jackson like a stone wall', leading to the general's famous sobriquet of 'Stonewall' Jackson.

At about 1:30 p.m., the Union forces were finally able to begin their attack on Henry House Hill. It was a bloody affair, with both sides sending in reinforcements. Both sides were engaged in a fierce firefight and the Union used artillery at close range, although it would cost them two batteries as a result. The fight over the plateau had drawn virtually all of the troops from the Stone Bridge but Tyler never pressed the attack, contenting himself with occupying the

The First Battle of Manassas cost the Union nearly 2500 killed and wounded while the Confederacy suffered close to 2000 casualties. After such a battle, the field would have been a bleak place, with both the damage caused by the fighting and the bodies strewn about.

northern bank of the Bull Run. By mid-afternoon, the Union forces were in a position to use their superior numbers and turn the Confederate left when the last of the troops from Winchester arrived by train and marched directly into the fight. This prevented the Union flanking manoeuvre and when, at about 4:00 p.m., forces from the Confederate right joined them, the Union troops had finally had enough and broke. Once the retreat began, there was no hope of rallying the inexperienced Union regiments. The troops fled towards Washington, sweeping up picnickers who had stopped to watch the battle. An artillery round from a Confederate gun overturned a wagon on the bridge at Cubs Ford, leading to the abandonment of a number of Union artillery

pieces and wagons. Although, by now, there was virtually no organized resistance left, eight companies of US regulars were able to serve as a rearguard. In the event, it turned out that this was not really necessary. Although the Confederate forces had won the battle, they too were inexperienced and exhausted, and a pursuit would have been, most likely, a disaster for them. The First Battle of Manassas (also known as the First Battle of Bull Run) had been won because the Confederate commanders were better able to coordinate the movements of their troops than were their Union counterparts. While McDowell was plagued by delays and uncoordinated attacks, Beauregard and Johnston were able to move troops where they were needed at critical moments.

Monuments to fallen comrades quickly appeared on Civil War battlefields. The first monument raised at Manassas went up only six weeks after the battle. The monument depicted was erected after the war on 11 June 1865 at Henry House Hill and is ornamented with artillery shells. The inscription reads, 'In memory of the patriots who fell'.

FORT DONELSON
12–16 FEBRUARY 1862

CONTROL OF THE MAJOR RIVERS WAS AN IMPORTANT STRATEGIC OBJECTIVE IN THE CIVIL WAR. FORTS EQUIPPED WITH POWERFUL ARTILLERY COMMANDED THE RIVER PASSAGES AND HAD TO BE REMOVED BEFORE OPPOSITION FORCES COULD MAKE USE OF THE WATERWAY. MANY MAJOR OPERATIONS REVOLVED AROUND THESE FORTRESSES.

WHY DID IT HAPPEN?

WHO 27,000 Union troops under Brigadier-General Ulysses S Grant (1822–85) vs. 21,000 Confederates under Brigadier-General John B Floyd (1806–63).

WHAT Union forces surrounded the fort and probed the defences, prompting a Confederate breakout attempt.

WHERE Fort Donelson, on the Cumberland River in Tennessee.

WHEN 12–16 February 1862.

WHY Forts Donelson and Henry commanded the Cumberland and Tennessee Rivers, and provided the Confederacy with a secure base from which to threaten Kentucky. Union operations were launched to remove the Confederate presence.

OUTCOME The breakout was unsuccessful and the trapped Confederates were forced to surrender.

At the outset of the Civil War, not all states declared for either the Union or the Confederacy. One that remained undecided was Kentucky. Kentucky had the third-largest population of all the slave-owning states and held much in common with both sides. The state refused to furnish troops to assist the Union in putting down the Confederacy, but neither would it join the rebellion.

Internal politics were rather vigorous, with various parts of the state aligned with the two factions. Kentucky at first proclaimed strict neutrality, which was eminently acceptable to the Union. Lincoln

(1809–65) himself believed that Kentucky would in time come over to the Union side. Whatever happened, he knew, Kentucky must not join the Confederacy.

Both sides thus courted Kentucky, and eventually matters came to a head. The state government declared for the Union, but large elements of the state forces went south to fight for the Confederacy. The state was contested by regular and irregular military forces and divided in its loyalty.

Confederate sympathizers formed their own provisional state government in December 1861, which then declared secession and was welcomed into the

Rather than a professional military staff, General Grant gathered a select group of men he knew and trusted from civilian life. None had military experience but they worked well together and served Grant admirably.

Confederate States of America. The Union could not tolerate this situation. Kentucky was necessary to both sides and might swing either way. The obvious answer was to demonstrate control of the state by chasing the Confederate field armies out, so in the winter of 1861–62 the Union advanced through Kentucky and pushed the rebels southwards.

By the beginning of 1862, the main Confederate threat to Kentucky was represented by Fort Donelson and Fort Henry, on the Cumberland and Tennessee rivers respectively. These forts would provide a base for rebel forces advancing to renew the campaign for Kentucky and in addition commanded their respective waterways. Union strategy called for an advance down the Mississippi to split the Confederacy in two, but the tributaries had to be cleared first – including the Cumberland and Tennessee.

Thus the elimination of the Confederate presence at Henry and Donelson served two purposes: political and strategic. The job was given to a commander who was relatively unknown at the time – Brigadier-General Ulysses S Grant.

On 6 February 1862, General Grant attacked Fort Henry. His plan was to advance with two divisions overland while gunboats under Flag Officer Andrew H Foote (1806–63) covered the attack by bombarding the fort.

In the event, things went better than Grant could have hoped. The Tennessee River was rising, and the fort turned out to be badly sited. As the floodwaters inundated the fort and the gunboats approached, the fort commander, Brigadier-General Lloyd Tilghman (1816–63), was forced to surrender. Thus Grant took possession of the first fort without his army having to fire a shot. He would not have it so easy at Fort Donelson, however.

GRANT ADVANCES
As Grant marched overland towards Fort Donelson, the Confederate position was not good. The fort was a strategic asset but in order to defend it, it would be necessary

to funnel in more troops than could be spared. If the Confederate Army was defeated at Fort Donelson, it might mean the loss of central Tennessee, including the armament factories at Nashville.

Nevertheless, the decision was made to fight for the fort. Twelve thousand troops marched quickly up to reinforce the 5000 already there, and additional forces deployed in Kentucky were pulled back to bring the force at Fort Donelson up to about 21,000. Command was offered to Lieutenant-General PGT Beauregard (1818–93), who had taken charge of the operation against Port Sumter. Beauregard was ill at the time, so Brigadier-General John B Floyd was appointed instead.

FORT DONELSON

LOCATION

In the vast North American interior, rivers provided a route for resupply and troop movement. Many of the battles of the Civil War were fought over control of a river. The Battle of Fort Donelson was no exception.

FORT DONELSON

Floyd was a politician rather than a career officer, as were many commanders on both sides. Despite having just come from a less than inspiring stint with the Army of Northern Virginia, he was senior, so command passed to him. There were serious doubts in the Confederate command as to whether Donelson was defensible, especially after the disaster at Fort Henry.

There were also doubts on the Union side. Major-General Henry Halleck (1815–72), the theatre commander, considered Grant to be something of a loose cannon and was unsure as to whether Fort Donelson could be taken. The clash of personalities played a part in the campaign; Grant was determined to achieve as much as he could before Halleck lost his nerve, which Grant thought was likely if he took too long or suffered any real setbacks.

Grant initially thought that he could reach and capture Fort Donelson, then return to Fort Henry, all by 8 February. With only 18km (12 miles) between the two, it seemed feasible. However, bad weather slowed the operation down. Grant was not ready to commence hostilities against Donelson until 12 February.

On the eve of battle, Grant held a council of war, as was fashionable at the time. All but one of his generals agreed with the plan, and Grant was determined to press ahead. Such councils were most common when a commander was unsure of his own judgment, and it is significant that this was the last one that Grant held.

THE FIRST DAY

Grant had about 15,000 men under his command at this point, with reinforcements coming up. In addition to the two divisions deployed at Fort Henry, Grant was forming a third as the units to create it came in. He also had eight batteries of artillery and two regiments of cavalry available.

Opposite Grant's force, the Confederates had created a semicircular defensive position with Fort Donelson and the town of Dover at the corners. The position backed onto the Cumberland River. The Confederate forces included nine batteries of field artillery and a heavy artillery battery that commanded the river. There were also

three cavalry regiments under Colonel Nathan Bedford Forrest (1821–77).

The Confederate position was fairly strong, with the fort situated some 30m (100ft) above the level of the river and the infantry entrenched on a ridge, with their position improved by obstacles placed to impede an assault.

Much of the first day was spent by the Union force in reaching the field and getting into position. Forrest's cavalry

Union naval officer Andrew H Foote later in life. Foote was highly commended for his brave and successful attack on Fort Henry, in the run-up to the encounter at Fort Donelson.

brigade harassed the deployment, causing delay. The Southern cavalry were highly skilled in the traditional screening role, and carried it out well. All the signs were that Floyd was going to make an aggressive defence of the fort. The first of the Union gunboats arrived during the day and exchanged fire with Fort Donelson for a time before withdrawing. Grant himself established his headquarters and assessed the situation, laying his plans for the

coming battle, which by now, he knew, would not be a walkover like Fort Henry.

THE SECOND DAY

Grant wanted detailed reconnaissance of the enemy positions and, contrary to his reckless reputation, gave orders for probing attacks only. No general engagement was to be initiated. The first probe was to be made by two brigades on the Union left. After some skirmishing, this attack stalled, degenerating

In this painting, Confederate cavalry under the command of Colonel Nathan Bedford Forrest gallop through woods near Fort Donelson.

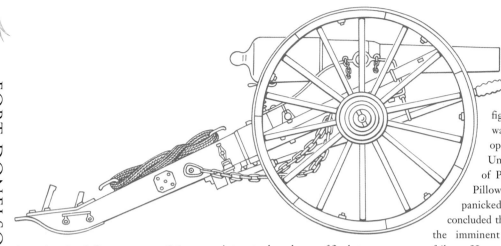

A recent invention, the Parrott gun was a rifled muzzle-loader. The commonest version was a 10-pounder with superior range and accuracy to the smoothbore 12-pound 'Napoleon'. Heavier guns were also built.

into a steady exchange of fire between troops remaining carefully under cover.

However, on the Union right, Brigadier-General John A McClernand (1812–1900), the only one of Grant's commanders to disagree about the attack, launched his own assault without orders. This was aimed at removing an artillery battery that was irritating McClernand's force. The attack was a confused affair involving three regiments from two different brigades, and it was not made clear to the officers involved who was in overall command.

The resulting chaos robbed the attack of any chance it might have had, and the three regiments were halted well short of their objective by intense fire. Casualties were heavy, and many of the wounded who might otherwise have survived perished when the grass they lay in caught fire.

The second day ended with a blizzard. Many of Grant's troops lacked coats or blankets due to supply issues on the march, and campfires could not be built as they highlighted soldiers for enemy marksmen.

THE THIRD DAY

During the bitter night of 13/14 February, Floyd held his own council of war, which came to the consensus that the fort could not be held. The forces trapped within the defensive line were vital to the defence of Tennessee, and in particular Nashville, and must be preserved. The only option was to break out and escape.

Brigadier-General Gideon J Pillow (1806–78) was given the task of leading the breakout from Donelson. An aggressive

fighting commander, Pillow was a good choice but the operation was delayed when a Union sharpshooter killed one of Pillow's aides close to him. Pillow may or may not have panicked, but in any case he concluded that the enemy was aware of the imminent operation, ensuring its failure. He postponed the breakout, to Floyd's annoyance.

The day dawned and the pattern of sniping and probing continued until midday, when another Union brigade arrived overland. Shortly afterwards, more gunboats came up, along with several thousand more Union soldiers aboard steamers. This was precisely the sort of development that the riverine forts were supposed to prevent.

Foote's gunboats went in to attack the fort at about 3:00 p.m. This time, however, things were different from how they had been at Fort Henry. Heavy artillery including 10 32-pounder smoothbores and two rifled cannon opened up at a range of about 480m (525 yards), pounding the Union gunboats. The fight was short, with the four Union boats taking about 170 hits between them. Two were disabled and all were damaged. There were three more boats available but these were 'timberclads', armoured more lightly (with thick timbers rather than iron) and even less able to withstand the devastating fire from the fort.

Grant realized that the naval assault was not going to work this time, and weighing up the odds he concluded that a land attack was not guaranteed to succeed either. He informed his superior, Halleck, that a siege might be necessary.

Armies have always foraged on the march, and here Grant's men appear to have located furniture rather than food. It seems likely that these benches were 'borrowed' from a small town's church or school.

THE OPPOSED FORCES

FEDERAL
riverine force comprising:
– 4 ironclads
– 3 timberclad gunboats
Total: **27,000**

CONFEDERATE
fortress artillery and troops
Total: **21,000**

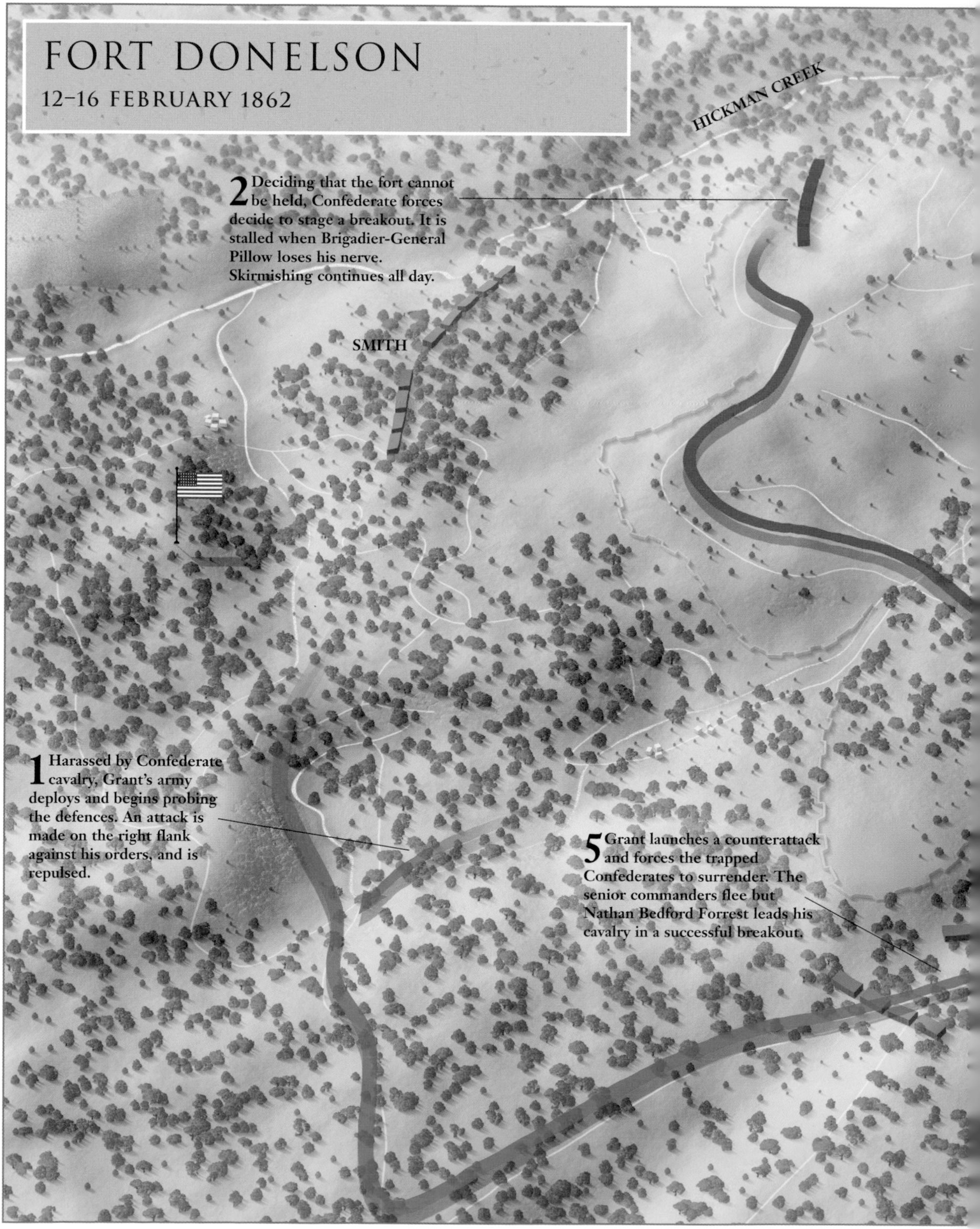

FORT DONELSON
12–16 FEBRUARY 1862

HICKMAN CREEK

2 Deciding that the fort cannot be held, Confederate forces decide to stage a breakout. It is stalled when Brigadier-General Pillow loses his nerve. Skirmishing continues all day.

SMITH

1 Harassed by Confederate cavalry, Grant's army deploys and begins probing the defences. An attack is made on the right flank against his orders, and is repulsed.

5 Grant launches a counterattack and forces the trapped Confederates to surrender. The senior commanders flee but Nathan Bedford Forrest leads his cavalry in a successful breakout.

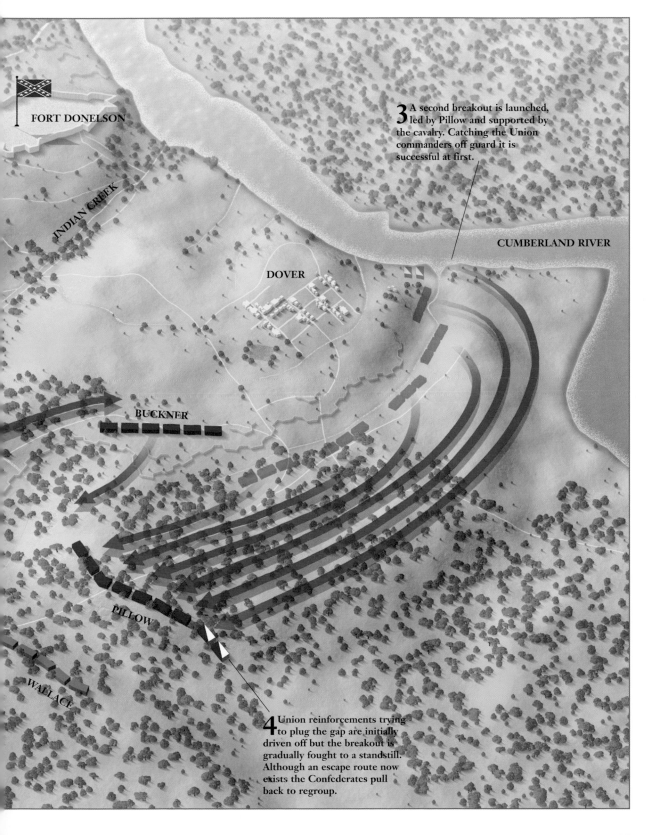

FORT DONELSON

INDIAN CREEK

CUMBERLAND RIVER

DOVER

BUCKNER

PILLOW

WALLACE

3 A second breakout is launched, led by Pillow and supported by the cavalry. Catching the Union commanders off guard it is successful at first.

4 Union reinforcements trying to plug the gap are initially driven off but the breakout is gradually fought to a standstill. Although an escape route now exists the Confederates pull back to regroup.

FORT DONELSON

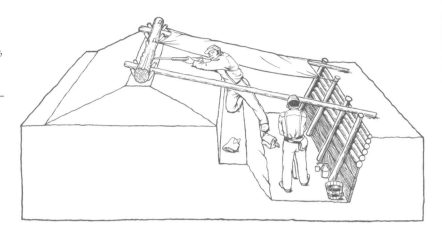

This illustration shows a typical entrenchment of the period. Well-prepared entrenchments would include such features as a headlog resting on top of blocks, with a firing slit beneath, a firing step, and supported trench walls.

THE FOURTH DAY

After another council of war, Floyd decided that his breakout plan was still the only viable option. Pillow was again detailed to lead it, and this time the assault went ahead.

At first light on 15 February, the Confederates came storming out of their positions and fell on McClernand's division at the right-hand end of the Union line. The foul weather actually worked to the Union troops' advantage; it was so cold that many men were awake trying to keep warm. Thus rather than a few sleepy sentries, Pillow's men were opposed by a larger number of wakeful, if chilled, troops.

Grant himself was caught off guard. Not expecting any real activity among the defenders, he had gone to visit the naval commander and, as the attack opened, was aboard Foote's flagship.

The Confederate attack achieved considerable success in the first two hours. Supported by Forrest's cavalry, who fought dismounted as often as not, Pillow's division pushed McClernand's back and aside, opening up a gap to escape through. The Union forces fell back in reasonably good order but they were under severe pressure.

McClernand knew he was in trouble and sent for help. But Grant had failed to delegate command to anyone in his absence and, without his authority, Brigadier-General Lew Wallace (1827–1905), commanding the newly formed Third Division, was reluctant to respond.

Things became steadily worse for the right flank. Ready ammunition was running out, and there was no resupply available. The previously orderly fighting retreat was beginning to crumble. McClernand sent a second messenger to Wallace, with a desperate entreaty for help, any sort of help – and soon. Wallace finally responded, shifting two brigades across to bolster the right. However, they were quickly flanked and forced back.

The Confederates were also suffering command problems. Seeing the Union flank turned, Forrest pushed for a headlong general assault, but all he got was a measured advance. Meanwhile, Pillow had realized that Brigadier-General Simon Bolivar Buckner's (1823–1914) division was not attacking. He demanded support, which

In this stylized illustration, Union troops attempt to storm a heavily defended Confederate redoubt at the Battle of Fort Donelson.

resulted in an exchange of hot words before Buckner finally got moving.

Buckner's division joined Pillow's and drove the Federal troops back, but the advance was slowing. McClernand's division was in disarray but enough of Wallace's men were engaged that a defensive line of sorts could be formed, and this bought McClernand some time to re-form his units. After three assaults on the Union line, the Confederates pulled back somewhat to regroup. This was about 12:30 p.m. The trap had been forced open, however. It was now possible to break out and escape.

About 30 minutes later Grant reached Wallace's headquarters, having been summoned from his conference with Foote. His command was in chaos, but Grant quickly took charge. First he sent a messenger to Foote, ordering him to advance with his gunboats and make as much noise as possible. Grant hoped the sounds of naval gunfire would encourage his wavering men. The Union commander also learned that some of the Confederate troops were carrying knapsacks, and correctly deduced that this was a breakout attempt rather than an attempt to win the battle. He began planning an attack, and the opposition obliged by handing him a splendid opportunity.

Despite the fact that he had opened the way for a breakout, Pillow did not exploit it. Instead, he was determined to regroup his force and bring up supplies before marching out. For some reason he concluded that this was best done in his original positions, and withdrew his division to their trenches. Floyd, in overall command of the Confederate force, decided to pull his entire command back in.

Grant ordered Brigadier-General Charles F Smith (1807–62), commanding the Union Second Division, unengaged on the left flank, to make the decisive attack. His orders were to do no less than take Fort Donelson, and Smith began an advance with two brigades. A lone regiment of Tennessee infantry attempted to resist the assault but was pushed out of its positions. Smith consolidated his gains and beat off several counterattacks late in the day.

Meanwhile, Wallace had managed to re-form some units and, with three brigades

(one from each division), he began to advance. Wallace's force was able to advance back to more or less where McClernand had started the day.

THE FINAL DAY

The night of 15/16 February was marked by another snowstorm, which killed many of the wounded. Although Grant had not actually plugged the gap that Pillow had made in his lines and the way was open for

Brigadier-General Lew Wallace commanded the newly formed Third Division at the Battle of Fort Donelson.

a Confederate breakout, he had decided to attack again in the morning. Meanwhile, Pillow and Floyd were congratulating one another and sending telegraphs to Nashville with news of a victory.

Sanity returned to the Confederate camp, assisted by Buckner, who gloomily informed Floyd that he could not hope to stop a renewed assault for even an hour. Sanity was then quickly displaced by defeatism, and Floyd turned over command

to Pillow. Floyd was wanted in the Union for corruption and supporting secession, and so feared capture.

UNCONDITIONAL SURRENDER

Pillow did not like the prospect of capture any better than his superior. Turning over command to Buckner, he escaped across the river in a small boat. Floyd's departure was a little more honourable, in that he left aboard a steamer with two regiments of

Union troops advance against prepared Confederate positions dimly seen through the smoke of battle. Casualties in an assault were always high, even before the attacking troops reached the enemy line.

troops and could, at least, pretend to have been trying to salvage something from the defeat rather than blatantly fleeing. Colonel Forrest was unimpressed by these less than heroic gestures and led his surviving cavalry in a successful breakout.

Buckner sent a note to Grant asking for surrender terms. The two had served together in happier times, but Grant was not inclined to be merciful. He demanded full surrender, and thus gained his nickname of 'Unconditional Surrender' Grant. Buckner knew he had no option. Smith was established within the Confederate position and ready to make an assault that Buckner knew he could not stop. Able to do nothing more than protest Grant's hard line, Buckner surrendered his command, ending the Battle of Fort Donelson.

AFTERMATH

The Battle of Fort Donelson cost Grant almost 3000 casualties. The Confederates lost 2000 killed and wounded. However, the defeat at Donelson was particularly costly to the Confederacy, as the Confederate Army was not merely routed; more than 12,000 men became prisoners and were lost to the war effort. This led to an inability to defend Tennessee properly and a retreat southwards that would eventually lead to the bloody clash at Shiloh. Nashville, with its arms factories and transport hub, was abandoned at the end of the month.

The Union could now begin the long drive down the Mississippi but, more importantly, the Confederate threat to Kentucky was gone and most of Tennessee would soon be under Federal control.

As the Civil War went on, procedures for locating casualties and bringing them to aid stations were implemented. Were this grisly but necessary task not undertaken, men who might well fight again would often die on the battlefield, sometimes days after the fighting ended.

KERNSTOWN
23 MARCH 1862

VIRGINIA'S SHENANDOAH VALLEY WAS CRITICAL TO THE CONFEDERACY BOTH AS AN AGRICULTURAL BREADBASKET AND AS A POTENTIAL INVASION ROUTE INTO THE NORTH. IN THE SPRING OF 1862, MAJOR-GENERAL THOMAS 'STONEWALL' JACKSON CONDUCTED A BRILLIANT CAMPAIGN THERE, USING SUPERIOR STRATEGY AND HARD MARCHING TO DEFEAT A MUCH LARGER FEDERAL FOE.

WHY DID IT HAPPEN?

WHO Confederate forces under Major-General Thomas 'Stonewall' Jackson (1824–63) battled the much larger Federal forces of Major-Generals Banks, Shields and Fremont.

WHAT Jackson defeated the Federals in a series of battles, including Kernstown (23 March), McDowell (8 May), Front Royal (23 May), Cross Keys (8 June) and Port Republic (9 June).

WHERE The Shenandoah Valley, Virginia.

WHEN March to June 1862.

WHY Jackson used interior lines and hard marching to defeat the uncoordinated Federal armies.

OUTCOME Jackson's success caused President Lincoln (1809–65) such concern for the safety of Washington that he withheld troops earmarked for Major-General George B McClellan's (1826–85) Peninsula Campaign.

From the very beginning of McClellan's planning for an operation on the Virginia Peninsula, events in the Shenandoah Valley had been of great importance. Terminating on the Potamac River just 48km (30 miles) northwest of Washington, the Valley represented a potential Confederate avenue of approach into the Federal capital.

President Abraham Lincoln had demanded that McClellan leave an adequate force behind to guarantee Washington's safety. Pursuant to this requirement, McClellan issued instructions to Major-General Nathaniel Banks (1816–94) on 16 March 1862, ordering him to 'open your communications with the valley of the Shenandoah. As soon as the Manassas Gap Railway is in running order, intrench a

brigade of infantry, say four regiments, with two batteries, at or near the point where the railway crosses the Shenandoah. Something like two regiments of cavalry should be left in the vicinity to occupy Winchester and thoroughly scour the country south of the railway and up the Shenandoah Valley. The general object is to cover the line of the Potomac and Washington.'

In reality, the defensive-minded General Joseph E Johnston (1807–91) was certainly not contemplating a Confederate offensive against Washington. He was beginning to feel very vulnerable with his position at Manassas, especially since the coming warm spring weather would dry the roads and make it possible for McClellan to attack with superior numbers. Johnston had no intention of waiting around long enough for

Few locations saw more of the Civil War than the Shenandoah Valley town of Winchester, Virginia. Three battles were fought there and formal possession of the town went back and forth between Federals and Confederates 14 times.

this to happen. On 7 March, he ordered all of his troops east of the Blue Ridge Mountains, some 42,000 effectives, to withdraw to the Rappahannock River, nearly half the distance to Richmond. Only Jackson's 5400 men would remain in the Shenandoah Valley to threaten the right flank of any Federal advance.

Unaware of McClellan's plans for an amphibious turning movement, Johnston expected the Federals to march directly south to Richmond. Accordingly, he ordered Jackson's Valley Army to fall back in line with the main army, protect its flank, secure the Blue Ridge passes and slow or stop enemy progress up the Shenandoah. Of greatest importance was the fact that Johnston needed Jackson to prevent Banks from reinforcing McClellan. Johnston could not have expected much from Jackson's small Valley Army. As it turned out, the Shenandoah Valley Campaign would be nothing short of a masterpiece.

KERNSTOWN

When McClellan learned of Johnston's withdrawal, he ordered his armies to push forward on all fronts. Cautiously, Banks and his 38,000 men moved up the Valley and occupied Winchester on 12 March, only to find that Jackson had departed the previous day. Jackson had fallen back to Mount Jackson, 56km (35 miles) to the south, where he learned from Colonel Turner Ashby's (1828–62) cavalry reports that part of Banks's army was preparing to head east to reinforce McClellan as he prepared to embark on his Peninsula Campaign. Indeed, on 20 March, Brigadier-General Alpheus Williams (1810–78) and his 7000 men had started for Manassas and Brigadier-General James Shields's (1810–79) 9000-man division had dropped back from Strasburg and was prepared to follow.

Jackson's mission was to hold Banks in place, so the Confederate began hurrying his forces north. In the meantime, Ashby's troopers clashed with Shields's pickets just south of Winchester on 22 March. Shields was wounded in the fighting, but he developed a solid plan before he left the

field. He ordered part of his division to move south of Winchester during the night, and another brigade to march north, to give the appearance of abandoning Winchester. However, that brigade would then halt and remain ready to return when Jackson approached. That same night, Confederate loyalists from Winchester mistakenly told Ashby that Shields had left only a four-regiment rearguard and even these were under orders to depart for Harpers Ferry the next day.

At about 2:00 p.m. on 23 March, Jackson rode into Kernstown, 6km (4 miles) south of Winchester, where Ashby told him the good news. Jackson was faced with a dilemma. His men were tired from marching 40km (25 miles) on 22 March and a further 26km (16 miles) on 23 March. Already some 1500 stragglers trailed behind. Even more

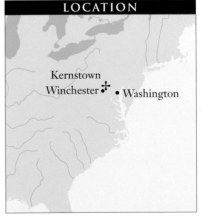

LOCATION

Kernstown
Winchester ✚ • Washington

Geography gave the Shenandoah Valley great military significance. Its southwest to northeast direction made it an ideal Confederate invasion avenue into the Federal capital in Washington.

KERNSTOWN

Between March and June 1862, Major-General Thomas 'Stonewall' Jackson led his 'foot cavalry' to victory over numerically superior but uncoordinated Federal armies in several battles.

THE OPPOSED FORCES

FEDERAL
Total: 60,000

CONFEDERATE
Total: 16,000
(under Jackson)

distressing to Jackson was the fact it was a Sunday. Traditionally, the pious Jackson rigorously adhered to the Sabbath – even considering government mail delivery on Sunday to be a violation of Divine Law and urging Congress to end such activity.

On the other hand, Jackson had a fleeting opportunity to defeat an isolated part of the Federal Army. He could not wait a day and still accomplish his mission of holding Banks in place. Although the decision distressed him, Jackson attacked Shields at Kernstown on Sunday, 23 March. He explained to his wife, Anna, who was also troubled by the action: 'You appear much concerned at my attacking on Sunday. I was greatly concerned too, but I felt it my duty to do it, in consideration of the ruinous effects that might result from postponing the battle until morning. So far as I can see, my course was a wise one; the best that I could do under the circumstances, though very distasteful to my feelings; and I hope and pray to our Heavenly Father that I may never again be circumstanced on that day.'

In fact, Kernstown was a tactical defeat for Jackson in which he suffered 718 casualties compared to 568 Federal losses. Against far superior numbers, the Confederates ultimately ran low on ammunition and were forced to withdraw 7km (4.5 miles) south to Newtown.

Strategically, however, Kernstown was a huge Confederate victory. Jackson's presence and aggressive action caused the Federal authorities to halt plans to shift forces to McClellan. Instead, Banks was held in place, Brigadier-General Louis Blenker's (1812–63) division was withdrawn from McClellan and sent to oppose Jackson, and Major-General Irvin McDowell's (1818–85) First Corps was withheld from McClellan. The Federals then established three separate and independent commands: the Department of the Rappahannock, under McDowell; the Department of the Shenandoah, under Banks; and the Mountain Department, under Major-General John Fremont (1813–90). These three commanders reported directly to

Washington, and no general on the scene was charged with synchronizing their operations. This uncoordinated command structure would ultimately contribute to Jackson's success.

GREATER POSSIBILITIES

In April, Major-General Richard S Ewell (1817–72) arrived to reinforce Jackson with 8500 men. Jackson also received permission to use Brigadier-General Edward 'Allegheny' Johnson's (1816–73) small division, which brought Jackson's total strength to 17,000. Jackson left Ewell to hold Banks in place, while Jackson, keeping his own plans secret even from his subordinates, went on the move.

As President Jefferson Davis' military advisor, General Robert E Lee (1807–70) had already seen an opportunity to use Jackson in the Valley to threaten McClellan's plans for the Peninsula. On 21 April, Lee wrote to Jackson: 'I have no doubt an attempt will be made to occupy Fredericksburg and use it as a base of

Brigadier-General Alpheus Williams commanded a division under Major-General Nathaniel Banks, whose brief was to safeguard Washington during Major-General George B McClellan's Peninsula Campaign of 1862.

operations against Richmond. Our present force there is very small.... If you can use General Ewell's division in an attack on General Banks and drive him back, it will prove a great relief to the pressure on Fredericksburg.' While Lee was trying to buy time to concentrate forces on the

Peninsula, the immediate Confederate response to McClellan's Peninsula Campaign was actually Jackson's effort in the Valley.

Banks thought Jackson was headed for Richmond, but on 8 May Jackson suddenly appeared at McDowell, 51.5km (32 miles) west of Stanton. There, he defeated the 6000 Federals commanded by Fremont. Jackson knew Fremont's army was closing in from the Allegheny Mountains, west of the Shenandoah Valley, and a junction between Fremont and Banks would have been disastrous to Jackson. Instead, the victory secured Jackson's left flank, and he then hurried back into the Valley to join Ewell for a concentrated effort against Banks.

By mid-May, part of Banks's army was again preparing to depart to join McClellan

In 1857 the United States Army fielded a new 12-pounder gun-howitzer. This multipurpose piece was designed to replace existing guns and howitzers. It could fire canister and shell like the 12-pounder howitzer and solid shot at an effective range of 1535m (1680 yards) like the 12-pounder gun.

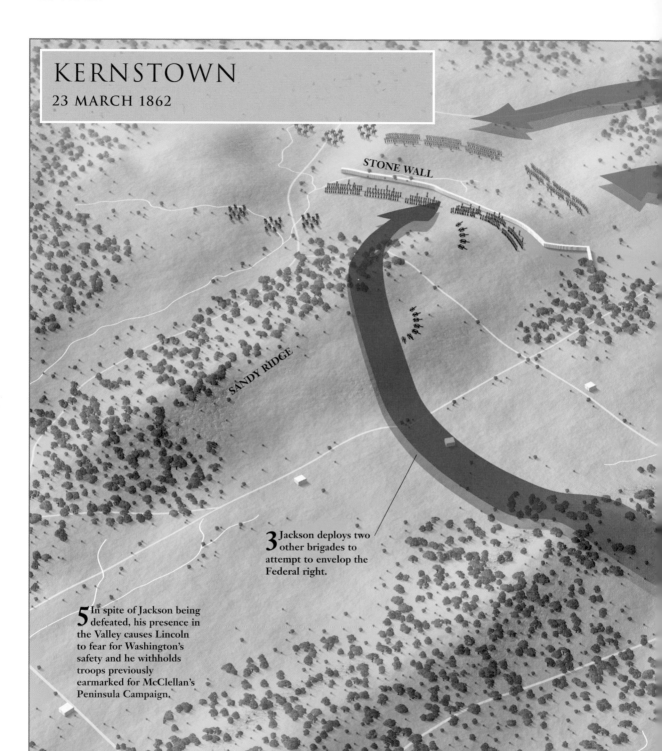

KERNSTOWN
23 MARCH 1862

STONE WALL

SANDY RIDGE

3 Jackson deploys two other brigades to attempt to envelop the Federal right.

5 In spite of Jackson being defeated, his presence in the Valley causes Lincoln to fear for Washington's safety and he withholds troops previously earmarked for McClellan's Peninsula Campaign.

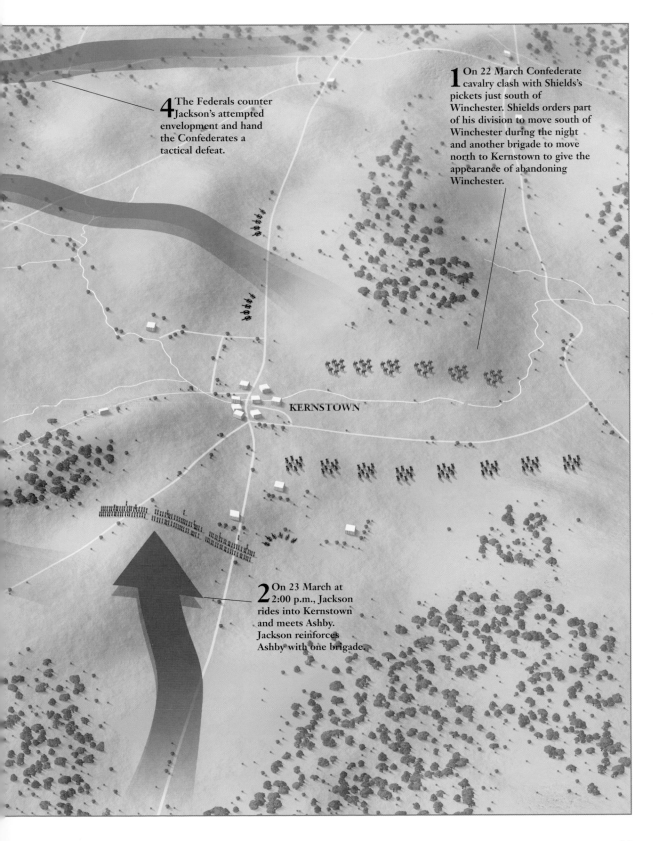

4 The Federals counter Jackson's attempted envelopment and hand the Confederates a tactical defeat.

1 On 22 March Confederate cavalry clash with Shields's pickets just south of Winchester. Shields orders part of his division to move south of Winchester during the night and another brigade to move north to Kernstown to give the appearance of abandoning Winchester.

KERNSTOWN

2 On 23 March at 2:00 p.m., Jackson rides into Kernstown and meets Ashby. Jackson reinforces Ashby with one brigade.

KERNSTOWN

Yorktown before the evacuation. Brilliant in its own right, the larger significance of Jackson's Shenandoah Valley Campaign lay in the effect it had on diverting resources from McClellan's Peninsula Campaign.

outside Richmond. Jackson used a cavalry screen to make Banks think Jackson was headed toward Strasburg. Instead, the Confederate general turned unexpectedly across the Massanuttens, joined with Ewell at Luray, and with their combined 16,000 men struck the unsuspecting 1000 Federals at Front Royal on 23 May. Jackson tore through the town and the Federals fled towards Strasburg. Then Banks and Jackson began a race to Winchester. On 25 May, the two armies collided in what became another victory for Jackson.

EFFECT ON THE PENINSULA

These events were occurring right as General McClellan's efforts were beginning

to bear fruit on the Peninsula, with the Confederates evacuating Yorktown on 3 May, withdrawing towards Richmond and, in the process, abandoning Norfolk. On 18 May, McClellan had received a telegram from Secretary of War Edwin Stanton (1814–69) announcing that McDowell's First Corps would be marching from Fredericksburg, where it had been held previously for fear of Washington's safety, and would soon join him. But Jackson's success in the Valley was beginning to have a much broader impact. President Lincoln, who had never been comfortable with McClellan's provisions for Washington's safety, was now seriously worried. On 24 May, Lincoln telegraphed

McClellan: 'In consequence of Gen. Banks' critical position I have been compelled to suspend Gen. McDowell's movement to join you.'

McClellan complained that 'the object of Jackson's movement was probably to prevent reinforcements being sent to me' rather than to attack Washington. McDowell agreed, stating that 'It is impossible that Jackson can have been largely reinforced. He is merely creating a diversion and the surest way to bring him from the lower valley is for me to move rapidly on Richmond.' Such arguments failed to convince Lincoln, and the order stood. Disgustedly, McDowell lamented: 'If the enemy can succeed so readily in disconcerting all our plans by alarming us first at one point then at another, he will paralyze a larger force with a very small one.' This is exactly what Jackson had succeeded in doing.

At first Jackson's operations had caught the authorities in Washington off guard. Now Lincoln and Stanton became obsessed with the idea of trapping Jackson. They ordered McDowell and his 40,000-man corps to join Fremont's at Strasburg. At the beginning of June, Banks, Fremont and Shields began converging on Jackson from the west, north and east in the hopes of bagging him at Strasburg.

To take full advantage of his central position in the Shenandoah Valley, Jackson had developed an excellent routine for his marches. His men would march for 50

In the Shenandoah Valley, 'Stonewall' Jackson faced vastly superior Federal armies commanded by Nathaniel Banks (shown here), Irvin McDowell and John Fremont. Each of these three officers operated independently, which hindered Federal unity of effort.

minutes, halt for a 10-minute rest, and then resume the march. At midday, they would have an hour for lunch. The role of the chain of command was clearly articulated: 'Brigade commanders will see that the foregoing rules are strictly adhered to, and for this purpose will, from time to time, allow his command to move by him, so as to verify its condition. He will also designate one of his staff officers to do the same at such times as he may deem necessary.' This strict regime and the accompanying results caused Jackson's command to become known as the 'foot cavalry'.

Now Jackson employed these techniques to march his men 80.5km (50 miles) in two days to escape the Federal trap closing in on Strasburg and then fell back to Harrisonburg. Fremont and Shields pursued on parallel roads that would eventually meet at Port Republic. Jackson positioned Ewell 6km (4 miles) to the northwest at Cross Keys and stationed his own men on the rolling hills of Port Republic.

Ewell selected a line astride the Port Republic Road on a high, wooded ridge. At 9:00 a.m. on 8 June, Fremont's men, advancing down Port Republic Road, met Ewell's pickets. Fremont launched a weak

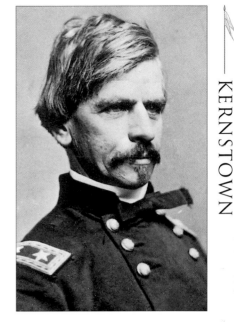

Although a tactical defeat for the Confederates, Kernstown was a strategic victory because Jackson's presence and aggressive action caused Lincoln to fear for the security of Washington.

KERNSTOWN

attack against Ewell's right flank, but was easily repulsed. Casualties on both sides were light, with Ewell losing 288 and Fremont 684, but Fremont withdrew from the field. Ewell left a few men to watch Fremont and then withdrew during the night to assist Jackson at Port Republic.

There, Jackson was in a close fight with Shields, but Ewell arrived just in time to turn the tide. Fremont could hear the fighting and took up the pursuit, but Ewell's rearguard had burned the bridge that Fremont needed to cross. Fremont could only watch as Jackson and Ewell defeated Shields and forced him to withdraw.

Jackson's victory at Port Republic was the climax of the Valley Campaign. He had defeated portions of four Federal armies totalling over 60,000 men. In the process he was changing events on the Peninsula as well. When Lee replaced Johnston, the new commander of the Army of Northern Virginia took advantage of the opportunity created by Jackson's success in the Valley. On 8 June, Lee wrote to Jackson: 'Should there be nothing requiring your attention in the valley so as to prevent your leaving it for a few days, and you can make arrangements

Opposite: Surrounded by his staff, Thomas 'Stonewall' Jackson is saluted by his men during the Shenandoah Valley campaign. Jackson had previously served with distinction in the Mexican War (1846–48).

to deceive the enemy and impress him with the idea of your presence, please let me know, that you may unite at the decisive movement with the army near Richmond.'

Three days later, Lee further explained that Jackson would 'sweep down between the Chickahominy and Pamunkey, cutting up the enemy's communications, etc., while this army attacks General McClellan in front. He will thus, I think, be forced to come out of his intrenchments where he is strongly posted on the Chickahominy and preparing to move by gradual approaches on Richmond.'

'The sooner you unite with this army the better,' Lee told Jackson on 16 June. Jackson's Valley Campaign had been the Confederates' first response to McClellan's offensive by diverting Federal resources from the Peninsula. Now Jackson's success would allow him to join Lee, giving him the numbers he needed to go on the offensive.

Until the advent of breech-loading rifles, loading from the prone was a slow and difficult process. Early breech-loaders were technically unsatisfactory because gas and flame escaped from the breech. Eventually, however, a good breech-loader, the Sharps, was developed at Harpers Ferry.

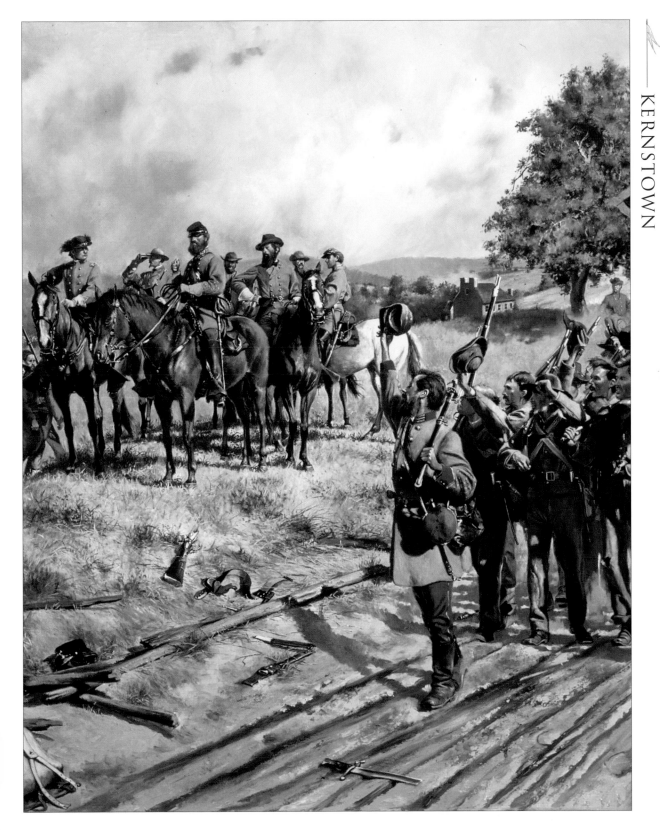

SHILOH
6–7 APRIL 1862

GENERAL ALBERT SIDNEY JOHNSTON'S ATTACK AT SHILOH WAS A CHANCE TO CRUSH A UNION FORCE BEFORE THE ARMIES OF THE OHIO AND TENNESSEE COULD EFFECT A JUNCTION. ONCE THESE FORCES COMBINED, THE REBELS WOULD BE AT A SIGNIFICANT NUMERICAL DISADVANTAGE. FAILURE TO WIN AT SHILOH RESULTED IN THIS HAPPENING ANYWAY AND, THEREAFTER, THE CONFEDERACY WAS ON THE DEFENSIVE IN THE WEST

WHY DID IT HAPPEN?

WHO Union Army of the Tennessee under Major-General Ulysses S Grant (1822–85) and Union Army of the Ohio under Brigadier-General Don Carlos Buell (1818–98), making a total of 62,000 vs. Confederate Army of Mississippi under General Albert Sidney Johnston (1803–62) totalling 44,000.

WHAT The Confederates attacked and pushed Grant's army back all day on 6 April, but were driven off the following day after Union reinforcements arrived.

WHERE 40km (25 miles) north of Corinth, Mississippi, at Shiloh on the Tennessee River.

WHEN 6–7 April 1862.

WHY The Confederate Army launched a surprise attack against Grant's command, hoping to destroy it before it was reinforced by Buell's force. This was necessary to prevent a concentration and thereby to protect the rail junction at Corinth.

OUTCOME After a day of hard-won successes in which Johnston was killed and replaced by Lieutenant-General PGT Beauregard (1818–93), the Confederates were forced to retire and ultimately to evacuate Corinth.

In the first months of the Civil War, both sides were convinced that the matter could be settled fairly quickly, and neither the Union nor the Confederacy was ready for a long war. The slaughter at Shiloh was an early indication that the struggle would be long and bitter.

Although towns and forts changed hands, many of the strategic objectives of the war, which led to eventual victory for the Union, were important as hubs or conduits of transportation rather than having political significance. Railway junctions and rivers, permitting rapid movement of supplies and forces, were of critical importance. One

such was the rail junction at Corinth, Mississippi, which linked the east–west Memphis and Charleston Railroad with the north–south Mobile & Ohio Railroad. If the Confederacy could be deprived of Corinth, its logistics capabilities would be dealt a serious blow.

The highly motivated but poorly trained forces on both sides had clashed to the north of Corinth over the winter of 1861–62, and the Confederates had come off worst. With the loss of Forts Henry and Donelson, the Rebel army under Johnston had been pushed out of southern Kentucky and most of Tennessee. Johnston pulled

William Tecumseh Sherman with his staff. Wars in Europe had demonstrated the value of a well-trained, trusted and reliable staff to support a general officer. Good staff work tended to be the exception rather than the rule in the inexperienced armies of 1862.

SHILOH

further back and established a new line to protect the vital railroads, which linked Richmond to Memphis and allowed forces to be brought forward from the far south.

Johnston's army was a little more experienced and better trained now, and he decided that he must strike rather than awaiting a Union move. Using the railroad to marshal supplies and men at Corinth, Johnston marched out on 2 April 1862. His plan was to fall on Grant's Army of the Tennessee and destroy it before reinforcements in the form of Buell's Army of the Ohio could arrive. Despite reorganization and some training, the Confederate Army was still inexperienced and this, combined with very bad roads, slowed the march down.

GRANT SITS TIGHT
On the Union side, Grant was not expecting any serious Confederate activity. While Buell was moving his force up to make contact, Grant's army was drilling in camp near Shiloh. Despite a certain amount of sickness (mainly diarrhoea), morale was good in the Union camp, partly due to the successes of the previous few months.

Grant asked his superior, Major-General Henry Halleck (1815–72), for instructions and was told that once Buell arrived, he was to advance on Corinth, but in the meantime he was to 'sit tight'. Grant's sub-commanders, including William Tecumseh Sherman (1820–91), were certain that there was not a 'Reb' nearer to the Union army than Corinth. They were still certain of this on the night of 5 April, despite the fact that 44,000 Confederate soldiers were camped just a few kilometres away.

That night, Beauregard, Johnston's second-in-command, feared that the Union army had been alerted. With the element of surprise lost, Beauregard thought the Federal army too numerous. He asked his commander to call off the operation, but Johnston disagreed, stating that he would fight even if the enemy turned out to have a million men ranged against him.

OPENING MOVES
The Confederate force was in position on 6 April when Union pickets stumbled on its massed brigades. They fled back in the

direction of their camps and Johnston's army rolled after them, moving quickly through the wooded terrain and achieving almost total surprise. Brutal close-range firefights broke out as the Rebels stormed through one stunned Union unit after another. Many were caught in camp and totally unready to fight.

Stumbling half-dressed from their tents and bivouacs, Federal troops grabbed for their weapons and tried to make sense of the chaos. Officers were not always nearby, and many of them had no real idea what was

LOCATION

Jackson• ✝Shiloh

The Battle of Shiloh was instigated by the Confederates in an attempt to defeat the larger Union army in detail. The location was not especially significant; what mattered was bringing the enemy swiftly to battle and defeating him.

More representative than accurate, this painting nevertheless gives some idea of the extreme close-quarters fighting that took place at Shiloh. Heavy casualties were inevitable at such short ranges.

THE OPPOSED FORCES

FEDERAL

Army of West Tennessee	48,894
Army of the Ohio	17,918

CONFEDERATE

Army of Mississippi	44,699

going on, either. There were problems with ammunition, which had not been issued in any quantity, as nobody was expecting action. Nor were the camps fortified; the need had not been perceived.

Lack of physical preparation was one thing but even worse was the psychological effect of being attacked out of nowhere. The first positions fell quickly, and for many units further back the only warning of the assault was the arrival of frightened comrades pursued by mobs of Rebel troops.

By mid-morning, it seemed that the Army of the Tennessee was about to be chased into the river. The Union army seemed to be dissolving rapidly under the assault but this was only partially true. Here and there, units rallied more or less intact, and small groups fought back as best they

could. The attack was also becoming disorganized, and on the Federal right something resembling a defensive line was being established.

STAND AND FIGHT

Around Shiloh church, the Federals made a stand. For the entire day this force, composed of a mix of formed units and men who had rallied and fallen in with their comrades, was subjected to a steady hammering by the inexperienced but determined Confederates. With little idea what was happening elsewhere, the Union troops clung on, with heavy casualties on both sides.

The stubborn fight around Shiloh Church stalled Johnston's left flank and, while the Confederates gradually pushed them back, the Union force was still fighting at the end of the day.

Meanwhile, on the Confederate right, the assault had been brought to a standstill by a force under the command of Brigadier-General Benjamin Prentiss (1819–1901), who had gathered every man he could find and was clinging grimly to a sunken road in front of an oak thicket that became known as the Hornet's Nest because of the sound bullets made passing through the leaves and branches. This position linked to a peach orchard to the south, where more Federals were making a fight of it.

Word came to Prentiss from Grant: 'Hold the sunken road at all costs', and for the next six hours, his thrown together command tried its best to do just that.

AT THE HORNET'S NEST

The Confederate army was now in as much confusion as its Union foes, but it was slowly gaining ground. Recognizing the Hornet's Nest as the key to the Federal position, the Rebels threw in 11 attacks, each one repulsed with heavy casualties on each side.

The Union line was bent back in places and pierced now and then, but the situation was restored each time, and as the day went

on Prentiss obeyed Grant's urgent instructions to hold out. Finally, Johnston found a way to break the Union line. Assembling 62 cannon, the largest 'grand battery' deployed in the war, he ordered a massive bombardment that tore through the oak thicket. Under the cover of the cannon fire, Johnston led the final attack in person.

Johnston's assault finally succeeded, but only at great cost. Even as the remnant of Prentiss' force scattered or surrendered, leaving the exhausted Confederate infantry in possession of the sunken road, Johnston was seen to be swaying in the saddle. His clothing was shot through and he was bleeding from a major leg wound. Before his personal surgeon could arrive – he had been sent off to look after wounded men from both sides – Johnston succumbed.

THE FIRST DAY ENDS

General Johnston's death left Beauregard in command of a chaotic but very nearly victorious Confederate army. Grant's force had been squashed into a small area around Pittsburg Landing, with its back to the river, and the army was badly shaken. A final hard blow might have settled the matter, but the Confederates were exhausted as well, and badly disorganized.

General Albert Sidney Johnston was an experienced professional officer and a good choice for army command. His compassion in sending off his personal surgeon to treat wounded proved his downfall when he bled to death from an easily treatable leg wound.

Although more advanced guns were available, the smoothbore 12-pound 'Napoleon' was still the mainstay of field artillery. At close range, firing canister, it was more effective than a rifled gun as the smooth bore produced a more even cone-shaped area of effect.

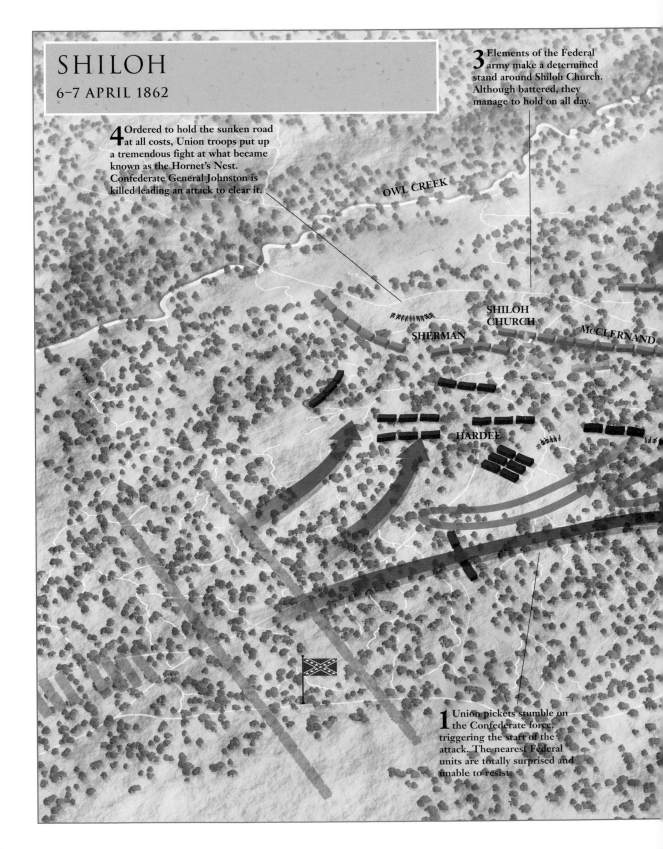

SHILOH
6–7 APRIL 1862

3 Elements of the Federal army make a determined stand around Shiloh Church. Although battered, they manage to hold on all day.

4 Ordered to hold the sunken road at all costs, Union troops put up a tremendous fight at what became known as the Hornet's Nest. Confederate General Johnston is killed leading an attack to clear it.

OWL CREEK

SHILOH CHURCH

SHERMAN

McCLERNAND

HARDEE

1 Union pickets stumble on the Confederate force, triggering the start of the attack. The nearest Federal units are totally surprised and unable to resist.

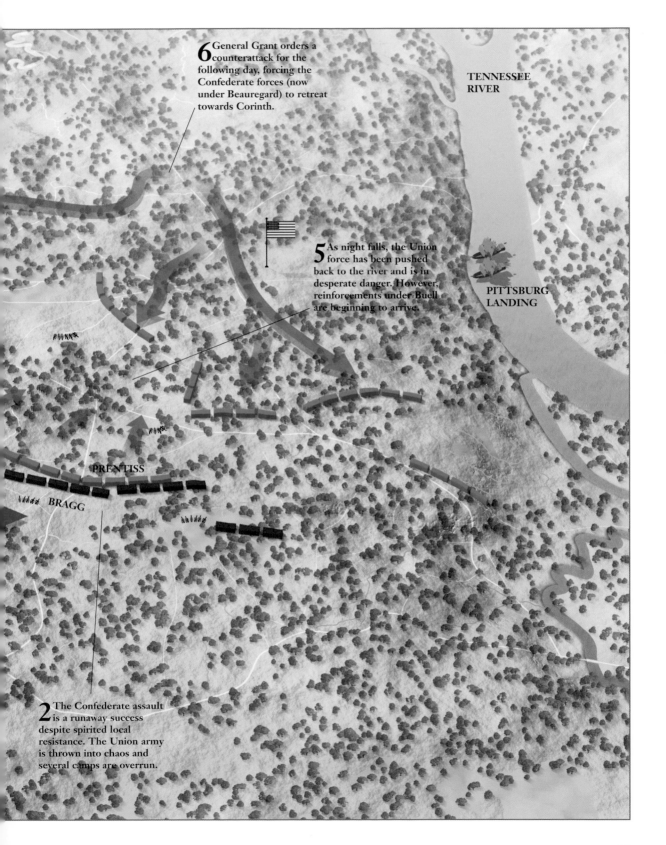

TENNESSEE RIVER

6 General Grant orders a counterattack for the following day, forcing the Confederate forces (now under Beauregard) to retreat towards Corinth.

5 As night falls, the Union force has been pushed back to the river and is in desperate danger. However, reinforcements under Buell are beginning to arrive.

PITTSBURG LANDING

PRENTISS

BRAGG

2 The Confederate assault is a runaway success despite spirited local resistance. The Union army is thrown into chaos and several camps are overrun.

Opposite: William Tecumseh Sherman was a graduate of West Point who was superintendent of the Louisiana Military Academy at the outbreak of war. Although the state seceded, Sherman decided to fight for the Union and waged his own version of total war against the South.

Right: Officers direct their companies to their positions on the firing line, struggling to maintain cohesion and control despite enemy fire and casualties on the ground. Once a unit became disorganized it was very difficult to re-form under fire.

Beauregard put in a somewhat half-hearted attack on the final Union position, but Grant had by now managed to establish a solid defensive line. He was supported by two gunboats operating on the river and by a powerful artillery battery. Even better, he had heard that Buell, who up to that point had not been hurrying, was coming up fast and was about to begin ferrying his troops across the Tennessee River.

Beauregard thought he had won, and telegraphed Richmond to that effect. He had good reason to think so: the army he had just inherited now occupied all but one of the Union camps. Johnston's promise that the Confederates would sleep in the

enemy's camp that night had come true. The Union force had its back to the river and could be annihilated in the morning.

THE NIGHT
After a day of desperate defence that left the battlefield carpeted with dead and wounded, Grant decided to strike back when morning came. His own forces were reinforced by Buell's men, and had gained a further advantage.

Major-General Lew Wallace (1827–1905), out on the Union right, had been too far away to take part in the first day's fighting but arrived during the night. His force was

Mounted raiders could range far and wide, causing damage to the enemy and distracting his attention from more major campaigns. Many raids were made by regular cavalry units while others were little more than excuses for banditry.

Amidst the closely wooded terrain of the Tennessee River, General Albert Sidney Johnston rallies the 13th Arkansas Regiment at the battle of Shiloh.

organized, relatively fresh and in a position to open hostilities.

The two gunboats shelled suspected Confederate positions during the night as Buell's men came ashore, and a heavy rainstorm added to the general misery. There was no system in place to collect the wounded from the battlefield, so they were left where they were. Many died of their wounds in the cold and wet.

GRANT COUNTERATTACKS

In the grey dawn of 7 April, Wallace's force attacked the Confederate left and caused the sort of confusion that had beset the Union camps the day before. The Rebels were still scattered and badly disorganized, and as the fighting spread along the length of the line, Beauregard managed to rally about 30,000 men and begin fighting back.

However, Grant had over 20,000 fresh reinforcements plus the survivors of the previous day's fighting. The numerical advantage, plus the psychological blow dealt when the troops who were expecting to attack on their own terms were themselves assaulted, was too much for the Rebels, who were gradually pushed back.

THE CONFEDERATE RETREAT

Beauregard realized that he was beaten and ordered a retreat towards Corinth, which was partially covered (and partially hindered) by a storm. Along the way, Beauregard organized a rearguard of about 12,000 men under Brigadier-General John C Breckinridge (1821–75).

Grant's army pursued as best it could, and inflicted about 3000 casualties on the rearguard, but it was not able to turn the retreat into a rout and thereby win a strategic victory. The Federal army was too shaken, tired and disorganized for an effective pursuit, so it retired to the shattered camps it had previously occupied and began dealing with the dead and wounded.

AFTERMATH

The sudden assault and near-disaster had shocked the Union army, and gave rise to the realization that the war was going to be long and hard, with colossal numbers of dead on both sides. About 13,000 Union troops were dead and missing, and the Confederates had lost about 10,500. This appalling death toll was equivalent to the Battle of Waterloo. Unlike Waterloo, however, it was not the cataclysmic end to an era of war, but merely the first of many such slaughters.

However, despite the vast casualty figures, nothing had really changed. Both armies were still 'in being' and the overall strategic situation was not greatly altered. That alone made Shiloh a decisive moment in the course of the war. The Confederacy needed a victory to protect the rail links and to keep the Union forces off balance, and it had failed to achieve one. The long-term prospects were not good, and the operation had been conceived to address that situation. There would not be another chance, and of course the able General Albert Sidney Johnston had been killed, making him the highest-ranking officer on either side to be killed in action.

Now Corinth and the rail links were in danger, and after Corinth the Union would be able to push on to Memphis and Vicksburg. Grant began preparations to advance on Beauregard's army and capture Corinth, but the operation was delayed by the arrival of Halleck, who outranked Grant and therefore assumed overall command. This short pause was enough for the Confederate army to ready itself for further combat, and led to a more protracted campaign. However, in due course, the Rebels were forced to abandon Corinth.

The fall of Corinth stemmed directly from the failure to win at Shiloh, and robbed the South of the only all-weather rail link from Richmond to Memphis. In time, Vicksburg too would fall, opening up the Mississippi to the Union and effectively splitting the Confederacy in half. It was such losses, as much as defeats in great battles like Gettysburg, that spelled the doom of the Confederacy.

With only a fraction of the industry and manpower available to the Northern (Union) states, the Confederacy was always at a strategic disadvantage. From Shiloh onwards, it was on the defensive in the west and that could only end one way. The North could afford to grind its enemy down but the South needed decisive victories. Shiloh was almost, but not quite, the masterstroke that gave the South a fighting chance at victory in the west.

John C Breckinridge had experience commanding volunteers in the Mexican War (1846–48) and had served as Vice-President of the United States. He was unsuccessful in running for president in 1860 but served the Confederacy well in both military and political capacities.

NEW ORLEANS
APRIL–MAY 1862

NEW ORLEANS WAS IMPORTANT TO THE SOUTH AS A PORT, A SHIPBUILDING CENTRE, AND A KEY CITY ON THE MISSISSIPPI RIVER. AS SUCH, IT WAS A PRIME TARGET FOR THE FEDERAL BLOCKADE. THE CITY SURRENDERED ON 25 APRIL 1862 AFTER ADMIRAL DAVID FARRAGUT CONDUCTED A DARING RUN PAST THE TWO FORTS THAT WERE SUPPOSED TO SAFEGUARD IT.

WHY DID IT HAPPEN?

WHO Confederate forces under Major-General Mansfield Lovell (1822–84) defended New Orleans, a key Confederate port, shipbuilding centre and wealthy Mississippi River city, against a Federal naval force led by Flag Officer David Farragut (1801–70).

WHAT Farragut ran his fleet past the powerful Forts Jackson and St Philip, compelling New Orleans to surrender, and then army troops under Major-General Benjamin Franklin Butler (1818–93) moved forward to occupy the city.

WHERE New Orleans, Louisiana.

WHEN 25 April to 1 May 1862.

WHY The Confederate defences were plagued by a low priority, a lack of unified effort and a mistaken assumption of the direction of the true threat. Farragut's bold plan to run past the forts was made possible by the presence of Butler's army troops to isolate the forts from New Orleans as Farragut proceeded to the city.

OUTCOME The South lost its most populated city and a key port, but the Federals were unable to seize the advantage and take Vicksburg.

By 1861, every shipyard in New Orleans was busy building, converting or repairing some type of vessel connected to the war effort. It was a largely decentralized enterprise with few of the ships actually earmarked for the fledgling Confederate Navy, but three ironclads were under construction. The *Manassas* was a private venture built to be a profit-making privateer. The *Louisiana* and the *Mississippi* were being built under separate contracts authorized by Confederate Secretary of the Navy Stephen Mallory (1813–73). It was, in most cases, a confused and competing effort that did not efficiently use the scarce Confederate resources. Nonetheless, New Orleans was a hubbub of shipbuilding

activity and rumours of Confederate ironclads there raised concerns in the Federal Navy office.

The Confederate first in charge of the New Orleans defences was Major-General David Twiggs (1790–1862), who arrived in the city on 31 May. Twiggs's hopes rested on Fort Jackson and Fort St Philip, which guarded the Mississippi River approaches 121km (75 miles) south of New Orleans. Fort St Philip was a citadel built by the Spanish in the 1790s and expanded two decades later. Fort Jackson, on the other hand, was a more modern and powerful structure built in a pentagonal design. These strongholds gave the Confederates an exaggerated feeling of security.

David Porter, shown in the centre of this photograph, commanded 19 mortar boats as part of his foster brother Flag Officer David Farragut's naval assault on New Orleans. Porter fired 2997 shells at Fort Jackson but was unable to compel the fort to surrender by his bombardment alone.

FAULTY ASSUMPTION

Early in the war, the Confederacy was most concerned with an attack on New Orleans from the south, but soon a competing point of view gained ascendancy. Faith in Forts Jackson and St Philip, as well as the broad inland bayous and a string of fortifications known as the New Orleans' Chalmette defence line, led local observers like George Cable (1844–1925) to believe that 'Nothing afloat could pass the forts. Nothing that walked could get through the swamps.' Instead, Federal ironclad construction upriver at places such as Cincinnati, Carondelet (near St Louis) and Mound City caused many to think the real threat would be from the north.

As for the southern approach, Twiggs anticipated the Federal Navy would use only wooden warships there and that Forts Jackson and St Philip were capable of defending against such a threat.

Indeed, in the first naval encounter below New Orleans, the Confederates had reason to believe the Federal Navy was not very powerful at all. As progress towards building the ironclads proceeded at a frustratingly slow pace, Confederate Commander George Hollins (1799–1878) finally lost his patience. He commandeered the *Manassas*, and, along with six lightly armed riverboats he already had, struck the remarkably complacent Federal fleet at Head of the Passes, where the main stem of the Mississippi River branches off into three distinct directions at its mouth in the Gulf, in the early morning hours of 12 October. Federal Captain John Pope (1798–1876) was thoroughly surprised and routed. The fiasco was derisively dubbed 'Pope's Run', but while the Confederate 'victory' embarrassed the Federals and boosted Confederate morale, it did no permanent damage other than to Pope's career.

Not long before, Twiggs would have been on solid ground in thinking that wooden ships were no match for heavy fortifications, but recent events at Port Royal Sound, South Carolina, had proven otherwise. There Captain Samuel DuPont (1803–65) had used steam power and superior weaponry to defeat two Rebel forts. If Twiggs had missed this lesson, Commander David Dixon Porter (1813–91)

had not. He saw no reason to believe that he could not do on the Lower Mississippi what DuPont had done at Port Royal.

Porter obtained an audience with Secretary of the Navy Gideon Welles (1802–78) and briefed him on his plan to precede the proposed attack with a 48-hour mortar bombardment of Forts Jackson and St Philip. By mounting these mortars on modified schooners, there would be no need for a large cooperating land force. In fact, with the Navy providing most of the firepower, the only support required from the Army would be a few thousand soldiers to garrison the captured forts and occupy

New Orleans was a key port on the Mississippi River and the South's largest city. Federal planners identified early in the war that its capture was critical to their success.

PETTY OFFICER, US NAVY

The Federals enjoyed a huge naval advantage over the Confederates, possessing over 90 warships at the outbreak of the Civil War. In contrast the fledgling Confederate Navy inherited just five vessels from the seceded states. Secretary of the Navy Gideon Welles and Assistant Secretary of the Navy Gustavus Fox (1821–83) provided very effective administrative leadership of the Federal Navy and seasoned sailors such as David Farragut, Samuel DuPont, Louis Goldsborough (1805–77) and Andrew Foote (1806–63), the first rear-admirals in the US Navy's history, provided solid command at sea. The Federals' naval superiority allowed them not just to mount an effective blockade of Confederate commerce but also to conduct amphibious operations with the Army along the Confederate coast at places such as Fort Fisher, North Carolina, and to project power up rivers to reach places such as Vicksburg, Mississippi.

In the LOCATION map: Jackson • Atlanta • New Orleans

David Twiggs, the Confederate general first responsible for the defences of New Orleans, was a senior military officer with service dating back to the War of 1812. By the time of the Civil War, however, he was past his prime and soon relinquished his command to Mansfield Lovell.

THE OPPOSED FORCES

FEDERAL

Navy:	**24 wooden vessels**
	19 mortar boats
Army:	**15,000**

CONFEDERATE

Navy:	**8 vessels**

(River Defense Fleet and Louisiana State Navy)

	6 vessels

(Confederate Navy, including the ironclads *Louisiana* and *Manassas*)

Army:	**4000**

the city. Welles was convinced and, together with Porter, he obtained President Abraham Lincoln's (1809–65) approval. To lead the operation, Welles employed Captain David Farragut. On 9 January 1862, Welles gave Farragut command of the newly constituted West Gulf Blockading Squadron and on 19 March, the Senate confirmed Farragut's appointment to flag officer.

While the Federal plans and command arrangements were solidifying, those of the Confederates were falling apart. By this time the prevalent opinion in the Confederate high command was that an attack would come from upriver. Thus,

Secretary Mallory sent Hollins and his small fleet upriver to join in the Confederate defence of Columbus, Kentucky. The move left New Orleans without naval protection. To add to the turmoil, on 5 October, Twiggs asked to be relieved of his command.

LOVELL ARRIVES

Even before Twiggs had tendered his resignation, the War Department had dispatched Mansfield Lovell to New Orleans to serve as Twiggs's assistant. When Lovell arrived on 17 October, he learned he was the new commander and had been promoted to major-general. Before Lovell

Samuel Colt (1814–62) was the most prolific manufacturer of handguns during the Civil War. His .36 calibre Navy model (pictured here) was especially popular in the South.

left Richmond for New Orleans, he spoke with both President Jefferson Davis (1808–89) and Secretary of War Judah P Benjamin (1811–84) and argued that the only proper way to defend New Orleans was to unify the land and naval commands. Davis chose to leave the commands divided, but encouraged Lovell to maintain 'unrestrained intercourse and cordial fraternization' with the Navy. In the end, a lack of unity of effort between the Confederate Army and Navy would plague the defence of New Orleans.

In the meantime, Lovell set out on an inspection tour of his new command and found inferior ammunition, antiquated cannon, manpower shortages, unimpeded river approaches, unfinished lines, incompetent officers and dilapidated fortifications. He worked diligently to correct these deficiencies, including scavenging loose chain and anchors from across the South to strengthen the defensive log boom across the Mississippi River. Lovell now had a barrier securely chained to both banks, held in place by 15 anchors weighing 1134–1814kg (2500–4000lb). Obviously proud, Lovell wrote: 'This raft is a complete obstruction, and has enfilading fire from Fort Jackson and direct fire from Saint Philip.'

But as fast as Lovell could improve things, the War Department seemed to unravel them. Part of the problem was the low priority New Orleans was receiving

New Orleans 1862. One of the important characteristics of New Orleans was its status as a shipbuilding centre. Especially threatening to the Federals were the ironclads being built there.

from Richmond. Medical supplies, clothing, rifles and even some of the big naval guns were being siphoned off for service in Virginia, South Carolina and Tennessee. Neither Davis nor Benjamin considered New Orleans in imminent danger of attack. Even after Lovell raised and trained a force of 10,000 infantry, the Secretary of War sent half of them to reinforce General Albert Sidney Johnston's (1803–62) Army of Mississippi at Corinth after the loss of Forts Henry and Donelson.

Lovell, however, knew there was a threat much closer to home. He could see the

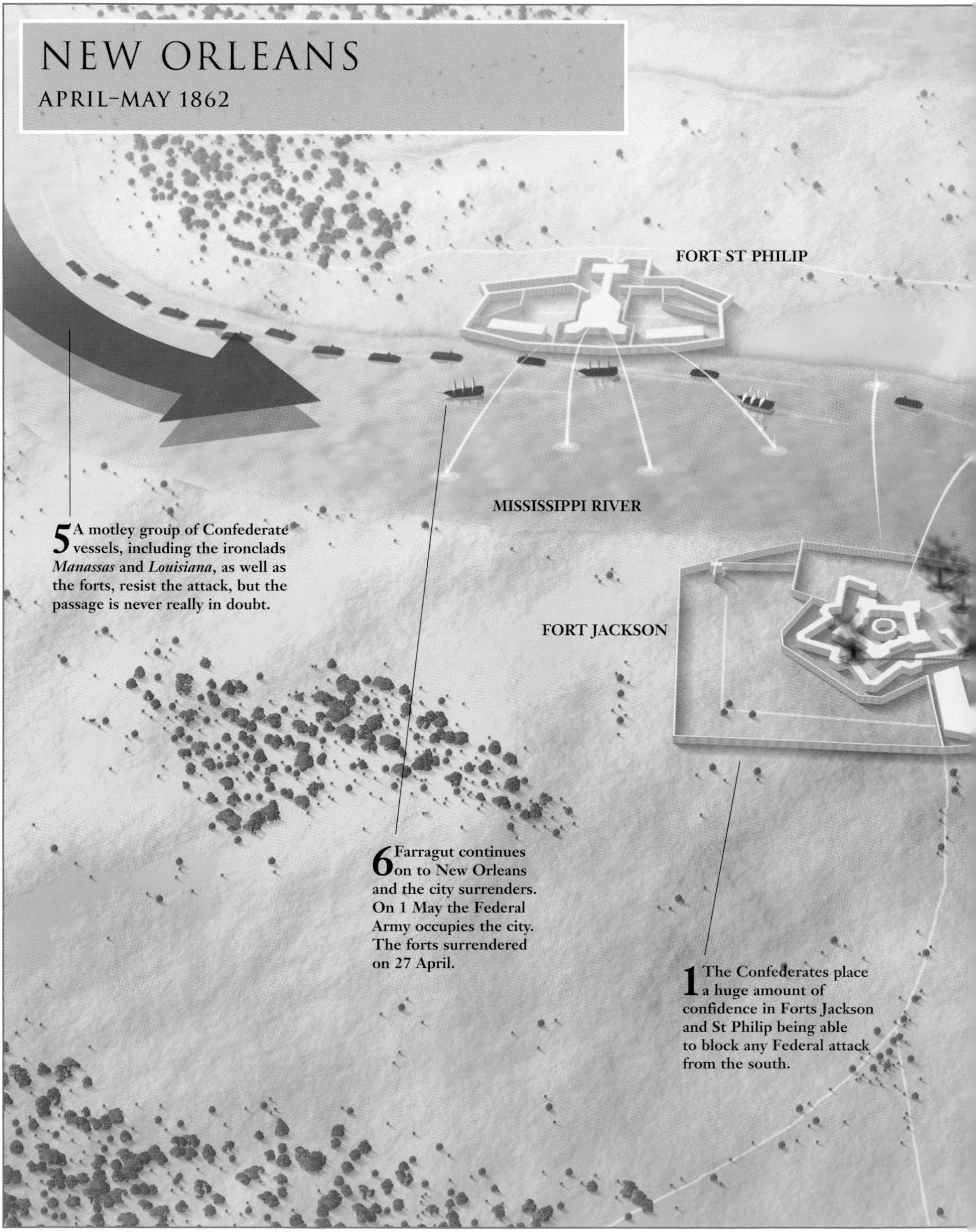

NEW ORLEANS
APRIL–MAY 1862

FORT ST PHILIP

MISSISSIPPI RIVER

5 A motley group of Confederate vessels, including the ironclads *Manassas* and *Louisiana*, as well as the forts, resist the attack, but the passage is never really in doubt.

FORT JACKSON

6 Farragut continues on to New Orleans and the city surrenders. On 1 May the Federal Army occupies the city. The forts surrendered on 27 April.

1 The Confederates place a huge amount of confidence in Forts Jackson and St Philip being able to block any Federal attack from the south.

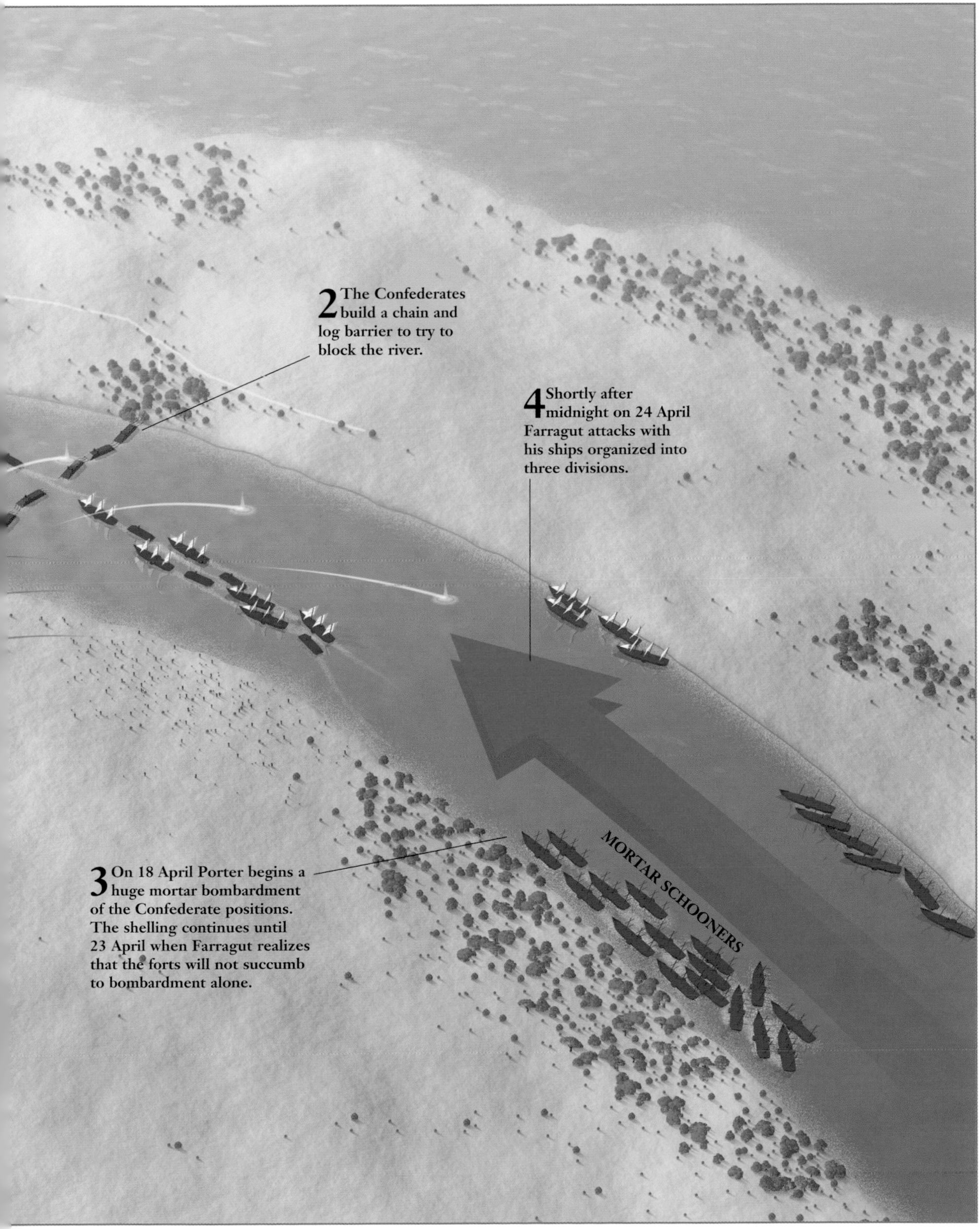

2 The Confederates build a chain and log barrier to try to block the river.

4 Shortly after midnight on 24 April Farragut attacks with his ships organized into three divisions.

3 On 18 April Porter begins a huge mortar bombardment of the Confederate positions. The shelling continues until 23 April when Farragut realizes that the forts will not succumb to bombardment alone.

MORTAR SCHOONERS

David Farragut was selected by Secretary of the Navy Gideon Welles to command the newly created West Gulf Blockading Squadron. The broad appointment helped conceal the more specific Federal plan to attack New Orleans.

about the lack of naval cooperation to Benjamin, who promptly ordered Lovell to impress 14 specific ships into public service. These became known as the River Defense Fleet, a grandiose name for what was in fact merely another distraction for the already-harried Lovell, who had to divert scarce resources, including his attention, in order to man, arm and clad it. The defence of New Orleans continued to spiral into a confused mess.

On 13 March 1862, Major-General Benjamin Butler arrived at Ship Island with the final instalment of his 15,255 Federal soldiers. In the meantime, Farragut was building his fleet there and preparing for the attack. The *Brooklyn* occupied Head of the Passes, light-draught steamers moved upriver to reconnoitre the forts, and Porter positioned his mortar schooners. The Federals were obviously up to something, but Confederate defensive preparations hardly kept pace. Even Lovell seemed ambivalent. On 15 April, he wrote a letter to the new Secretary of War George W Randolph (1818–67) stating 'no harm done. Twenty-seven vessels in sight from forts.' The defenders of New Orleans continued in their ignorant bliss.

PORTER'S BUMMERS

The vessels Lovell had observed were of Porter's mortar flotilla. On 16 April, Porter towed three schooners to a marker 2743m (3000 yards) from Fort Jackson and lobbed a few shells to test the range. The next day, all 21 of Porter's vessels, derisively called 'bummers' by the 'real' sailors in the fleet, were at anchor in carefully determined positions. Then on 18 April, at 9:00 a.m., Porter began his huge bombardment. For 10 straight hours, each schooner fired a round every 10 minutes for a total of nearly 3000 shells. Porter had predicted his mortars could reduce the forts in two days, and by nightfall he realized that was not going to be the case.

Still, Farragut let Porter continue his efforts until the morning of 20 April, when the former signalled his officers to his flagship to announce his new plan.

Farragut was convinced that mortars alone would not cause the forts to surrender. With Butler and 7000 of his men now across

Federal force unloading troops on Ship Island, a narrow stretch of sand some 21km (13 miles) southwest of Biloxi, Mississippi, and a convenient staging location for any operation against New Orleans. With Hollins' fleet still upriver, Lovell had only two small naval vessels operating on Lake Pontchartrain to help defend New Orleans against a landing. Lovell took his concerns

Farragut ran his fleet past the powerful Confederate forts Jackson and St Philip and pressed on to New Orleans. Once the forts realized New Orleans had been captured, they also surrendered.

the bar, Farragut had other options. Farragut's plan was to destroy the chain barrier, run past the forts with his warships and, once above the forts, land Butler's troops to seize the forts. Porter's mortars, much to their commander's chagrin, would remain in position.

The first part of Farragut's plan began on the night of 20 April, when a force under Captain Henry Bell (1808–68) departed on a mission to break the chain. The Confederates tried to disrupt the operation by launching a fire raft, but Bell and his men were ultimately successful in clearing the obstacle. Still, Farragut allowed Porter to continue his bombardment, but by 23 April the promised results had not yet come. The commander asked for still more time. 'Look

here, David,' Farragut replied, 'We'll demonstrate the practical value of mortar work.' Farragut then ordered his signal officer to wave a red pennant every time a shell landed inside Fort Jackson and a white one for every shell that missed its target. The results spoke for themselves, as time and again the white flag was unfurled. 'There's the score,' Farragut conceded, 'I guess we'll go up the river tonight.'

THE FEDERAL ATTACK

Farragut began his attack shortly after midnight on 24 April. Although the Federal fleet took fire from both the forts and the Confederate ram *Manassas*, the passage never really was in doubt. Farragut had organized his ships into three divisions for the run. Singly or in small groups, they all made it except for the *Varuna*, which was sunk, and three gunboats from the rear division that were forced to turn back.

Farragut now sent word to Porter to demand the surrender of the forts, and to

Butler to bring up the Army transports from Head of the Passes. Farragut then pushed on towards New Orleans and anchored for the night 24km (15 miles) below the city.

Before dawn on 25 April, Farragut was up and moving towards New Orleans. Lovell had torched the levee and retreated from the city, leaving the inhabitants in a state of panic. As Farragut pulled alongside New Orleans, he hammered it with broadsides.

Then Farragut dispatched his marines to take possession of the Federal mint, post office and customs house and replace the Confederate flag with the Stars and Stripes on all public buildings. Captain Theodorus Bailey (1805–77), commander of Farragut's Red Division, worked his way through an angry mob and demanded the city's surrender, but the mayor claimed to be under martial law and without authority. When Farragut threatened a bombardment, the mayor and Common Council declared New Orleans an open city.

The forts had refused Porter's demand to surrender, so he resumed his bombardment. He made a second offer two days later but still the forts refused. Finally, as word drifted downriver of New Orleans' fate, morale broke. At midnight on 27 April, the fort troops mutinied. Brigadier-General Johnson Duncan (1827–62) had no choice but to surrender. Commander John Mitchell (1811–89) held out a little longer aboard the *Louisiana*, but ultimately blew her up and surrendered the remnants of the naval command.

On 1 May, Butler and the Army came up from their landing at Quarantine and began a controversial occupation of New Orleans. A debate would develop between Butler and Porter over their relative contributions to the victory. In fact, while the Navy did do the fighting, the Army's presence was critical to the Navy's success. Without Butler's force to isolate Forts Jackson and St Philip and pacify the hostile New Orleans population, Farragut could have remained in New Orleans just a short time. Instead, Farragut was able to run past the Confederate forts and then land Federal Army troops to cut the defenders off from New Orleans.

UNREALIZED POTENTIAL

New Orleans was indeed a great victory for the Union. One of the South's premier cities and the mouth of the Mississippi River were now under Federal control. Still, it was a limited victory in that this strategic momentum was not maintained. The logical sequence after New Orleans was to move up the Mississippi to capture the river port city of Vicksburg.

Belatedly, Farragut did make minor attempts to do so, but by then the opportunity had been lost. The Federals would not be able to wrest Vicksburg from the Rebels until Major-General Ulysses S Grant (1822–85) did so on 4 July 1863 after a lengthy campaign of manoeuvre and siege.

New Orleans was the greatest single victory of the Civil War for the Federal Navy. Not only was the Confederacy's largest city captured, the Federals now had control of a large stretch of the lower Mississippi River.

GAINES' MILL
27 JUNE 1862

ON 17 MARCH 1862, MAJOR-GENERAL GEORGE MCCLELLAN ADVANCED 90,000 FEDERAL SOLDIERS TOWARDS RICHMOND UP THE VIRGINIA PENINSULA. HOWEVER, WHAT BEGAN AS A BOLD MANOEUVRE QUICKLY LOST ITS MOMENTUM AS MCCLELLAN FELL VICTIM TO HIS OWN OVERCAUTION AND THE SUPERIOR ABILITIES OF GENERAL ROBERT E LEE. IN A SERIES OF HARD-FOUGHT BATTLES COLLECTIVELY KNOWN AS THE SEVEN DAYS, LEE DEFEATED MCCLELLAN AT PLACES SUCH AS GAINES' MILL AND FORCED HIM TO ABANDON THE OFFENSIVE.

WHY DID IT HAPPEN?

WHO Federal forces under Major-General George B McClellan (1826–85) battled Confederates first under General Joseph E Johnston (1807–91) and then General Robert E Lee (1807–70).

WHAT McClellan conducted an amphibious turning movement in an attempt to avoid a frontal assault on Richmond.

WHERE The Virginia Peninsula.

WHEN March to July 1862 with the Battle of Gaines' Mill occurring 27 June.

WHY McClellan was overly cautious and gave Lee a chance to build enough of a force to launch an audacious counteroffensive. In the process, Lee was aided by Major-General 'Stonewall' Jackson's (1824–63) brilliant Shenandoah Valley Campaign, which caused forces earmarked for McClellan to be withheld to help defend Washington.

OUTCOME McClellan was repulsed and withdrew from the Peninsula, while Lee built on his momentum and moved north to attack at Second Manassas.

McClellan's goal was to avoid a frontal assault against General Joe Johnston's entrenched Confederates around Manassas and Centreville. To this end, McClellan proposed a bold, amphibious turning movement from Annapolis, Maryland, through Chesapeake Bay to the mouth of the Rappahannock River. The landing site would be the small hamlet of Urbanna, which lay about 96.5km (60 road miles)

northeast of Richmond. From there, McClellan would march on Richmond.

However, Johnston began feeling vulnerable with his position at Manassas, and on 7 March 1862 he ordered all of his troops east of the Blue Ridge Mountains, some 42,000 effectives, to withdraw to the Rappahannock River, nearly half the distance to Richmond. Only Major-General 'Stonewall' Jackson's 5400 men would

Against protected defenders, Civil War artillery could not get close enough to have the desired effect with canister without exposing the gunners to the long-range fire of the defenders' rifles. Therefore most artillery battles, such as Malvern Hill during the Seven Days, were defensive.

remain in the Shenandoah Valley to threaten the right flank of any Federal advance. Johnston's move completely negated the basis of the Urbanna Plan. Instead of turning the Confederates and getting between them and Richmond, McClellan now faced an enemy who had occupied the very area from which he proposed to begin his operation.

By this time, however, McClellan was committed to an amphibious campaign. Instead of Urbanna, he decided on Fort Monroe as a landing site. Fort Monroe guarded the strategic Hampton Roads on the tip of the Virginia Peninsula and had the advantage of being garrisoned by 10,000 Federal troops, but it did not offer the opportunity to cut off the Confederates as the Urbanna Plan would have done. The campaign would now require a slow, toilsome march ending in a toe-to-toe fight at Richmond.

Standing in the way of McClellan's plan was the *Merrimack*, a former US steam frigate that the Federals burned and scuttled and which the Confederates had raised and converted to an ironclad. On 8 March, the *Merrimack*, now rechristened the *Virginia*, sailed down the Elizabeth River into Hampton Roads and made short work of five of the Federal blockade ships lying at anchor. The next day, the Federal ironclad,

the *Monitor*, arrived on the scene. The two ironclads fought to a tactical draw, but the overall result was a strategic Federal victory. Although the *Virginia* was still a threat, anxiety over the vessel's potential to destroy single-handedly the Federal fleet was abated. At least one obstacle had been lessened along the way of McClellan's Peninsula Campaign.

THE PENINSULA CAMPAIGN

The embarkation itself began on 17 March and was fully effected on 5 April. It was a colossal move, eventually totalling 90,000 men and leading one British observer to liken it to 'the stride of a giant'. By 4 April, McClellan felt he had enough forces on the ground and began to advance on Yorktown.

However, after a brief encounter with Major-General John Magruder's (1807–71) Warwick River defensive line, McClellan decided to cease manoeuvre and initiate siege operations. These lasted until 3 May, when the Confederates abandoned Yorktown and withdrew up the Peninsula on their own terms. Major-General James Longstreet (1821–1904) covered the Confederate withdrawal with a sharp delaying action at Williamsburg.

As Johnston traded space for time, Robert E Lee, then serving as President Jefferson Davis' (1808–89) military advisor,

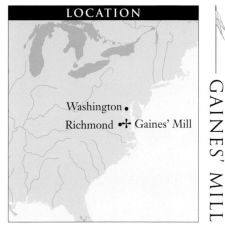

Washington

Richmond ✠ Gaines' Mill

Gaines' Mill lay about 16km (10 miles) northeast of the Confederate capital of Richmond, which was McClellan's objective during the Peninsula Campaign.

FIRING VOLLEYS

Each Civil War soldier carried paper cartridges containing sealed powder and a Minie ball, a cylindro-conoidal bullet. One end of the bullet was hollow, and when the rifle was fired, expanding gas widened the sides of this hollow so that the bullet gripped the rifling and created the spinning effect needed for accuracy.

To load, the soldier poured the powder and ball down the barrel, then wadded the paper and dropped it too down the barrel, using his ramrod to compact the contents. Then he placed a percussion cap over the small nipple at the base of the hammer, cocked the hammer, aimed and fired. A well-drilled soldier could fire three rounds a minute.

Lee's plan for a turning movement at Mechanicsville failed because of the late arrival of 'Stonewall' Jackson. Instead Federal Major-General Fitz John Porter (1822–1901) made good use of the terrain to repulse the Confederate attack.

THE OPPOSED FORCES

FEDERAL
Seven Days 104,300
Gaines' Mill 34,214

CONFEDERATE
Seven Days 85,000
Gaines' Mill 57,018

effected a 're-concentration' of forces that would ultimately turn the tables on McClellan's offensive. However, of greater concern to the immediate situation, Johnston's withdrawal up the Peninsula forced the Confederates to abandon Norfolk. This left the *Virginia* without a home port. Her draught of 8m (22ft) was too deep for her to withdraw up the James River and, finally, on 11 May, she was abandoned and blown up.

With the *Virginia* gone, the James was open as an avenue of attack to Richmond. Federal Flag Officer Louis Goldsborough (1805–77) attempted to project a naval force up the river only to be repulsed by Confederates at Drewry's Bluff, less than 13km (8 miles) south of Richmond.

SEVEN PINES

On 28 May, Johnston learned that Jackson's Shenandoah Valley Campaign had caused such concern for the safety of Washington that Abraham Lincoln (1809–65) had withheld Major-General Irvin McDowell's

(1818–85) corps that had been earmarked to join McClellan. This news changed the strategic situation outside of Richmond dramatically. With the threat of McDowell's force removed, the Confederates could act more aggressively.

Reconnaissance informed Johnston that there were two vulnerable Federal corps south of the Chickahominy River. In the Battle of Seven Pines, Johnston tried to isolate and destroy these corps, but he failed. Johnston mismanaged the battle, issuing unclear instructions and failing to synchronize his forces. Over two days of fighting, the Confederates lost 6134 killed, wounded or missing, and the Federals 5031. Johnston accomplished none of his objectives and, after midnight on 2 June, the Confederates retreated to the west. During the fighting, Johnston was wounded and, on 1 June, Lee arrived with orders from President Davis to take command.

Lee quickly took advantage of the opportunity created by Jackson's success in the Valley. On 8 June, he wrote to Jackson, asking him if he could bring his forces to the Peninsula. Then Major-General JEB 'Jeb' Stuart (1833–64) rode completely around McClellan's army between 12 and 15 June. The cavalryman returned with news that the Federal right flank near Mechanicsville did not extend far enough north to block the roads that Lee planned to use to bring Jackson's troops to the battle. Moreover, the Federals' primary supply line, the Richmond & York River Railroad, was vulnerable. If Lee could turn McClellan's flank, he could threaten the Federal communications at the same time. 'The sooner you unite with this army the better,' Lee told Jackson on 16 June.

The result was the Battle of Mechanicsville, the first of a series of battles known collectively as the Seven Days. At

Mechanicsville, Union forces used superior terrain around Beaver Dam Creek to inflict over 1500 dead and wounded, compared to less than 400 Federal casualties. Jackson, no doubt exhausted from the Valley Campaign, was uncharacteristically late, turning Lee's planned flanking manoeuvre into a costly frontal attack. But when McClellan finally ascertained Jackson was advancing, the Federals panicked and decided to retreat. Lee had lost the battle, but, thanks to McClellan's loss of nerve, was on his way to winning the campaign.

GAINES' MILL

When McClellan decided to retreat, crossings over the swampy terrain became of critical importance to him, so he ordered Major-General Fitz John Porter to pull

Federal troops rest near Gaines' Mill, seen in the background. Joe Johnston was wounded at Seven Pines and Robert E Lee assumed command. Lee would go on to become the heart and soul of the Army of Northern Virginia. Johnston himself confessed, 'The shot that struck me down is the very best that has been fired in the Confederate cause yet.'

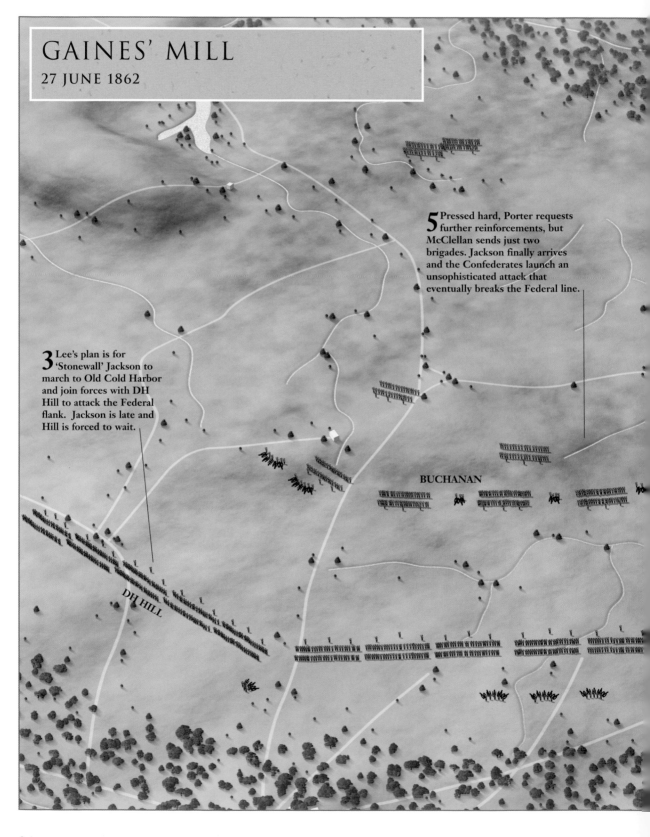

GAINES' MILL
27 JUNE 1862

5 Pressed hard, Porter requests further reinforcements, but McClellan sends just two brigades. Jackson finally arrives and the Confederates launch an unsophisticated attack that eventually breaks the Federal line.

3 Lee's plan is for 'Stonewall' Jackson to march to Old Cold Harbor and join forces with DH Hill to attack the Federal flank. Jackson is late and Hill is forced to wait.

BUCHANAN

DH HILL

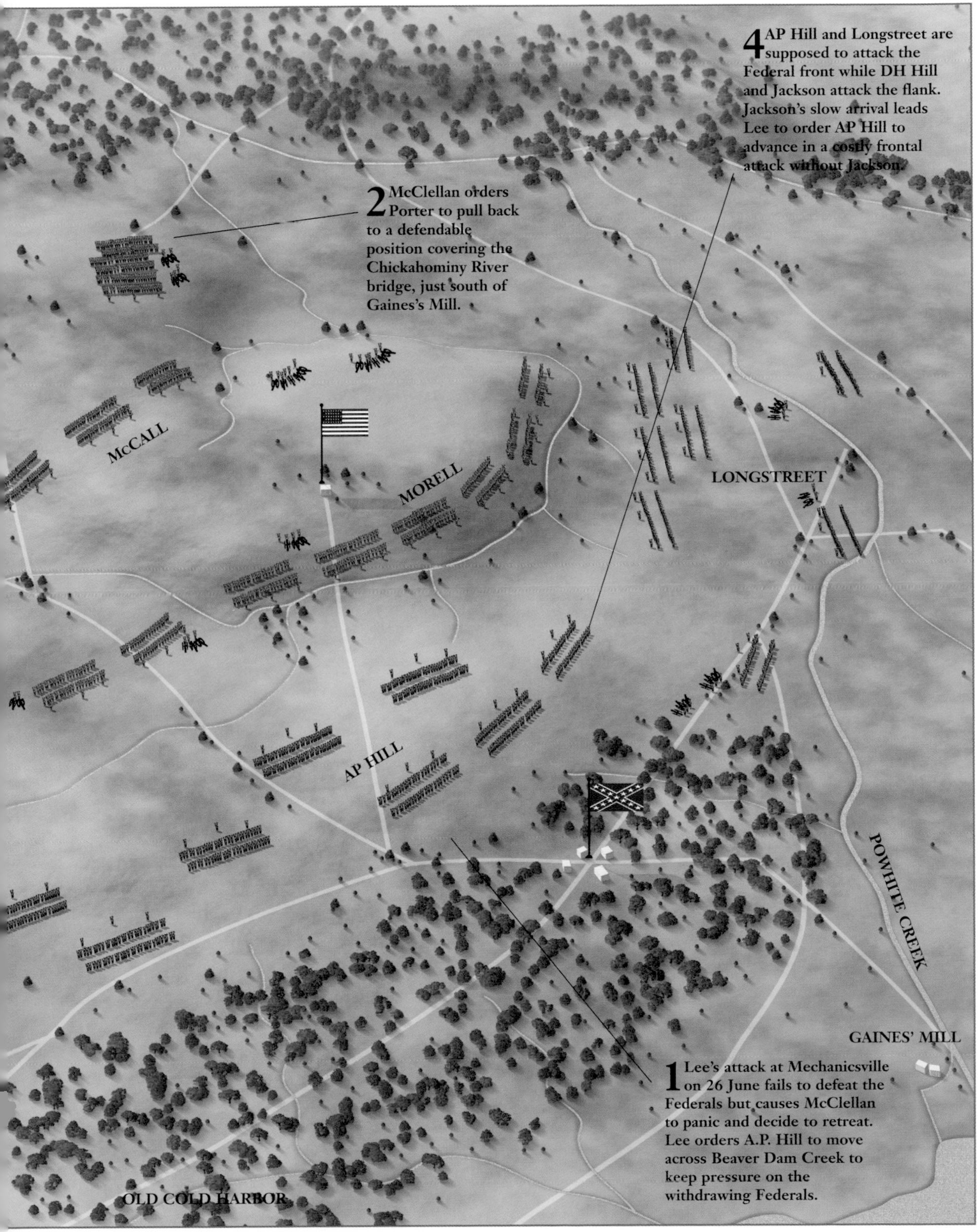

4 AP Hill and Longstreet are supposed to attack the Federal front while DH Hill and Jackson attack the flank. Jackson's slow arrival leads Lee to order AP Hill to advance in a costly frontal attack without Jackson.

2 McClellan orders Porter to pull back to a defendable position covering the Chickahominy River bridge, just south of Gaines's Mill.

McCALL

MORELL

LONGSTREET

AP HILL

POWHITE CREEK

GAINES' MILL

1 Lee's attack at Mechanicsville on 26 June fails to defeat the Federals but causes McClellan to panic and decide to retreat. Lee orders A.P. Hill to move across Beaver Dam Creek to keep pressure on the withdrawing Federals.

OLD COLD HARBOR

Among the technological innovations of the Civil War was the use of observation balloons. Thaddeus Sobieski Constantine Lowe (1831–1913) became the father of the US Balloon Corps and George McClellan made frequent use of Lowe's services during the Peninsula Campaign.

back to a defendable position covering the Chickahominy bridges. The general area was a largely open, oval-shaped plateau, varying in height from 12–24m (40–80ft). The highest elevation was known locally as Turkey Hill, although the battle would be named for Gaines' Mill, around 1.6km (1 mile) away.

Beginning at the northeastern corner of the plateau, and curving around its northern and western sides before emptying into the Chickahominy, was Boatswain's Swamp. Its banks and bottomlands were heavily overgrown and towards its mouth it was steepsided and particularly marshy. Boatswain's Swamp was not the obstacle Beaver Dam Creek was, but it would prove to be rough going for the Confederates.

To the north and west of the plateau, the ground was largely open and sloped down towards the swamp. On the Federals' side, it rose more steeply. Porter placed his corps in a 3km (1.75-mile) crescent facing north and west. Major-General George Morell's (1815–83) division was on the left or western flank, and Brigadier-General George Sykes's (1822–80) was on the right or northern flank. These were arranged in two lines, one near Boatswain's Swamp and the other halfway up the hillside. Major-General George McCall's (1802–68) division constituted a third line, the reserve, at the crest of the plateau. In all, Porter had 27,160 men in position for the Battle of Gaines' Mill. Seventeen Federal batteries, 96 guns in all, were positioned in line, or in reserve, across the plateau. Additionally, three batteries from Major-General William Franklin's (1823–1903) Sixth Corps south of the river could range any assault against Porter's left flank. As at Beaver Dam Creek, Porter had found excellent defensive terrain and used it to his advantage.

MCLELLAN'S RESPONSE

Lee knew that McClellan was defensive-minded, but he did not suspect the magnitude of McClellan's response to Mechanicsville. Rather than completely abandoning the campaign, Lee believed that McClellan would merely reposition to defend his supply line to White House. Thus Lee intended to keep up the pressure, and he ordered Major-General AP Hill (1825–65) to move across Beaver Dam Creek as soon as he learned Porter had abandoned his position. He believed that the Federals would withdraw to Powhite Creek, the next good defensive position.

When Lee finally made contact with Jackson at 10:30 a.m. on 27 June, he formed a plan for an envelopment. Jackson was to march northeast on the Old Cold Harbor Road across the headwaters of Powhite

Creek to Old Cold Harbor, where he would be joined by Major-General DH Hill (1821–89). Hill was already conducting his own wider turning movement over the Old Church Road further north. When joined, Jackson and DH Hill would have 14 of the Army of Northern Virginia's 26 brigades. While AP Hill and Longstreet kept the Federals busy from the front, Jackson and DH Hill would threaten the enemy communications with the Richmond & York River Railroad. Major-General Benjamin Huger (1805–77) and Magruder would be left to defend Richmond.

As it turned out, Lee would face some of the same problems in synchronizing the attack at Gaines' Mill that he had faced at Mechanicsville. DH Hill reached Old Cold Harbor well before Jackson and found himself prematurely joined in battle between noon and 1:00 p.m. Hill, however, had run into a larger force than he had expected. Furthermore, he appeared to be at the enemy's front rather than its flank. He decided to wait for Jackson. As at Mechanicsville, however, Jackson would be painfully slow in arriving.

While DH Hill was waiting, AP Hill had advanced down Telegraph Road towards Gaines' Mill and New Cold Harbor beyond it. At New Cold Harbor, AP Hill's lead brigade under Brigadier-General Maxcy Gregg (1814–62) encountered a severe Federal artillery barrage. Lee and Hill quickly moved to Gregg's position and learned that the Federals had not made their stand at Powhite Creek but had occupied a considerably stronger position further east. This was at Boatswain's Swamp, a feature that did not appear on Lee's map.

Under McClellan, Federal artillery batteries were assigned to divisions, with each division then relinquishing two batteries to form a corps reserve. Control of the guns under this system was inconsistent. In September 1862, Henry Hunt (1819–89) became the Chief of Artillery for the Army of the Potomac, and within a year, he effected a reorganization of the artillery and centralized its command.

To meet this new situation, Lee ordered the rest of AP Hill's division and that of Longstreet to move up and form a line. Porter could observe these developments from his headquarters on the hilltop and requested reinforcements. In response, Major-General Henry Slocum's (1827–94) division from Sixth Corps was sent forward to cross the Chickahominy River at Alexander's Bridge.

At 2:30 p.m., AP Hill gave the order to advance. Most of his men would have at least 400m (440 yards) of open ground to cross before they reached Boatswain's Swamp. They would be facing three batteries of Federal artillery posted on the lower slopes of the plateau and several higher up on the crest. For nearly two hours, Hill's men struggled against these odds and got nowhere.

In the course of the day Hill would lose 2154 men, and most of these losses would occur right here. For Hill, it was Beaver Dam Creek all over again. He was taking a furious pounding in a frontal assault across open ground into Federal artillery. Moreover, Jackson was nowhere to be found.

WRONG DIRECTION

In fact, Jackson had obtained a guide at Walnut Grove Church and apparently told him only that he wanted to go to Old Cold Harbor. He did not impress upon the guide that he wanted to arrive at Old Cold Harbor by a route that would approach the Federals from the flank. It was not until 5km (3 miles) into the march, just short of Powhite Creek, that the guide discovered Jackson's intent.

At that point, there was no choice but to backtrack to Old Cold Harbor Road. By the time Jackson's lead division under Major-General Richard S Ewell (1817–72) reached Old Cold Harbor, Lee's aide Colonel Walter Taylor (1838–1916) was there to meet him. Lee was concerned by AP Hill's vulnerability to a counterattack and had sent Taylor to direct Jackson's men to the battlefield. Ewell hurried his brigades into action, committing them piecemeal. The Federals defeated each in turn.

By now, Slocum's reinforcements were reaching Porter, and Porter would use them

Brigadier-General George Sykes commanded one of the divisions in Major-General Fitz John Porter's Fifth Corps at Gaines' Mill. While 'Stonewall' Jackson was late in arriving at the battle, Sykes held off a Confederate attack from DH Hill.

Left: Carrying their regimental colours, soldiers from the 28th Massachusetts Volunteers and the Irish Brigade engage with Confederate forces at Gaines' Mill.

Smoothbore muskets had a range of 100–200m (110–220 yards), while rifles were effective from 400–600m (440–660 yards). This new range and accuracy served to strengthen the defence during the Civil War.

Volunteer soldiers formed a critical part of both armies. However, their individualistic nature and lack of formal military training frustrated many professional officers like George McClellan.

to plug gaps in the Federal lines. He was under increasing pressure as Longstreet was now launching diversionary attacks on the right to try to afford some relief for AP Hill. Porter reported to McClellan that 'I am pressed hard, very hard' and, unless reinforced, 'I am afraid I shall be driven from my position.'

McClellan had no plan as to how he might meet this situation. Instead of acting, he non-committally asked his subordinates if they had any troops to spare. In the end, McClellan responded by sending Porter two brigades from Major-General Edwin Sumner's (1797–1863) Second Corps. This was a mere one-tenth of the forces available to McClellan on the south side of the Chickahominy, where he was being paralyzed by nothing more than a demonstration by Magruder.

While McClellan was so parsimoniously reinforcing Porter, Jackson's belated arrival was providing Lee with additional men. Daylight was beginning to fade, and there was time for just one more large-scale attack

before darkness. Both Lee and Jackson had gravitated to the centre of the battlefield and ultimately met on Telegraph Road. 'Ah, General, I am very glad to see you,' Lee said. 'I had hoped to be with you before.' Jackson only nodded at the gentle rebuke.

The result of the meeting was that Jackson would add Major-Generals Chase Whiting's (1824–65) and Charles Winder's (1829–62) divisions to the fight, attacking on Longstreet's left. After combat, ineffective units were removed and two of Winder's brigades and one of Longstreet's were allocated to the reserve. Lee had 32,100 men in 16 brigades to throw against Porter's 34,000 remaining effectives.

CLIMAX

The climax of the Battle of Gaines' Mill was a confused mêlée. DH Hill advanced with his five brigades on the left. To his right was Ewell, then Whiting, then Longstreet. There was no nuance about the attack, but, in the end, Confederate persistence ultimately carried the day. Brigadier-General John Bell Hood's (1831–79) brigade of Whiting's division is traditionally credited with being the first to break the Federal line. Indeed, Lee had earlier sought out Hood. 'This must be done,' he told him, explaining the situation. 'Can you break this line?' 'I will try,' Hood promised. On Whiting's instructions, Hood and Brigadier-General Evander Law (1836–1920) advanced their brigades without pausing to fire, covering the open ground to Boatswain's Swamp as quickly as possible. Hood had split his men, making the charge on both flanks of Law's brigade.

Hood's and Law's brigades suffered staggering casualties. Between them, they lost 1018 men at Gaines' Mill, at least two-thirds of whom were from this charge. Nonetheless, the Federals, able to fire at best three shots a minute, were unable to keep up with the swift pace of the attack. The Federal line broke.

Employing generalship based on audacity and manoeuvre, Lee launched a counteroffensive to McClellan's Peninsula Campaign that removed the Federal threat to Richmond.

It was soon the same everywhere. Almost simultaneously, Porter's defence cracked. There was no choice now but to retreat towards the Chickahominy crossings. Darkness covered the Federal move.

Gaines' Mill would prove to be the largest and most costly battle, not just of the Seven Days but also of the entire Peninsula Campaign. A total of almost 100,000 men had been on the field. In less than nine hours of fighting, Porter had suffered 6837 total casualties and Lee 7993. The Federal failure is best explained by the fact that McClellan did not fight the battle to win. He had left 64,000 men idle on the south side of the Chickahominy while Porter fought alone. Although victorious, the Confederates suffered high casualties, and this too can be explained by an inability to get forces into the fight.

The setback caused McClellan to announce to his lieutenants what he had privately already decided. He would abandon the campaign and shift his base from White House to Harrison's Landing, where he would be under the protection of Flag Officer Goldsborough's Navy gunboats. As McClellan withdrew, there would be sharp fighting at Savage's Station (29 June), White Oak Swamp (30 June) and Malvern Hill (1 July).

Lee had turned the Federals back from Richmond, but he was unable to defeat them decisively. Safe at Harrison's Landing, McClellan consolidated his forces until they were withdrawn to northern Virginia to support Major-General John Pope (1822–92) and the threat he was then facing at Second Manassas. The Peninsula Campaign was over.

SECOND MANASSAS
28–30 AUGUST 1862

THE SECOND BATTLE OF MANASSAS (ALSO KNOWN AS THE SECOND BATTLE OF BULL RUN) WAS THE HIGH POINT FOR THE CONFEDERACY'S ARMIES. GENERAL ROBERT E LEE TOOK AN INCREDIBLE RISK IN DIVIDING HIS FORCES IN THE FACE OF SUPERIOR NUMBERS, BUT WAS ABLE TO GAIN A DECISIVE ADVANTAGE THAT RESULTED IN A TOTAL VICTORY.

WHY DID IT HAPPEN?

WHO Union Army of Virginia (63,000 men) under Major-General John Pope (1822–92) opposed by the Confederate Army of Northern Virginia (55,000 men) under General Robert E Lee (1807–70).

WHAT Pope attacked Major-General Thomas 'Stonewall' Jackson's (1824–63) corps in a disjointed fashion and was unable to defeat it before Lee arrived with the remainder of the Confederate army.

WHERE Near Manassas, Virginia, 42km (26 miles) southwest of Washington DC.

WHEN 28–30 August 1862.

WHY Lee wished to prevent a junction between Pope's army and the Union Army of the Potomac under Major-General George B McClellan (1826–85). He advanced against Pope's supply line and drew the Army of Virginia into a fight on approximately equal terms.

OUTCOME After some initial successes, Pope's force was soundly defeated. Pope was dismissed from army command. Lee's victory opened the way for an invasion of the North.

The ground around Manassas was not auspicious for the Union forces. It was here, in July 1861, that a Union army had broken on the bulwark of Jackson's brigade and thus earned the Southern general his nickname of 'Stonewall'. More recently, three independent Union forces had been unable to defeat a badly outnumbered Jackson in the Shenandoah Valley.

Nonetheless, victory here was necessary. Washington was just 42km (26 miles) away and had to be protected, while the Confederate capital at Richmond was also within striking distance. To bring about this much-needed victory, the Union forces in the region were combined under the command of Major-General John Pope, who managed to antagonize his own side as well the enemy. Even Robert E Lee, a man

not normally given to animosity even towards his enemies, took a personal dislike to the Union commander.

Pope's newly formed Army of Virginia was a serious threat to Lee, who was already outnumbered by the 90,000 strong Army of the Potomac under Major-General George McClellan. If the two Union forces made a junction, Lee was in real trouble. It would have to be prevented.

Lee knew that McClellan was much given to procrastination and was unlikely to make a decisive move any time soon, so he decided to hit Pope hard before McClellan realized what was going on. He sent Jackson north against Pope with just 12,000 men, then ordered Major-General AP Hill (1825–65) to support Jackson, bringing another 24,000 men under Jackson's hand.

Thomas Jonathan Jackson was a strong-willed and eccentric man with deeply held religious beliefs. Although a staunch Christian who disliked fighting on a Sunday, he was also a fearsome battle commander.

The three Union corps that had been formed into the Army of Virginia were still dispersed, and Jackson decided to defeat them in detail by use of a central position from which to lunge against each one in turn. However, Jackson was so concerned with secrecy that he did not fully brief his commanders (including AP Hill) and disorganized his own force in the process.

Jackson's force ran into the Union corps under Major-General Nathaniel Banks (1816–94) at Cedar Mountain and was driven back by a very aggressive assault until Hill's force arrived on the field. Banks had neglected to request reinforcements and could not cope with the setback; his force was soundly defeated.

However, by now McClellan was moving to reinforce Pope. This was a slow business, but Lee knew that his time was limited. He decided to crush Pope as quickly as possible, using Clark's Mountain to conceal his advance until he could launch a decisive attack on Pope's eastern flank. This was more than a tactical flanking movement; if successful, it would drive a wedge between Pope and McClellan, and also knock Pope off his line of retreat to Washington.

Things did not quite go according to plan. Lee's staff was slow to organize the attack, and then his cavalry commander Major-General JEB 'Jeb' Stuart (1833–64) was almost captured when his headquarters was attacked. His adjutant was taken, and in his possession was a copy of Lee's entire battle plan. Stuart struck back with a raid on Pope's headquarters and came back with dire news: in five days McClellan's forces would be in position to aid Pope, bringing the Union army up to 130,000 against Lee's 55,000 or so. Pope already had 75,000 men but if Lee was going to act, it had to be now, before things got any worse.

UNCONVENTIONAL MOVES

Even though he knew that conventional strategy became the norm because it worked, and that those who ignored the rules invited disaster, Lee threw away convention and caution (and, some said, sanity), and split his forces in the face of a superior foe. It may be that he had no choice – it was either this desperate gamble or certain defeat by superior forces.

PRIVATE, IRON BRIGADE

First known as Rufus King's Brigade and later as 'that damn Black Hat Brigade', the formation that became known as the Iron Brigade was composed mainly of units from Wisconsin, plus one from Indiana and, later, one from Michigan. The unit's nickname came from its ability to stand 'like iron' under intense fire – one reason why the formation suffered very high casualties during the war.

Before the Second Battle of Manassas the Iron Brigade was able to muster 2100 men of all ranks. Afterwards, only 1250 answered the roll call. The brigade was recruited back up to just under 1900 in time for Gettysburg but suffered a staggering 1212 casualties there. Some of the units of the brigade took 75–80 per cent casualties.

Whatever the reasoning, Lee sent Jackson's corps, supported by Stuart's cavalry, off on the morning of 25 August. They marched first to Salem (42km/26 miles) and, after covering a remarkable 58km (36 miles) the following day, fell on the Union depot at Manassas on the night of 26 August, destroying the supplies found there.

POPE'S REACTIONS

Pope now found himself in the central position, with 75,000 men available. He could move against Jackson's 24,000 or Major-General James Longstreet's (1821–1904) corps of 30,000, leaving a small force to cover the other. Pope had already

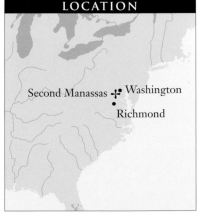

LOCATION

Second Manassas ✛ Washington
Richmond

Lying just 42km (26 miles) from Washington, about midway between the Union and Confederate capitals, Manassas Junction was a critical point that had already seen heavy fighting earlier in the war.

THE OPPOSED FORCES

FEDERAL
Total: 63,000
(troops of all arms)

CONFEDERATE
Total: 55,000
(troops of all arms)

begun redeploying his forces to counter Jackson's move, and now had a real chance to smash the Confederate corps. However, Jackson was a master of what would come to be known as deception operations. Manoeuvring his forces in a manner designed to mislead and confuse Pope as to his intentions, Jackson moved to Sudley Mountain and reformed his corps on Stony Ridge. His forces were in position by midday on 28 August.

Pope was thoroughly confused by Jackson's movements and did not have adequate reconnaissance information to hand. The captured Confederate battle plan did not help at all. Pope's men reached Manassas too late to catch Jackson and wasted more time in confused movements. Pope then heard that there were Confederates in Centreville and jumped to the conclusion that he had found his enemy.

He sent his entire force racing towards Centreville to engage the enemy. He had been so busy trying to intercept and destroy Jackson that he forgot about Longstreet, permitting the two Confederate forces to make a junction.

ACTION AT GROVETON

Late in the day on 28 August, Jackson's forces attacked Union troops moving down the turnpike towards Centreville. Jackson did not want the Federal forces to take up good defensive positions in Centreville, so

Troops from one of the many New York regiments to fight at Second Manassas pose for the camera. The Civil War was the first conflict to be extensively photographed. Posed images like this one were a novelty at the time, as were the newspapers they appeared in soon after being taken.

The opening of the Second Manassas Campaign came on 9 August in the shadow of Cedar Mountain in northern Virginia, where Brigadier-General Nathaniel Banks's corps fought with Major-General Thomas J. 'Stonewall' Jackson's Second Corps. The battle cost the Federal forces 314 killed, 1445 wounded and 662 missing, totalling 2381 of the 8000 troops engaged. The Confederate forces suffered casualties of 241 killed, 1120 wounded and 4 missing for 1365 of the 16,800 troops employed.

he accepted the risk inherent in making his position known to Pope (who was still groping around for him) and fired on elements of Brigadier-General Rufus King's (1814–76) division as they moved down the Warrenton Turnpike.

Six thousand Confederates attacked about 2300 Union troops under Brigadier-General John Gibbon (1827–96). The Union troops were green but Gibbon was an experienced and determined commander who led his men at the advancing Confederate force. Lines shook out and the firing started. For over two hours the opposing lines stood, in places just 100m (110 yards) apart, and blazed away at one another. There was no attempt at flanking or manoeuvre, just raw firepower poured into the enemy in the hope of breaking them. Gibbon's brigade was reinforced during the battle, bringing his strength up to about half that of the Confederates. At nightfall, the battle petered out, leaving about 1300 casualties on each side. The Confederate force withdrew. Pope misconstrued the action as evidence that Jackson was retreating towards the Shenandoah Valley. He ordered his army to concentrate at Groveton, ready to annihilate Jackson.

SECOND MANASSAS OPENS

Pope was wrong about his opponents' intentions, but Jackson's position was not all that good. He had 20,000 men, who were positioned behind an unfinished railroad line, with the cut as a defensive obstacle. Longstreet was on his way but was still some hours out. Despite his mistakes thus far, Pope had a real chance to pulverize Jackson's force. The first attack went in on the morning of 29 August.

Pope's force advanced against Jackson in a disjointed fashion, making repeated attacks that caused heavy casualties but did not drive Jackson back. About an hour into the fighting, Longstreet's corps came up on Jackson's right and began extending the Confederate line to the south.

On the Union side, Major-General Fitz John Porter's (1822–1901) corps did make a probing attack against what seemed to be Jackson's right flank. In fact, Porter's troops, who were moving up from Manassas Junction, had encountered Longstreet, whose flank was, in turn, held by Stuart's cavalry. After a minor skirmish, Porter withdrew and refused an order to attack, presumably thinking he was unlikely to succeed. He led his force to join the main Union body.

Proving that mistakes were not the sole preserve of the Union army, Longstreet did not attack once he was in position. A dangerous gap had opened up in the Union army, and Longstreet was ideally positioned to exploit it. However, his thinking was defensive at the time and although the Confederates did press forward somewhat as their opponents fell back, there was no

John Pope held general rank more or less from the outset of the war and helped raise some of the earliest volunteer units to be recruited. Although successful in the west, he is mainly remembered for his defeat at Second Manassas and for his arrogant address upon assuming his new command in the east.

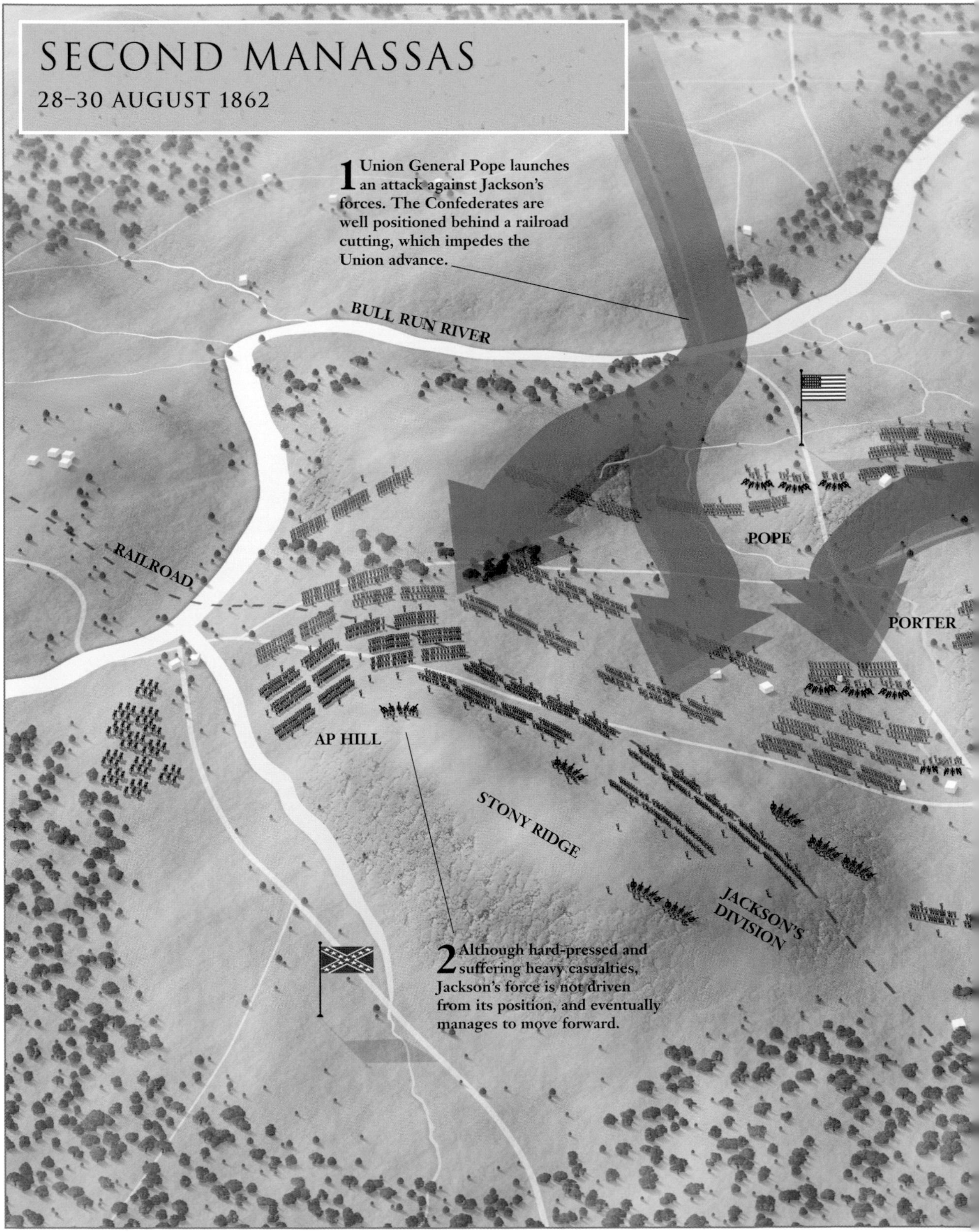

SECOND MANASSAS
28–30 AUGUST 1862

1 Union General Pope launches an attack against Jackson's forces. The Confederates are well positioned behind a railroad cutting, which impedes the Union advance.

BULL RUN RIVER

RAILROAD

POPE

PORTER

AP HILL

STONY RIDGE

JACKSON'S DIVISION

2 Although hard-pressed and suffering heavy casualties, Jackson's force is not driven from its position, and eventually manages to move forward.

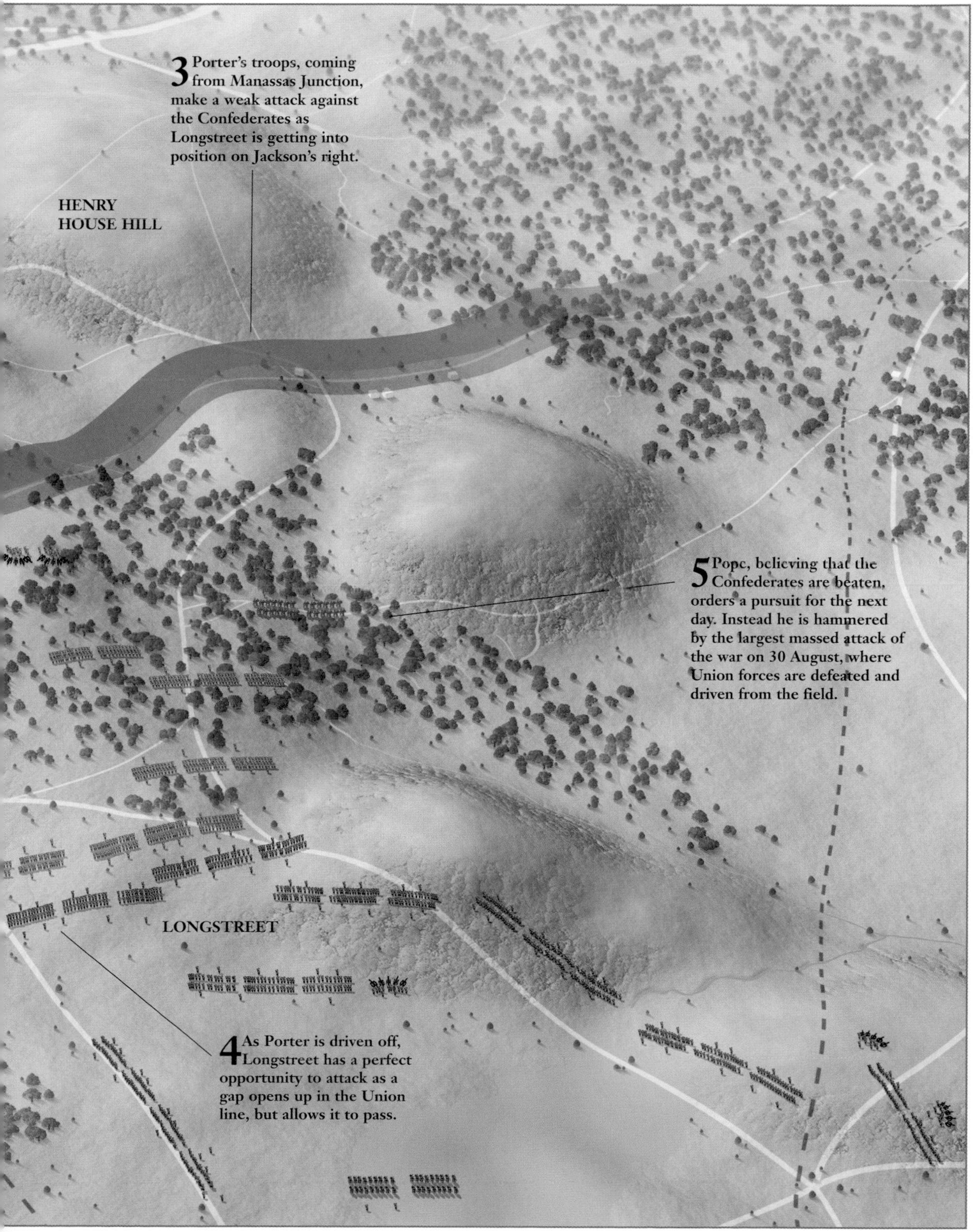

3 Porter's troops, coming from Manassas Junction, make a weak attack against the Confederates as Longstreet is getting into position on Jackson's right.

HENRY
HOUSE HILL

5 Pope, believing that the Confederates are beaten, orders a pursuit for the next day. Instead he is hammered by the largest massed attack of the war on 30 August, where Union forces are defeated and driven from the field.

LONGSTREET

4 As Porter is driven off, Longstreet has a perfect opportunity to attack as a gap opens up in the Union line, but allows it to pass.

SECOND MANASSAS

A Confederate Kentucky cavalryman fires his service revolver. Cavalry were mainly effective as scouts, raiders and skirmishers in the Civil War. Infantry firepower was such that a traditional sabre charge was unlikely to be effective. The cavalryman's combination of mobility and firepower made him an important asset all the same.

had reached the battlefield with his own force, ordered Longstreet forward against the Union left flank.

Longstreet had 28,000 men under his hand, who had thus far played little part in the battle. They were relatively fresh and were opposed by only weak forces. The advance, which was the largest massed assault of the entire war, smashed into the

pursuit or attempt to exploit the repulse of the Union army. Indeed, Jackson ordered his troops to withdraw from the ground they had taken and resume their previous defensive positions. Pope, as usual, misconstrued the move.

This time, Pope decided that the Confederates were in retreat, and ordered a pursuit for the following day. He still did not know that Longstreet was on the field, nor that Lee was coming up as well.

THE SECOND DAY

The second day opened with Jackson's force returning to its former positions and the Union army beginning a new series of attacks. Pope finally became aware of Longstreet's presence but still thought the Confederates were retreating. Skirmishing went on all day, with casualties mounting on both sides.

In the early afternoon, Pope decided to put in a decisive assault. This began at about 3:00 p.m., and was launched with great determination. Successive lines went forward and fierce close-range firefights broke out all along the Confederate line.

Jackson's corps had a good defensive position and confidence born of the previous day's victory. But the men were tired and the enemy far more numerous. Many battles of the Civil War were decided by raw firepower, with victory going to the side that hung on longest. Would the Rebels be broken first by the hammering they were receiving, or would the Federal troops run out of aggression and fall back? The crisis point had arrived.

THE DECISIVE MOMENT

Porter's force put in an attack, which was met with massed Confederate artillery fire and hurled back. Seeing that the moment had arrived, General Robert E Lee, who

weak Union line and flung it back. This endangered the flank of the forces assaulting Jackson, and resulted in a general movement towards the rear. For a time, it appeared that Pope's army was going to be chased from the field and devastated.

Despite the extremely aggressive advance of Longstreet's corps, elements of the Union force were able to rally and make a

stand on Henry House Hill, the same place where Jackson's brigade had broken the Union assault at the First Battle of Manassas. Although the rearguard was hard-pressed by determined Confederate attacks, it was able to hold out and prevent the total collapse of the Union Army.

As a result of the rearguard action, Pope's army came off the field at Second Manassas

defeated and bloodied but generally intact. It remained a viable fighting force, which was an improvement on the situation after First Manassas.

Below: The Confederate 5th Texas Regiment charge the Federal 5th New York Zouaves at the battle of Second Manassas.

SECOND MANASSAS

Left: Confederate commanders and staff at the Second
Battle of Manassas. Commanders on both sides relied
on mounted messengers to bring information and carry
orders to the commanders actually engaged. A
'galloper' who failed to find the recipient of his message
could tip a battle one way or the other.

Opposite: James Longstreet resigned a commission in
the US Army to serve the Confederacy. Although
controversy dogged his career there is no doubt that he
performed very well in battle.

PURSUIT (1 SEPTEMBER)

Following on from this success, Lee
continued to attack. He made a second large
flanking manoeuvre, hoping to cut off the
retreating Union army and obliterate it.
However, the going was slow even for
Jackson's hard-marching 'foot cavalry'.
Jackson's force reached Chantilly and there
encountered Union forces under Major-
General Isaac Stevens (1818–62) and
Major-General Philip Kearny (1815–62) on
1 September.

A sharp fight ensued, in which both
Union commanders were killed, but
Jackson was unable to complete his flanking
movement and the Union line of retreat
remained open. Pope was shaken by the
string of defeats and retired into the
defences of Washington, even though
reinforcements were available to him.

AFTERMATH

Lee had not quite managed to destroy
Pope's army, mainly due to Longstreet's
failure to attack on the first day and the
determined rearguard action on Henry
House Hill. Pope's decision to send troops
north to cover his flank, thus precipitating
the inconclusive but important fight at

Chantilly, also did much to stop a tactical
defeat becoming a strategic disaster. Pope
was blamed for the fiasco and relieved of his
command. Porter's career was also wrecked
by allegations that his refusal to attack
Longstreet was calculated to cause Pope's
defeat and McClellan's reinstatement as
overall commander.

Lee was not able to make an attempt on
Washington's defences with the forces he
had to hand, and McClellan remained a
threat. However, the way was now open for

an advance across the Potomac into the
North. Lee had shown that he could gamble
when he had to and that, overall, the
Southern forces were better led than their
Northern counterparts.

Victory at Second Manassas was a
turning point for the Confederacy. Not
long beforehand, Lee was facing certain
defeat; now the Union forces were in
disarray and there was a real chance of
winning the war.

Up until Second Manassas, the
Confederacy had been trying to stave off
defeat in Virginia, which would mean the
loss of the capital and probably the end of
the war. Now a new campaign opened,
which would lead to Antietam and another
turning point.

*Thanks to the stand at Henry House Hill, the Federal
army was able to cross the Bull Run and withdraw in
good order. Thousands of men were funnelled across
this narrow bridge.*

ANTIETAM
17 SEPTEMBER 1862

THE YEAR 1862 BEGAN WELL FOR THE UNION. IN THE WEST, UNION ARMIES ACHIEVED A NUMBER OF IMPORTANT VICTORIES, INCLUDING GRANT'S SUCCESS AT SHILOH. LIKEWISE, THE UNION NAVY WON SOME SIGNIFICANT GAINS, INCLUDING THE CAPTURE OF NEW ORLEANS AND THE USS *MONITOR*'S FORCING THE CONFEDERATE IRONCLAD *VIRGINIA* (FORMERLY THE UNION FRIGATE USS *MERRIMACK*) TO YIELD HAMPTON ROADS AND THE MOUTH OF THE JAMES RIVER TO FEDERAL CONTROL.

WHY DID IT HAPPEN?

WHO Major-General George B McClellan's (1826–85) Union Army of the Potomac (87,000) confronted General Robert E Lee's (1807–70) Confederate Army of Northern Virginia (45,000).

WHAT McClellan's army attacked while the Confederates were drawn up along Antietam Creek on the Maryland side of the Potomac River, inflicting some 10,300 casualties while losing 12,400 men.

WHERE Sharpsburg, Maryland, some 80.5km (50 miles) northwest of Washington DC.

WHEN 17 September 1862.

WHY McClellan's natural caution, his belief that he was outnumbered, plus poorly coordinated attacks allowed Lee to repulse Union attacks and withdraw to Virginia.

OUTCOME While the Army of Northern Virginia remained a significant force, Southern hopes of Maryland joining the Confederacy were dashed, as was the possibility of foreign intervention on their behalf. Lincoln also had the victory he needed to issue the Emancipation Proclamation.

Despite these successes on other fronts, the Union was unable to make significant progress in the central theatre of the war, that 161km (100-mile) front between the capitals of Washington DC and Richmond. Here, the main Confederate army of 60,000 men under General Joseph E Johnston (1807–91) faced the Union army of more than 100,000 under the command of Major-General George B McClellan. Under pressure from Lincoln (1809–65), McClellan came up with a plan for a grand flanking manoeuvre that required transporting his army to the Virginia Peninsula for an attack on

Richmond. By late March McClellan had concentrated a large army of nearly 100,000 on the Peninsula, but he was slow to act and so missed an opportunity to strike at Richmond from the Peninsula while he was opposed by a force of only 17,000 men. Johnston and his army moved to block McClellan's advance.

At this point, McClellan, noting that with the withdrawal of Johnston to the Peninsula Washington was no longer in danger, requested the release of a corps that had been left to defend Washington. He was thwarted by the advice of Robert E Lee, who suggested that Major-General Thomas

This is the railroad bridge at Harpers Ferry. The town was an important Union garrison and supply centre. The heights in the background were captured by Confederate troops and it is clear from the photograph how these dominate the town.

'Stonewall' Jackson's (1824–63) troops in the Shenandoah Valley make a feint to tie down Union forces. Jackson executed a masterful campaign, not only pinning, and defeating, large numbers of Union forces in and around the Valley, but also convincing Lincoln not to release the corps McClellan had requested.

Although McClellan would advance to within 8km (5 miles) of Richmond, he would be forced to retreat when Robert E Lee assumed command of the Confederate army there after Johnston had been wounded. During June and July, the two armies fought a number of engagements and, although the battles were indecisive and costly to the Confederacy, Lee's skilful manoeuvring forced the Union army to halt its efforts to seize Richmond.

POPE TO THE FORE

In early August, Lincoln decided to concentrate Union forces in northern Virginia under the command of Major-General John Pope (1822–92) as the Army of Virginia. He also ordered McClellan to begin withdrawing his forces from the Peninsula, intending for the two forces to join together and create a huge army to march on Richmond from the north. Lee reacted quickly, ordering a probing attack by Jackson against Pope and moving the bulk of his own forces north in support. At the Second Battle of Manassas (28–30 August), Pope's army was mauled by Jackson and by Longstreet, whom Lee had sent to support him.

Lee had hoped to annihilate the Army of Virginia, but Pope began an orderly retreat to Centreville, and the exhaustion of the Rebel troops, especially those of Jackson's command, a vigorous defence by the Union rearguard and impending arrival of Union reinforcements, made this impossible.

By the end of the summer, Confederate fortunes on the war's central front were on the rise. Lee had turned back a major Union effort against the Rebel capital, Richmond, and, in conjunction with Jackson, had counterattacked and won a significant victory. At the same time, Union forces in the western theatre had become bogged down and lost the initiative. It was at this point that the Confederacy planned a major

series of coordinated offensives against the Union forces both in the east and the west.

THE CAMPAIGN

The Union Army was in disarray. Pope and his subordinates blamed one another for the debacle at Manassas. President Lincoln was despondent because he was unable to find a commander who seemed capable of winning the decisive victory he so sorely wanted. In the event, he appointed, once again, George McClellan as the commander of the reinforced Army of the Potomac. Many in the Lincoln administration were against the general's reappointment, including Secretary of War Edwin Stanton (1814–69). Although Lincoln perhaps

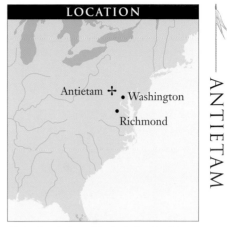

LOCATION

The battle took place in Maryland where Confederate forces could threaten the capital, Washington, as well as the rich farms and towns of Pennsylvania. It was further hoped that a Confederate army in Maryland would bring that state over to the Confederate cause.

1ST SOUTH CAROLINA REGIMENT OF RIFLES

Also known as Orr's Rifles, the regiment was formed in July 1861 and was engaged in many of the important battles of the war. At Antietam, it was part of Brigadier-General Maxcy Gregg's (1814–62) brigade of AP Hill's (1825–65) Light Division along with four other units of South Carolinians. The unit was involved in Hill's counterattack against Major-General Ambrose Burnside (1824–81). Hill notes that Gregg's brigade was composed of veterans and while engaging in a firefight, poured in 'destructive volleys' against the advancing Union troops. Three Confederate brigades, including Gregg and his South Carolina regiments, numbering only 2000 men, were able to drive off Burnside's corps.

This illustration shows the difficulty that faced the troops of Burnside's corps as it tried to push across the Rohrbach Bridge. Only one unit at a time could cross the bridge and so the Union forces were forced to launch piecemeal attacks rather than coordinated ones.

realized that McClellan's cautious nature made him less than ideal as an aggressive battlefield commander, McClellan had, nonetheless, demonstrated his skills as an excellent military administrator. After the defeat at Second Manassas, it was these skills that were needed to reforge the demoralized Union army.

While the Union forces were regrouping, the Confederacy was planning its coordinated offensives for the autumn of 1862. There were to be three separate campaigns launched. Two western armies under General Braxton Bragg (1817–76) and Major-General Earl Van Dorn (1820–63) were to invade Kentucky and Tennessee respectively. In the meantime, Lee and the Army of Northern Virginia were to move north through Maryland, pushing on to Harrisburg, the capital of Pennsylvania. If successful, the Confederacy would see a number of positive strategic

effects. First, it was hoped that the arrival of a Confederate army in Maryland, which was home to a number of Southern sympathizers, would bring that state within the Confederacy, providing both manpower and resources.

Secondly, Lee's army had suffered from the constant and arduous campaigning earlier in the year and his troops were in desperate need of all manner of supplies. Many of these could be procured in Pennsylvania. Lastly, Harrisburg was an important centre of communications that sat astride road and railroad lines that would allow Lee and his army to threaten a number of important Northern cities, such as Philadelphia, Baltimore and Washington, with either direct attack or by cutting their supply lines.

On 5 September, Lee led his Army of Northern Virginia across the Potomac River into Maryland. Unfortunately, it quickly became apparent to him that, despite the sympathetic leanings of many Marylanders, the state and its population were not actively going to support him or his army. One reason for this may have been the appearance of the Army of Northern Virginia. Although the troops were flushed

with victory and very confident, they hardly looked like a triumphant army. Few units had a uniform appearance and many of the troops' clothing was threadbare and their equipment was worn out.

HARPERS FERRY

Lee continued to move north towards Frederick, which he occupied. While there he learned that the Union forces in and around Harpers Ferry, about 13,000 men, had not retreated even though they were now cut off by his invasion force. Lee decided to have Jackson cross the Potomac with 15,000 men while two other divisions supported Jackson by occupying the heights on the Maryland side of the river. He would take the remainder of the army and move towards Hagerstown.

On 9 September, Lee had orders drawn up, Special Orders 191, outlining his plan, with copies sent to the pertinent commanders. This did not seem to be a particularly risky manoeuvre given McClellan's propensity for caution and his tentative movements. Lee believed that the army would be reunited before it faced a major engagement. Having received its marching orders, the Army of Northern

Virginia divided into four columns and departed the next day.

Unfortunately for Lee, McClellan moved more quickly than usual, perhaps spurred on by the panic that Lee's invasion had caused. On 7 September, the Army of the Potomac left Washington in pursuit of Lee's forces. The army's morale had not improved much since the defeat at Second Manassas a little more than a week before. But as the Union troops marched though western Maryland, a profound change occurred. Unlike Lee, the Union troops were met with great enthusiasm by the local population, who came out in large numbers to cheer them on and provide them with food and drink. For the first time, the Army of the Potomac was on the defensive, fighting on its own soil, and with the outpouring of support morale soared.

On 12–13 September, Confederate troops occupied the heights east of Harpers Ferry, facing only minor resistance, and,

after a brief bombardment, the town and its garrison, less 1500 cavalry who managed to break out, surrendered to Jackson the following day. But while Jackson was enjoying success at Harpers Ferry, fate struck a serious blow to the Army of Northern Virginia.

On 13 September, McClellan's army entered Frederick and received an enthusiastic greeting from the inhabitants. One Union regiment, the 27th Indiana, halted that morning at a farm just outside town. As troops fell out to rest, a corporal in the unit found an envelope containing three cigars wrapped in a sheet of paper. The soldier unwrapped the paper and discovered that it was a copy of Special Orders 191, detailing Lee's campaign plan. The captured document was quickly passed up the chain of command until it reached General McClellan's headquarters. But McClellan was indecisive; although he had the enemy's plans, he believed, as he all too

THE OPPOSED FORCES

FEDERAL
Army of the Potomac,
consisting of 7 army corps   **87,000**

CONFEDERATE
Army of Northern Virginia,
consisting of 2 army corps   **45,000**

Major-General Ambrose Burnside, seated in the centre with his legs crossed, commanded the Union army's Ninth Corps. He is shown with his staff. Photographs of commanders and their staffs taken either before or after a battle were very popular.

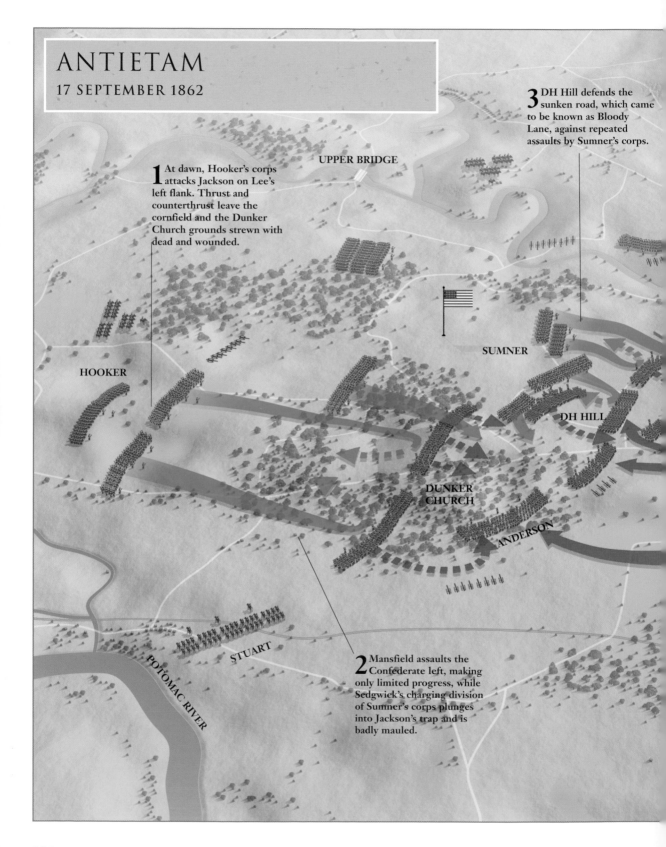

ANTIETAM
17 SEPTEMBER 1862

3 DH Hill defends the sunken road, which came to be known as Bloody Lane, against repeated assaults by Sumner's corps.

UPPER BRIDGE

1 At dawn, Hooker's corps attacks Jackson on Lee's left flank. Thrust and counterthrust leave the cornfield and the Dunker Church grounds strewn with dead and wounded.

SUMNER

HOOKER

DH HILL

DUNKER CHURCH

ANDERSON

STUART

POTOMAC RIVER

2 Mansfield assaults the Confederate left, making only limited progress, while Sedgwick's charging division of Sumner's corps plunges into Jackson's trap and is badly mauled.

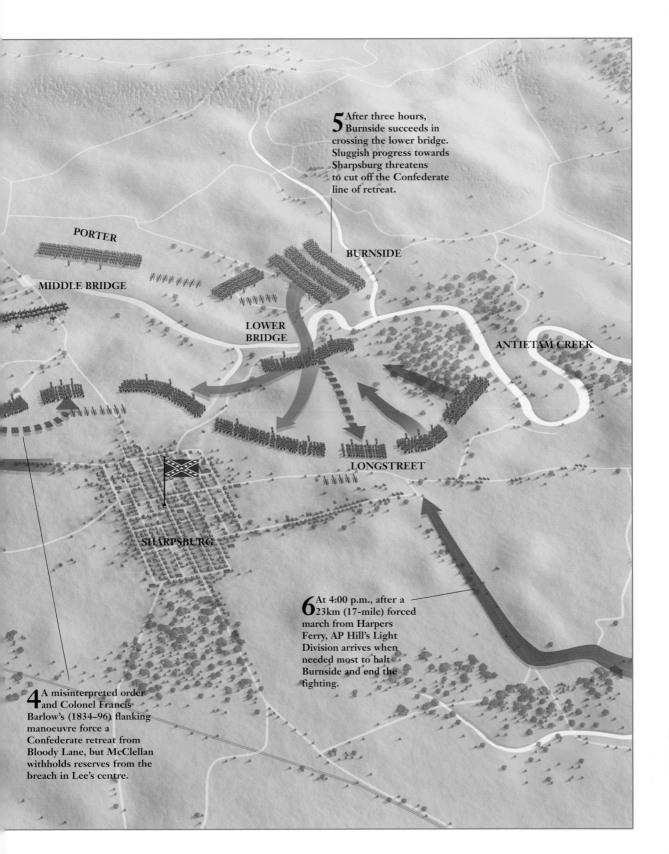

5 After three hours, Burnside succeeds in crossing the lower bridge. Sluggish progress towards Sharpsburg threatens to cut off the Confederate line of retreat.

PORTER

BURNSIDE

MIDDLE BRIDGE

LOWER BRIDGE

ANTIETAM CREEK

LONGSTREET

SHARPSBURG

6 At 4:00 p.m., after a 23km (17-mile) forced march from Harpers Ferry, AP Hill's Light Division arrives when needed most to halt Burnside and end the fighting.

4 A misinterpreted order and Colonel Francis Barlow's (1834–96) flanking manoeuvre force a Confederate retreat from Bloody Lane, but McClellan withholds reserves from the breach in Lee's centre.

Above: A soldier of a Zouave unit which formed part of Major-General Ambrose Burnside's Ninth Corps. His regiment had the distinction of being the Union unit which advanced farthest during the battle, attacking the outskirts of Sharpsburg in the afternoon.

often did, that Lee's force was much larger than it actually was. As a result, it took hours for orders to be drafted and the Union forces did not begin moving until the next morning.

Lee, however, received intelligence regarding the impending movement of the Union army. Colonel JEB 'Jeb' Stuart's (1833–64) cavalry scouts had noted the unusual activity among the Union units and a message was received from a Southern sympathizer that McClellan had obtained a copy of his orders. Had McClellan moved quickly on 13 September, he might have taken and held the passes in the South Mountain range. Lee, however, moved more quickly and blocked the three key passes with his available forces, perhaps 16,000 men. On 14 September, these forces were attacked by more than twice their number of Union soldiers. Although the fighting was fierce, the Southern troops were forced to yield the passes to the enemy.

Things looked bleak for Lee on the night of 14 September and he was planning to abandon the campaign and retreat back to Virginia when he received word that Harpers Ferry was about to surrender to Jackson. This strengthened his resolve and so Lee determined to make his stand where

he had received the message – Sharpsburg. This was a strong position, protected by a series of hills and Antietam Creek. At noon on 15 September, Lee received confirmation that Harpers Ferry had in fact surrendered and sent orders to all of his units to converge on Sharpsburg for what could be, if they were victorious, a decisive battle.

DISPOSITIONS

On 15 September, Lee had managed to gather some 18,000 troops at Sharpsburg, but they had not had the time to fully deploy. McClellan's forces began arriving that afternoon as well but, cautious as ever, he did not cross the unguarded Antietam Creek; indeed, he did not even make an effort to reconnoitre the far bank by sending out a cavalry screen. The next day, troops arrived on both sides. Lee's force increased to perhaps 25,000 men while McClellan had some 55,000 men deployed with another 14,000 or so men only a few

Hooker's First Corps launched a sustained attack along the Hagerstown Turnpike on the morning of 17 September and there was heavy fighting stretching the length of the road. The bodies are those of Confederate soldiers killed in the fighting.

ANTIETAM

kilometres away. But rather than attacking on 16 September, McClellan spent the entire day planning rather than moving. Once again, he assumed that Lee's forces were far stronger than they actually were and so he delayed attacking. This was a missed opportunity for the Union to defeat the Army of Northern Virginia while it was divided. By the time the battle began on the morning of 17 September Lee had gathered most of his available forces at Sharpsburg. Only Major-General AP Hill's division was not present, as it was on the march and expected to arrive later that day.

Lee had deployed his forces to the north and east of Sharpsburg along a ridgeline with both wings protected by water; the left rested on a bend in the Potomac River, while the right was anchored on Antietam Creek. Stuart's cavalry held the extreme left of Lee's line. The main body of the

Confederate left was composed of Jackson's corps, while Longstreet's corps held the Confederate right flank.

McClellan had finally sent troops across the Antietam on the evening of 16 September. He sent Major-General Joseph Hooker (1814–79) and his First Corps, later followed by Major-General Joseph K Mansfield's (1803–62) 12th Corps, as the right wing of his army. On the eastern bank of the Antietam, the remainder of his army was placed, beginning with Major-General William B Franklin (1823–1903) and his Sixth Corps, closely followed by Major-General Edwin Sumner's (1797–1863) Second Corps. Then came the Fifth Corps under Major-General Fitz John Porter (1822–1901) supported by Brigadier-General Alfred Pleasonton's (1824–97) cavalry division and, finally, Major-General Ambrose Burnside's Ninth Corps, which

This painting shows Union troops advancing at the double. Although tactics of the time, such as Hardee's Rifle and Light Infantry Tactics, emphasized firepower, moving forward at the double in order to come to grips with cold steel was seen as a possible counter to the infantry firefight.

In an era without radios and on battlefields that were quickly covered with billowing smoke, signal towers like the one shown provided both a vantage point as well as a way of communicating across the battlefield through the use of semaphores and heliographs.

formed the army's left flank. The plan called for 'Fighting Joe' Hooker supported by Mansfield and Sumner to sweep down the Hagerstown Turnpike and engage the Confederate left flank. Once this had been done and Lee's attention was fixed on his left, Burnside would force his way over the Antietam by the Rohrbach Bridge. The remaining two corps and Pleasonton's cavalry were to be kept in reserve.

THE BATTLE

The battle began at dawn with Hooker's First Corps quickly moving to the attack along the Hagerstown Pike. As the Union troops entered the cornfield that lay to the east of the Pike between two large woods, they became heavily engaged with Jackson's troops. The fighting was intense, with both sides suffering heavy losses. Particularly devastating was the artillery fire. Both sides engaged in stiff counterbattery fire and the Union artillery fired at point-blank range into the cornfield, inflicting massive casualties. For nearly two hours both sides fed divisions into the fray without gaining the advantage. It was not until 7:00 a.m. that troops from the next Union corps, Mansfield's 12th, joined the action. Sadly, this was to be typical for the battle –

McClellan's inability to coordinate attacks that would have allowed him to take advantage of his superiority in numbers. By the time Mansfield engaged the enemy, Hooker's division had been rendered nearly combat ineffective. Moreover, Lee used the time to move additional troops to support his left flank.

Once again, the Union troops of the 12th Corps attacked, but without much support and thus with limited success – when the troops did make a breakthrough they were unsupported. The only support came from one division of Sumner's corps, which, having crossed the cornfield and entered the West Woods without reconnoitring first, was ambushed and badly mauled.

Sumner's remaining two divisions advanced around 9:00 a.m., moving south to engage the centre of Lee's line. Here, the Confederates occupied an 800m (880-yard) stretch of road that had been eroded by years of use and provided a natural trench line for the Confederates holding it. For nearly four hours the Union troops launched attacks against the enemy in 'Bloody Lane' until, finally, they managed to take and hold it.

Once again, a lack of coordination, in this case not committing the troops held in reserve from the corps of Major-Generals Porter and Franklin, allowed an opportunity to be lost. It is clear that McClellan assumed that he needed to keep these troops in reserve to counter Lee's reserve forces – which did not exist.

While the Union army was hotly engaged in the cornfield, the West Woods, and then at Bloody Lane, Burnside, who was to have engaged in early assault, remained inactive. This allowed Lee to move units facing Burnside to other parts of the battlefield at critical moments. At 10:00 a.m., however, Burnside received direct orders to attack and he now faced a considerably reduced Confederate force. Although he outnumbered the enemy by more than three to one, Burnside was unable to force a crossing of the Antietam for several hours.

His actions at Rohrbach, soon to be evermore known as Burnside's Bridge, were both unimaginative and lethargic. He suffered heavy casualties by sending units to attack across the bridge. It was not until the early afternoon that some of his troops turned the Confederates' position by fording the creek downstream; and it was not until nearly 3:00 p.m. that he was prepared for a more general advance against the Confederate right and began forcing them back towards Sharpsburg, cutting off their line of retreat across the Potomac. But Burnside's lack of initiative proved costly since at 4:00 p.m. AP Hill arrived from Harpers Ferry with badly needed reinforcements and attacked Burnside's left flank, collapsing it.

Although Burnside's left flank was in serious trouble, his right continued to press the Confederates, driving them towards Sharpsburg, but McClellan refused to send in his reserves, assuming himself still to be outnumbered.

As night fell, both sides were exhausted and had suffered horrific casualties. On the morning of 18 September Lee could muster perhaps 30,000 effectives and had no hope of fresh troops. McClellan, meanwhile, had received some 13,000 reinforcements who, together with his uncommitted reserves, gave him more fresh troops than Lee had fit for duty in his entire army. But his belief that Lee had hidden reserves kept him from

engaging on 18 September, and so the Army of Northern Virginia was able to slip away unmolested that night.

Although McClellan had missed an opportunity to destroy Lee's army and likely end the war, the strategic effects of the Battle of Antietam were nonetheless significant. The Union had turned back a major Confederate offensive on to their soil and, in so doing, had kept Maryland out of the Confederacy. This also ended any hope of foreign intervention on behalf of the South. Finally, President Lincoln, who did not wish to appear desperate when he issued the Emancipation Proclamation, could now do so in the wake of a major strategic victory.

This photograph shows President Lincoln with Allan Pinkerton (1819–84), head of the Secret Service, and Major-General John McClernand (1812–1900). The victory at Antietam was important to Lincoln since it provided him with a much-needed success before announcing the Emancipation Proclamation.

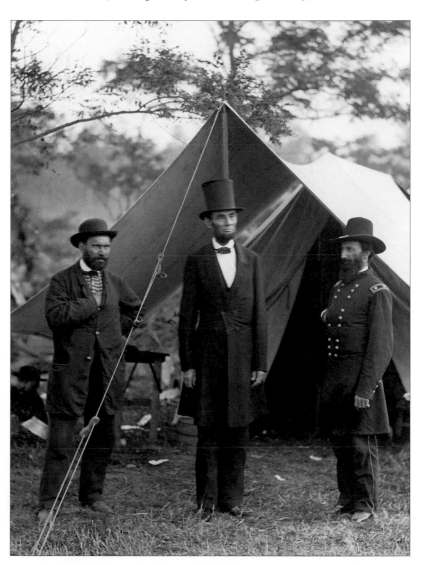

CORINTH
3–4 OCTOBER 1862

RAILROADS AND THEIR ABILITY TO MOVE TROOPS AND EQUIPMENT RAPIDLY OVER GREAT DISTANCES CATAPULTED THE OTHERWISE MODEST TOWN OF CORINTH, MISSISSIPPI, ONTO CENTRE STAGE OF THE CIVIL WAR. BOTH FEDERALS AND CONFEDERATES WANTED THIS STRATEGIC LOCATION AS A MEANS OF INFLUENCING OPERATIONS IN TENNESSEE. TWO BATTLES WERE FOUGHT OVER CORINTH, WITH THE FEDERALS ESTABLISHING PERMANENT CONTROL AFTER THE SECOND BATTLE ON 3–4 OCTOBER 1862.

WHY DID IT HAPPEN?

WHO Confederate and Federal forces sought to control the railroad system in the west in order to influence operations in Tennessee.

WHAT First a pending siege forced the Confederates to abandon Corinth. Then the Federals occupied and fortified the town and defeated a Confederate attack.

WHERE Corinth, Mississippi, where the Memphis and Charleston Railroad met with the Mobile and Ohio Railroad.

WHEN 3–4 October 1862.

WHY The Confederate attack was poorly planned and became progressively weaker as it lengthened while the Federal defences became stronger as they contracted.

OUTCOME The Confederates' ability to reinforce Tennessee was denied and Major-General Ulysses S Grant (1822–85) was then able to turn his attention to Vicksburg.

At the time of the Civil War, Corinth was still a young town. It was settled in 1854 and had a pre-war population of only 1200. Its business district consisted mostly of one- and two-storey, gabled, wood-frame structures. Corinth boasted the typical dry goods stores, blacksmith shops, livery stables, saloons, restaurants, drugstore, bakery, tailor's shop and picture gallery. The Aetna Insurance Company had a local office there, and there were three hotels, including the Tishomingo, renowned for its luxury of serving ice water. It was all relatively routine, save perhaps for the post office, which, rather than the standard whitewash, was painted pink.

What separated Corinth from any of the hundreds of other similar-sized towns throughout the Confederate west was the railroad. Railroads brought with them the important strategic concept of interior lines – the ability of one side to use superior lateral communications to reinforce their separated units faster than the enemy could reinforce theirs. Indeed, the Civil War would become the first great railroad war.

At Corinth, the Memphis and Charleston Railroad met with the Mobile and Ohio Railroad. Control of Corinth meant control of railroads from Columbus and Memphis, as well as those running south into Mississippi and eastwards to connect with Nashville and Chattanooga. Many Federal military and political leaders believed that if the Union could occupy two points in the South, the rebellion would

At Iuka, Major-General Edward Ord (1818–83), standing, centre, was unable to combine with Major-General William Rosecrans (1819–98) to trap the Confederates between two pincers. He would later command the 18th Corps during Grant's Overland Campaign in Virginia.

collapse. Obviously, one point was Richmond. The other was Corinth. Major-General Ulysses S Grant called Corinth 'the great strategic position at the West between the Tennessee and Mississippi Rivers and between Nashville and Vicksburg'. Confederate President Jefferson Davis (1808–89) considered the Memphis and Charleston Railroad the 'vertebrae of the Confederacy'. Corinth itself was known as 'the crossroads of the Confederacy'. It was all sufficiently important to cause Corinth to play a pivotal role in the preliminaries to the Battle of Shiloh, to host two battles itself and to facilitate the launching of the decisive Vicksburg Campaign.

CORINTH AND SHILOH

Grant's victories at Forts Henry and Donelson in February 1862 forced General Albert Sidney Johnston's (1803–62) Army of Mississippi out of Tennessee. Johnston then decided to concentrate his forces at the rail junction at Corinth. At the same time, Grant had assembled some 45,000 men at Pittsburg Landing, about 32km (20 miles) northeast of Corinth, where he would wait for the arrival of Major-General Don Carlos Buell's (1818–98) Army of the Ohio from Nashville. In times of peace, one of the ways goods reached Corinth from the Tennessee River was along a road from the wharf at Pittsburg Landing. Now Pittsburg Landing offered Grant a convenient staging area for a march south to attack Corinth.

Grant was quite sure that Corinth would be the next battlefield and that he would be the one initiating the action. He wrote to one of his generals: 'I am clearly of the opinion that the enemy are gathering strength at Corinth quite as rapidly as we are here, and the sooner we attack, the easier will be the task of taking the place.' Indeed, attack was all Grant had in mind. He failed to prepare any defences himself and responded to suggestions that the Confederates themselves might attack by saying: 'They're all back at Corinth, and, when our transportation arrives, we have got to go there and draw them out, as you would draw a badger out of a hole.'

CONFEDERATE CAVALRYMAN

In the Civil War cavalrymen were used to gather intelligence and conduct raids. They were especially skilled at attacking enemy lines of communications such as railroads. While Major-General Earl Van Dorn did not perform well at Corinth, he eventually found his calling as a cavalry commander. His December 1862 raid against Grant's supply depot at Holly Springs, Mississippi, caused Grant to restructure his plans for a railroad-centred campaign against Vicksburg. Nathan Bedford Forrest (1821–77) posed such a threat that Grant called him 'that devil Forrest'.

As a result, Grant was caught completely by surprise on 6 April, when Johnston attacked at Shiloh. The first day of the fighting was a close call for Grant's army, but the Federals recovered the second day and won the battle. In the process, Johnston, who some considered the Confederacy's greatest general at the time, was killed, and General PGT Beauregard (1818–93) assumed command. Beauregard retreated back to Corinth and began building heavy fortifications.

The Federals also experienced a leadership change. In spite of the overall victory, Grant's poor showing on the first day of Shiloh damaged his credibility, and he was replaced by Major-General Henry Halleck (1815–72). Thus it would be Halleck who would lead the Federal

LOCATION

The importance of railroads: Corinth's position at the junction of the Memphis and Charleston Railroad and the Mobile and Ohio Railroad made it 'the crossroads of the Confederacy'.

offensive against Corinth that Grant had been anticipating before General Johnston interrupted his plans.

FIRST BATTLE OF CORINTH

Halleck would eventually provide valuable service to the Union in an administrative capacity as General-in-Chief and then as Grant's chief of staff, but he was not an impressive field commander. His approach march towards Corinth was slow and deliberate. Every night he stopped and had his men dig in. After the horrific losses at

Opposite: Confederate troops charge Union trenches. The Confederates' lack of reserves prevented them from exploiting local successes at the Second Battle of Corinth.

Shiloh, Halleck was in no mood to risk additional heavy combat. As Captain EB Soper described: 'Every advance was made in line of battle preceded by skirmishers. When the popping on the skirmish line became hot, lines were dressed up at favourable positions, every other man holding two rifles, and his file-mate industriously using the shovel or axe, relieving each other every minute or two. A strong line of rifle pits was in this way speedily constructed.'

To make matters worse, Halleck had to corduroy many kilometres of roads (surface them with branches and small tree trunks laid side by side) to give him the dry, dependable and durable surface he needed to transport supplies by wagon. Thus Halleck crept along at a rate of less than

The dashing Pierre Beauregard won early fame in the Civil War as both the hero of Fort Sumter and First Manassas. He assumed command at Shiloh after General Albert Sidney Johnston was killed.

THE OPPOSED FORCES

FEDERAL
Army of the Mississippi — 23,000

CONFEDERATE
Army of Tennessee — 22,000

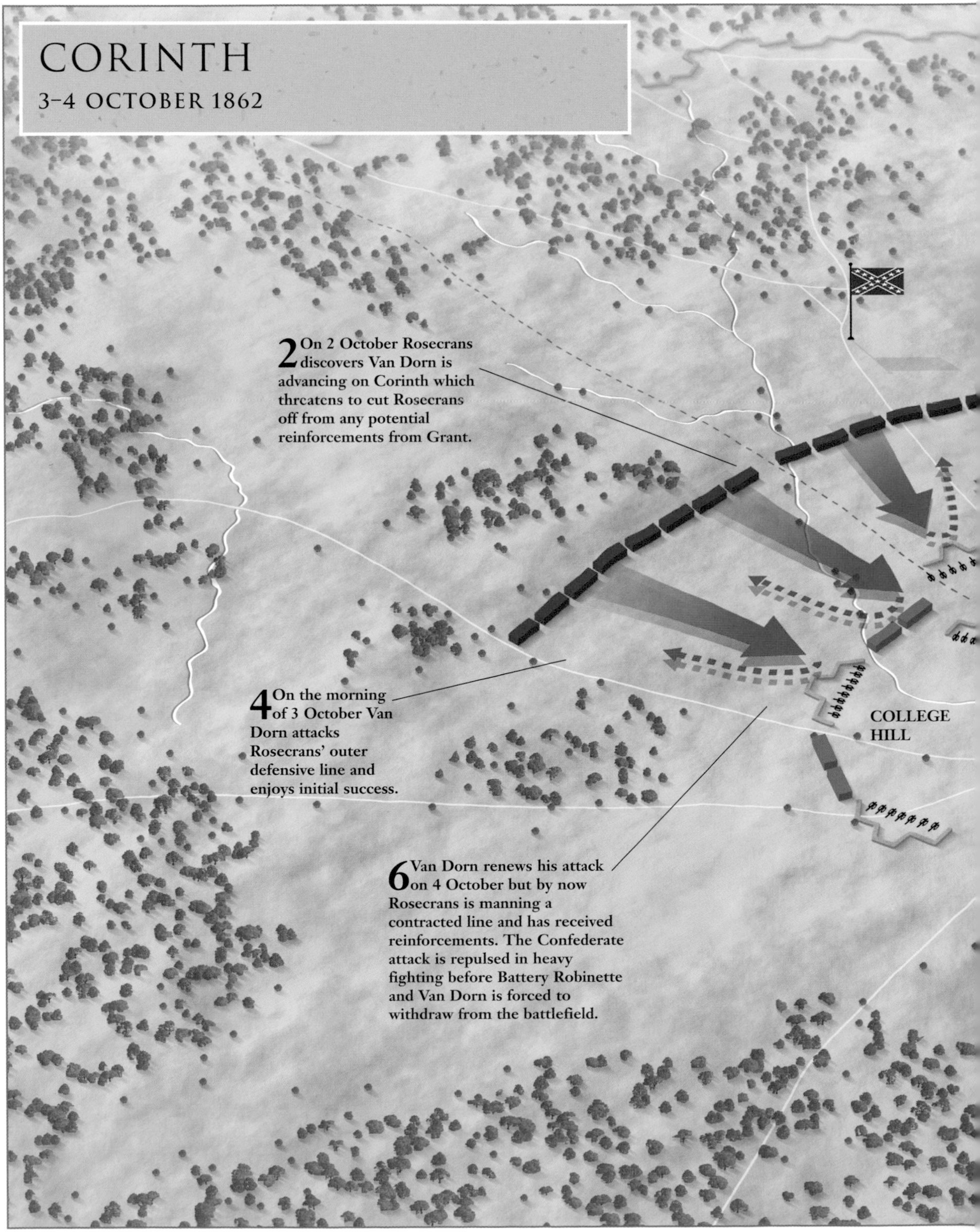

CORINTH
3–4 OCTOBER 1862

2 On 2 October Rosecrans discovers Van Dorn is advancing on Corinth which threatens to cut Rosecrans off from any potential reinforcements from Grant.

4 On the morning of 3 October Van Dorn attacks Rosecrans' outer defensive line and enjoys initial success.

COLLEGE HILL

6 Van Dorn renews his attack on 4 October but by now Rosecrans is manning a contracted line and has received reinforcements. The Confederate attack is repulsed in heavy fighting before Battery Robinette and Van Dorn is forced to withdraw from the battlefield.

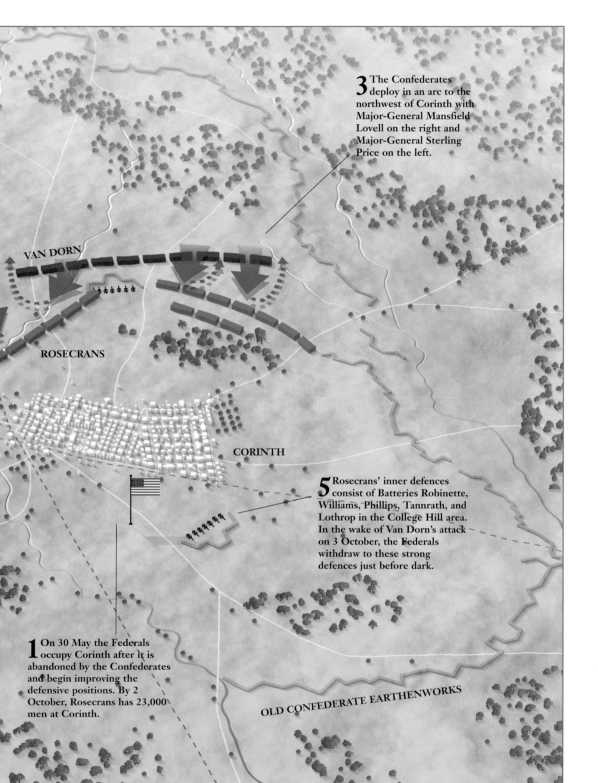

3 The Confederates deploy in an arc to the northwest of Corinth with Major-General Mansfield Lovell on the right and Major-General Sterling Price on the left.

VAN DORN

ROSECRANS

CORINTH

5 Rosecrans' inner defences consist of Batteries Robinette, Williams, Phillips, Tannrath, and Lothrop in the College Hill area. In the wake of Van Dorn's attack on 3 October, the Federals withdraw to these strong defences just before dark.

1 On 30 May the Federals occupy Corinth after it is abandoned by the Confederates and begin improving the defensive positions. By 2 October, Rosecrans has 23,000 men at Corinth.

OLD CONFEDERATE EARTHENWORKS

Opposite: The Federals occupied and improved the already strong positions left behind when the Confederates abandoned Corinth during the night of 29/30 May. By the time of the second battle, the Confederate forces faced successive inner and outer rings of entrenchments.

1.6km (1 mile) per day. The consequence was that Beauregard had plenty of time to prepare his defences and his plan.

The Confederate entrenchments formed an 11km (7-mile) line that covered the northern and eastern approaches to Corinth and extended in an arc about 2.4km (1.5 miles) from town. They were anchored east and west on the Memphis and Charleston Railroad and included rifle pits with battery emplacements at key points. It was a formidable line.

Still Beauregard knew that he was far outnumbered. He had withdrawn to Corinth with 30,000 of the 40,000 Confederates who fought at Shiloh, and later reinforcements brought his strength to 66,000. Halleck had begun his march from Shiloh with 90,000, and his ranks had swollen to 110,000 by the time he reached Corinth. By mid-May, Halleck was astride the Mobile and Ohio Railroad north of Corinth and had cut the Memphis and Charleston Railroad to the east.

Instead of subjecting himself to the lopsided siege that Halleck was planning, Beauregard resorted to a ruse to play on Halleck's cautious nature. As trains rolled into Corinth, Beauregard had his men cheer wildly as if reinforcements were arriving.

Halleck took the bait and proceeded with due caution. In reality, there were no reinforcements, and instead, on the night of 29/30 May, Beauregard loaded his men and equipment onto the trains and withdrew to Tupelo. By the time Halleck finally assaulted Corinth on the morning of 30 May, Beauregard and his army were gone.

Halleck had captured an important location without a fight, but he had let his enemy escape. This was of little concern to Halleck, who had always considered Corinth rather than Beauregard's army to be his true objective. Halleck wrote to his wife that he now possessed 'a most important military point'. Moreover, he had accomplished the feat with very little loss of life. He wrote: 'This to me is the great merit of the whole, although the public will be greatly disappointed that thousands were not killed in a great battle! I have won the victory without the battle! Military history will do me justice.' Grant, who assuredly would have used a more aggressive strategy in attacking Corinth, had a different opinion. 'The possession of Corinth by National troops', he wrote, 'was of strategic importance, but the victory was barren in every other particular.' Nonetheless, Corinth was now in Federal hands, and it would be the Confederates who would be doing the attacking at the next battle there.

IUKA

On 11 July 1862, President Abraham Lincoln (1809–65) ordered General Halleck to Washington, where Halleck finally found his calling as General-in-Chief. Grant

assumed Halleck's command more or less by default and inherited a widely scattered army that lacked the centralized striking force he wanted.

Moreover, Confederate forces in Mississippi under Major-General Earl Van Dorn (1820–63) and Major-General Sterling Price (1809–67) were a threat to General Grant's communications with Federal forces in Tennessee and represented possible reinforcements to the Confederate forces under General Braxton Bragg (1817–76) who were concentrating in Tennessee in preparation for Bragg's invasion of Kentucky.

Grant resolved to act, attacking Price at Iuka on 19 September. Grant had planned to trap Price in a pincer between Major-Generals William Rosecrans and Edward OC Ord, but the two Federal generals failed to act in concert and Price escaped. Price and Van Dorn joined forces near Ripley, southwest of Corinth, on 28 September. For his part, Grant ordered most of his army back to Corinth, which was now 'more than ever the centrepiece and linchpin of the Union position in northern Mississippi and West Tennessee'.

CORINTH AGAIN

Still Grant's army was relatively scattered, and Van Dorn considered Rosecrans' force at Corinth to be isolated enough to be a

Civil War defenders would often use chevaux de frise – sharpened rows of sticks that were especially effective obstacles against cavalry charges.

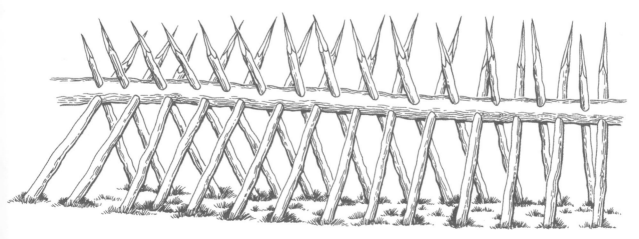

CORINTH

This illustration shows the elaborate regulation Confederate Army officers' sleeve design. From left to right: general, colonel, captain and lieutenant.

vulnerable target. Accordingly, Van Dorn planned to defeat Rosecrans, seize the railroad junction at Corinth, and use it to support a campaign into western Tennessee. It was not a particularly well-thought-out plan as events would demonstrate.

On the morning of 3 October, Van Dorn struck. Rosecrans had greatly improved the already-formidable defences the Rebels had vacated, and the Federal fortifications now consisted of successive outer and inner entrenchments. The sweeping arc of the outer defences stretched the Federals thin, but this initial line served its purpose even if it only delayed the attackers. After a day of hard fighting, the Federals withdrew to their inner defences, just before dark. Now Rosecrans was at his strongest defences, consisting of Batteries Robinette, Williams, Phillips, Tannrath and Lothrop in the College Hill area, just a few hundred metres

outside Corinth. These batteries were connected by breastworks and in some cases protected by abatis – trees that were felled and sharpened to create an obstacle for the enemy. Corporal Charles Wright of the 81st Ohio considered the College Hill line 'a splendid place to make the fight'. It was indeed an advantageous situation for the Federals. While the Confederates had been sapping their strength fighting through Rosecrans' defence in depth, Rosecrans was receiving a steady stream of reinforcements and improving his ability to support mutually his forces in his now contracted line. 'The line of attack was a long one,' Van Dorn noted, 'and as it approached the interior defences of the enemy that line must necessarily become contracted.'

The next day Van Dorn continued his attack, opening up with a pre-dawn bombardment that amounted to 'a real display of fireworks' according to one Federal. Many of the Confederate shells, however, landed long, exploding in Corinth itself and killing civilians and one wounded Federal soldier in the Tishomingo Hotel. Price launched an initial charge at about 10:00 a.m. that showed promise when the Confederates found a weak point in the Federal line and penetrated into Corinth, where house-to-house fighting ensued. Rosecrans himself seemed to have thought the day was lost and began issuing panicky orders to burn various stockpiles of supplies.

But Rosecrans need not have worried. In a pitched battle in front of Battery Robinette, the Federal line rallied and pushed back Brigadier-General Dabney Maurey's (1822–1900) division of Van Dorn's army. The Confederates had thrown all they had at the Federals, who had reserves that the Confederates did not. Van Dorn had reached his culminating point and he knew it. To continue the attack risked complete destruction, and that afternoon he began marching away from the battlefield.

Rosecrans was now in a good position to cut off the Confederate retreat, and Grant had high hopes for such a vigorous pursuit, but instead Rosecrans told his men to get some rest and be ready to go after Van Dorn in the morning. Major-Generals Edward OC Ord and Stephen Hurlbut (1815–82) did attempt a pursuit but without Rosecrans to press the Confederates from the southeast, the trap could not be closed. When Rosecrans finally got moving on 5 October, he advanced only 13km (8 miles) and went into camp.

The Second Battle of Corinth was over. It had been a costly affair for both sides. Federal casualties were 3090, while the Confederates suffered 4467. While Grant was disappointed that Van Dorn had not been destroyed, securing Corinth was still a major victory for the Federals.

CORINTH AND VICKSBURG

With Corinth safely in Federal hands, Van Dorn and Price could no longer reinforce Confederate forces in Tennessee. Grant was now free to concern himself with greater ventures. He explained: 'The battle relieved me from any further anxiety for the safety of the territory within my jurisdiction, and soon after receiving reinforcements I suggested to the general-in-chief a forward movement against Vicksburg.' The railroad had made Corinth worth fighting for, but, having won it, Grant was ready to move on.

Grant now held significant portions of the Mobile and Ohio, Mississippi Central, and Memphis and Charleston railroads, but he wanted to get out of the business of guarding railroads and depots and go on the offensive. 'By moving against the enemy,' Grant explained, 'into his unsubdued, or not yet captured, territory, driving their army before us, these lines would nearly hold themselves; thus affording a large force for field operations.' The object of these 'field operations' was to be Vicksburg.

SIGNIFICANCE

Corinth stands as a demonstration of how railroads influenced operations and strategy in the Civil War. It had already brought together the two great armies that clashed at Shiloh. In turn, the Rebels and Federals had defended and attacked it, struggling for its control. Now possession of this small railroad town was about to make possible one of the war's most decisive campaigns. As much as perhaps any other place in the western theatre, Corinth shows why the Civil War was a war of railroad strategy.

General Beauregard used a ruse to trick Halleck into thinking reinforcements were arriving at Corinth. Instead Beauregard withdrew to avoid Halleck's numerical advantage. By the time of the Second Battle of Corinth, Beauregard had been replaced by Braxton Bragg as commander of the Army of Tennessee and had assumed command of coastal defences in Georgia and South Carolina.

PERRYVILLE
8 OCTOBER 1862

PERRYVILLE DEMONSTRATED THE WEAKNESSES OF BOTH SIDES AT THIS STAGE OF THE WAR. THE REBELS WERE SKILLED AND EXPERIENCED BUT TOO FEW IN NUMBER; THE FEDERALS WERE INEXPERIENCED AND BADLY LED. THIS BATTLE WAS THE CIVIL WAR IN MICROCOSM: THE CONFEDERATES OUTFOUGHT THEIR OPPONENTS BUT LOST AT THE STRATEGIC LEVEL DUE TO THE ENEMY'S VASTLY SUPERIOR RESOURCES.

WHY DID IT HAPPEN?

WHO Union Army of the Ohio (37,000 men) under Major-General Don Carlos Buell (1818–98) opposed by the Confederate Army of the Mississippi (16,000 men) under General Braxton Bragg (1817–76).

WHAT A skirmish over water sources developed into a full-scale battle, in which the Confederates were tactical victors. However, the Rebel force was forced to retreat upon discovering that the Federals were much stronger than expected.

WHERE Perryville, Kentucky.

WHEN 8 October 1862.

WHY Confederate forces had invaded Kentucky, hoping to rally support in the state for the Rebel cause.

OUTCOME Although tactical victors, the Confederates were forced to retreat, entirely withdrawing from Kentucky.

Kentucky was important to both sides, and there was considerable support for the Rebel cause in the state even though it had officially declared for the Union. If Kentucky could be induced to switch sides, then the balance of power would shift dramatically. Such a shift was badly needed. After being driven out of Kentucky and most of Tennessee, the Confederacy had lost Nashville and Corinth, and was gradually losing the war in the west.

Major-General Edmund Kirby Smith (1824–93), commanding Confederate forces in eastern Tennessee, believed that the answer was to take the offensive, driving into Kentucky. If successful, the operation might bring the state into the Confederacy, which already recognized it as a member because of the considerable support there for secession.

Even if Kentucky did not change sides, the Union could not afford to risk losing the state and would have to oppose the invasion force, along with whatever local support rallied to it, and this would take pressure off Tennessee. President Jefferson Davis (1808–89) agreed and authorized Smith to

Philip H Sheridan (1831–88) never lacked aggression. He was suspended while at West Point for fighting with another cadet, but went on to become one of the North's most successful fighting commanders.

go ahead. He also confirmed General Braxton Bragg, who had assumed temporary command of the Confederate Army of the Mississippi, as permanent commander of that force.

The plan was for Bragg to move to protect Chattanooga, which was threatened by a large Union army under Major-General Don Carlos Buell, while Smith advanced into Kentucky with his command and some of Bragg's brigades. This operation called for a considerable logistics undertaking, with numerous units moving simultaneously on several different railroads. Critically, neither Bragg nor Smith was in charge of the other. Jefferson Davis himself confirmed Smith as an independent commander, and though there was an understanding that the two would support one another, there was no clear chain of command.

THE PLAN

Throughout the summer, regular and partisan Confederate forces caused chaos in Kentucky, Tennessee and Missouri, distracting the attention of the Federal forces. Meanwhile, Bragg and Smith met to discuss the campaign, drew up a plan of action and set about making it a reality.

Smith commanded about 21,000 men in four infantry divisions and a cavalry brigade, which were to advance and clear the Cumberland Gap of Union forces, opening the way to Kentucky. His force

was then to join Bragg's and move into middle Tennessee, cutting off Buell from Nashville and forcing him to retreat.

Buell was at this time making slow progress in Tennessee. Having advanced into enemy territory, he was reliant on the Memphis and Charleston Railroad for his supply line. First having to repair it, he was now constantly fighting off Confederate cavalry raids to keep the supply line open. Bragg's movement to Chattanooga forced Buell to reassess, and it soon became apparent that capturing Chattanooga was no longer practicable.

Buell decided to move to Murfreesboro, southeast of Nashville, ignoring the advice of Major-General George H Thomas (1816–70). This caused a rift between the two commanders at a time when close cooperation was vital. Buell changed his mind about intercepting Bragg's army and fell back on Nashville to defend it against the expected attack.

However, Bragg instead crossed the Cumberland River and entered Kentucky, where Smith was already operating. Smith had decided to ignore the plan to join up and retake Nashville, and instead marched his force through the Cumberland Gap and into Kentucky. Now his force and that of

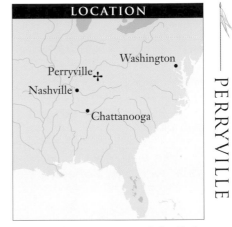

The western theatre is sometimes overshadowed by the great events in the east, but the hotly contested battles for Kentucky and Tennessee were a vital factor in the eventual Federal victory.

MARCHING ORDER

Troops on both sides did a lot more marching than fighting. 'Light Marching Order' was used for a short march with the expectation of picket duty, work or combat at the end. Troops carried their weapon, ammunition, canteen and haversack in light order but left cook pots and such like in camp.
'Heavy Marching Order' was used for changes of position and meant that troops had to carry everything they owned and needed with them. Troops would set out in neat columns of fours but within a kilometre or so this order would dissolve with men walking as they thought best. Straggling was common and many men became lost on a long march.

Bragg were both in Kentucky, forcing Buell to come after them.

CONFEDERATE SUCCESSES

On 30 August, Smith's command met and routed a green Union force of two brigades under Major-General William 'Bull' Nelson (1824–62). About 4300 of the 6500 Union troops fielded were taken prisoner. After resting for a day, Smith then advanced on Lexington and captured it. His cavalry pursued the remnants of the Union force towards Louisville while elements of his infantry moved up to threaten Cincinnati.

Responding to the desperate situation, neighbouring Union states threw together whatever units they could, mostly forming them from raw recruits, and appointed Major-General Horatio Wright (1820–99) to command the scratch force. Panic prevailed in Cincinnati and the frantic Union response eventually resulted in Wright having 70,000 men under his command. These men were very green, however, and many had not even completed basic training.

Smith was unable to achieve much more than he already had, however, mainly due to splitting his force up too much. After some skirmishing, Smith halted and then began to pull back towards Lexington.

Meanwhile, Bragg had positioned his army between Buell and Smith, cutting Buell off from Louisville. His position was good, but he allowed himself to be distracted by a rather bizarre incident. One of Bragg's subordinates attacked a Union bridge garrison under Colonel John Wilder (1830–1917) and was repulsed. Bragg just had to respond and marched his force to surround the garrison.

The newly appointed Colonel Wilder did not know what to do in the face of a demand for his surrender, and asked for advice from – of all people – Confederate Major-General SB Buckner (1823–1914). Buckner showed him the hopelessness of his position and Wilder wisely surrendered.

Bragg then weighed his options and decided to make a junction with Smith, enabling Buell to rush to Louisville. There, 'Bull' Nelson was bickering with a fellow officer, Brigadier-General Jefferson C Davis (1828–79), who ended up being sent to Cincinnati by Nelson and then back to Louisville by Wright. Arriving back in Louisville on 29 September, Davis entered into another argument with Nelson and eventually shot him.

Buell's efforts to reorganize his army and kick the Confederates out of Kentucky were further impeded by an order from the War Department to hand over command to Major-General George H Thomas. The latter resolved the situation by refusing to assume command, allowing Buell to deal with the crisis without the disruption brought about by a change in command.

THE ARMIES CONVERGE

Finally, Buell's Army of the Ohio marched out to confront Bragg on 1 October. It was now formed as three corps. The Third

A military academy graduate and veteran of previous wars, Don Carlos Buell was a stern disciplinarian. His career fell victim as much to political factors as his own actions, which were at times more headstrong than well considered.

Corps included Brigadier-General Philip Sheridan, and was commanded by Major-General Charles C Gilbert (1822–1903) instead of Nelson, who died shortly after being shot by Davis. Thomas went with the army as second in command.

Bragg and Smith held a ceremony on 4 October to inaugurate a Confederate governor for the Confederate state of Kentucky, but news that Buell was in the field caused the Confederates to fall back. They reached Perryville on 6 October. Sending out forces to scout for the enemy, Bragg discovered that the Union army was approaching Perryville along three roads.

The day of 7 October was spent preparing defensive positions, while the Union army made its dispositions for battle. Buell set up his headquarters about 8km (5 miles) from Perryville and gave his orders. He was suffering from the effects of a fall from his horse that day and was unable to ride during the battle.

THE BATTLE OPENS
In the early hours of the 8 October, Union forces were preparing to attack, with some units still far from their intended positions. Those that were in place began sending out parties to look for water. Rainfall had been sparse for months, and water was in short supply. The 10th Indiana, sent to set up a picket line on Peter's Hill to secure a water source in Doctor's Creek, were unaware for a time that they were in close to proximity

to the Confederate 7th Arkansas. When Major-General Alexander M McCook (1831–1903) sent a brigade up to reinforce the Indiana men, they ran into the Arkansas regiment instead and fighting broke out, which then spread to neighbouring troops.

Fierce combat took place between Sheridan's division and Brigadier-General St John Liddell's (1815–70) Confederate brigade for possession of Peter's Hill. Throughout this engagement, Sheridan's superior, the newly appointed Gilbert, bombarded him with instructions not to cause a general engagement and to stop wasting artillery ammunition.

THE CONFEDERATES ATTACK
The right wing of the Confederate army, under Major-General Leonidas Polk (1806–64), had been ordered by Bragg to attack the Union forces opposite it. However, Polk decided that, given the size of the force facing him, this was not practicable. He ordered his command to assume a defensive posture.

Bragg himself was convinced that the main Union force was located at Frankfort and that the main action would be fought there, and was thus not present at Perryville when the action opened. He expected to hear Polk's attack begin, and when he did not, he rode to Perryville in person. There, although he did not have accurate reconnaissance information, he ordered Polk's force to attack. A division under

These guns are rifled Parrott 30-pounders, capable of firing solid shot to destroy other guns or fortifications, or explosive fragmentation rounds for anti-personnel work. They were extremely accurate to about 2km (1.2 miles) and capable of hitting a target about three times as far away, with some luck.

THE OPPOSED FORCES

FEDERAL
Army of the Ohio   37,000

CONFEDERATE
Army of the Mississippi   16,000

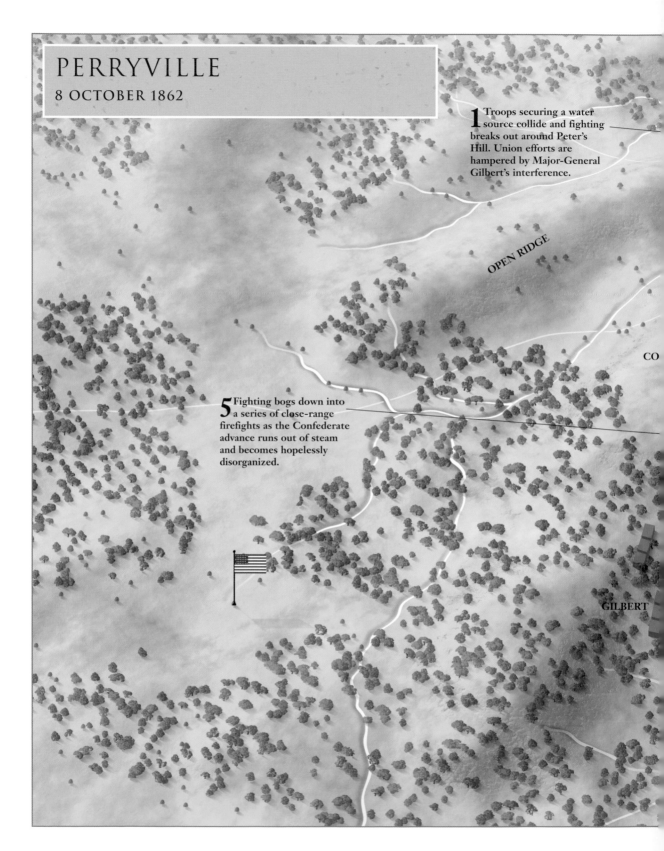

PERRYVILLE
8 OCTOBER 1862

1 Troops securing a water source collide and fighting breaks out around Peter's Hill. Union efforts are hampered by Major-General Gilbert's interference.

OPEN RIDGE

CO

5 Fighting bogs down into a series of close-range firefights as the Confederate advance runs out of steam and becomes hopelessly disorganized.

GILBERT

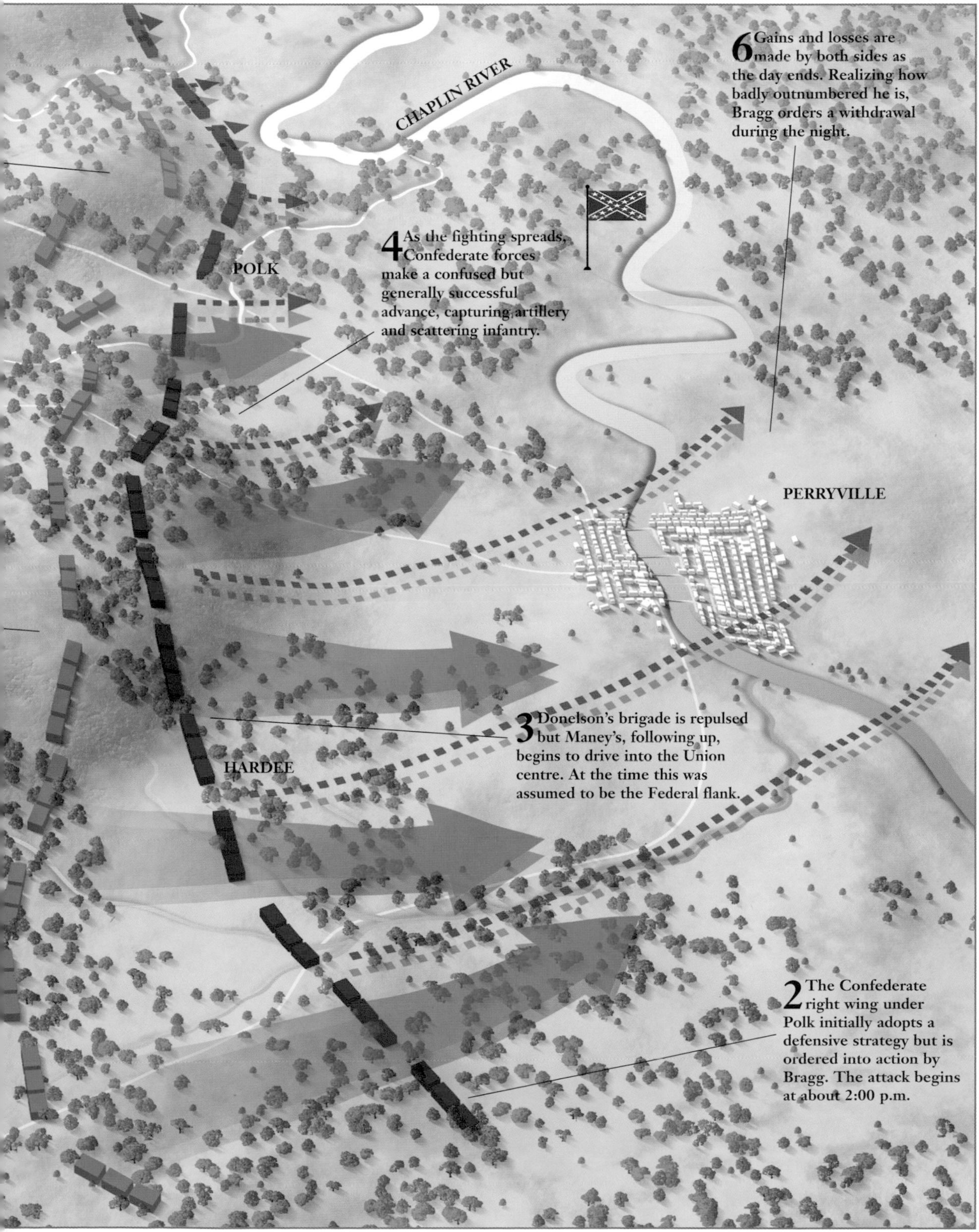

CHAPLIN RIVER

6 Gains and losses are made by both sides as the day ends. Realizing how badly outnumbered he is, Bragg orders a withdrawal during the night.

4 As the fighting spreads, Confederate forces make a confused but generally successful advance, capturing artillery and scattering infantry.

POLK

PERRYVILLE

3 Donelson's brigade is repulsed but Maney's, following up, begins to drive into the Union centre. At the time this was assumed to be the Federal flank.

HARDEE

2 The Confederate right wing under Polk initially adopts a defensive strategy but is ordered into action by Bragg. The attack begins at about 2:00 p.m.

127

The Colt Army Model 1860 was a state-of-the-art sidearm and popular with officers and cavalrymen on both sides. Although expensive it offered good firepower, reliability and man-stopping performance.

Many of the Union units at Perryville were composed entirely of raw recruits. Not yet used to army life, they were flung into desperate fighting against more experienced Confederate forces and suffered accordingly.

Major-General BF Cheatham (1820–86) began to advance a little after 2:00 p.m., crossing the river and clambering up the slopes beyond to assault what Bragg thought was the Union flank.

In fact, Cheatham's division had gone up against the centre of the Union line. Facing them was General McCook's force of some 22,000 men, and Cheatham's division was enfiladed by artillery batteries.

The first brigade to attack, that of Brigadier-General Daniel S Donelson (1801–63), was halted and driven back. The second, a veteran force from Tennessee under Brigadier-General George E Maney (1826–1901), began pushing the largely raw Federals back. They overran the Union artillery and captured several guns.

About an hour after Cheatham's division moved off, its supports began their own advance. This was a very confused affair due to revised orders that were not properly transmitted. Some formations followed their original orders, while others used the new ones. Amid the ensuing chaos, a protracted firefight broke out between troops using two parallel stone walls as cover, and this went on for some time.

Despite the confused orders, the attack was going well. Cheatham's division continued to advance after overrunning the artillery, scattering the raw 21st Wisconsin that was ordered up to halt it. Meanwhile, Brigadier-General Bushrod Johnson's (1817–80) Confederate brigade, now hopelessly disorganized by terrain, enemy action and its own orders, tried to put in a new attack but was halted by the 3rd Ohio.

Brigadier-General Patrick R Cleburne's (1828–64) brigade was ordered up to replace Johnson's and to allow it to re-form properly. At the same time, Brigadier-General Daniel W Adams' (1821–72) brigade was ordered to pass right across the front of Sheridan's division to take up a flanking position. Under normal conditions this manoeuvre would be shot to pieces, but Adams got lucky; command and control problems existed in the Union army, too.

UNION GENERALS

With Buell sitting in a house a few kilometres away, Thomas was in a position to make a real difference on the battlefield. By rights he should have been commanding this battle anyway but for his decision to leave Buell in charge. He did not make a great job of being second-in-command, however. As well as neglecting to report in person as ordered, he also failed to provide any advice about, or personal observations of, the situation to Buell.

Worse, Gilbert's constant badgering of Sheridan to stop wasting ammunition constrained him from interfering in the redeployment of Adams' brigade, which then fell on the flank of Colonel William Lytle's (1826–63) brigade. Lytle himself was wounded in the head and captured, though since the Confederates thought his wound would be fatal, he was not taken prisoner.

McCook's corps in the centre was under severe pressure, but reinforcements were available. One reason they were not transferred was the rather optimistic attack by Colonel Samuel Powell's brigade on what amounted to most of two corps. Gilbert hesitated to send reinforcements – even a single brigade – to McCook's aid while he was under attack. Buell finally realized that something major was going on late in the afternoon when a messenger

from McCook arrived requesting urgent assistance. By this time, it was rather late.

At the day drew to an end, sporadic attacks took place along the Rebel line. On the right, having driven the Union forces back, the brigades of Maney and Brigadier-General Alexander P Stewart (1821–1908) pulled back, allowing Union troops to retake the heights in front of them. New orders arrived, and the two brigades advanced again, regaining their former positions. Meanwhile, in the centre, a new

William S Rosecrans (1819–98) had served in the regular Army as an engineering officer until 1854, and returned from a successful civil engineering career to join the Union cause. Although overall a good officer, he had a tendency to micromanage his forces.

This photograph taken after the battle shows a lane near Perryville flanked by lines of chevaux-de-frise *and wooden palisades. This severely restricted the movement of enemy infantry – breaking up any charges – as well as ensuring enemy cavalry did not carry out flanking manoeuvres.*

Union line, with reinforcements coming up from Third Corps, managed to bring the Confederate advance to a standstill. Lack of ammunition was also a problem for the Rebel troops, which then pulled back.

On the Confederate left, Powell's brigade had also failed to make much impression against the vastly superior force it had attacked. As it retired, Union troops

and a half-dozen guns were able to advance into Perryville, presenting the Federals with a real opportunity to cut Bragg's line of retreat. Lack of coordination robbed them of the opportunity, however.

The last action of the day took place at about 6:30 p.m., when a final Confederate attack, in brigade strength, drove back the Union troops facing it. The fall of night prevented further gains from being made, and McCook's battered corps was reinforced by a fresh brigade soon after.

THE CONFEDERATE RETREAT

The Confederates had been on the offensive all day, despite Polk's initial decision to fight a defensive action. They

had delivered a splendid beating to McCook's corps and driven the raw, untried Union troops before them at every opportunity. However, they had also lost 510 killed and about 2900 wounded or missing. Union losses came to some 845 killed and about 3350 wounded or missing.

The day had been a clear victory for the Confederate Army, though only a tactical one. Nothing of strategic significance was gained. More importantly, Bragg became aware of the size of the force ranged against him at last, and ordered a retreat rather than continue the struggle for another day.

At about 1:00 a.m., on 9 October, the Confederate forces began retiring. The last units were pulled out of Perryville at midday. Buell made no attempt to interfere with the withdrawal, allowing Bragg to meet up with Smith and detached forces under Brigadier-General Humphrey Marshall (1812–72) at Harrodsburg, giving him a force nearly the same size as Buell's command, and far more experienced.

Smith wanted to turn and attack Buell, savaging the Union army, but Bragg decided that he had a good defensive position and preferred to await an attack. However, he soon began to worry that Buell would move to block his line of retreat and ordered his army to fall back. Buell did not so much pursue the retreating Confederate army as shuffle nervously after it. Finding his army once again in proximity to Bragg's new position at Bryantsville, Buell hesitated once more, as he considered undertaking a flanking movement.

Elsewhere, the Confederate Army of Northern Virginia was retreating from Sharpsburg, and other forces had failed to recapture Corinth. They would not now be moving to assist Bragg, and the hoped-for explosion of support for the Rebel cause in

Kentucky had not occurred. Bragg thus decided to retire into Tennessee. Buell did nothing to impede the movement.

AFTERMATH

The combined Confederate force dispersed again into two armies under Smith and Bragg, and a smaller force under Marshall. Buell ambled after the retreating Rebels for a while, then headed for Nashville. His army was reconstituted as 14th Army Corps and given to Major-General William S Rosecrans to command. Buell never commanded a major force again.

Bragg was also in trouble with his superiors. Notorious for being 'naturally disputatious', he had upset several of his subordinates and complaints had been made. He was summoned to Richmond to explain himself to President Jefferson Davis (1808–89), but retained his command.

The result at Perryville was more or less a victory by default for the Union, and effectively ended the Confederate threat to Kentucky. The initiative was now firmly with the Union in the western theatre.

This illustration shows Confederate infantry firing volleys into advancing Federal troops. Well-trained troops could fire on average 3–4 rounds per minute, causing devastation at ranges of up to 500m (560 yards). Most engagements between infantry took place at less than 200m (220 yards). Charging infantry were expected to cover 147m (160 yards) per minute, allowing the enemy to fire at least five rounds before engaging in hand-to-hand combat. Consequently, losses amongst charging troops could be staggering.

CHANCELLORSVILLE
1–5 MAY 1863

CHANCELLORSVILLE SEVERELY DENTED THE MORALE OF THE ARMY OF THE POTOMAC. ALTHOUGH POSSESSING SUPERIOR NUMBERS, IT WAS AGAIN DEFEATED BY LEE, WHO USED UNCONVENTIONAL TACTICS OUT OF NECESSITY. BOTH SIDES MADE RISKY MANOEUVRES IN THE HOPE OF GAINING AN ADVANTAGE. THE BATTLE IS CHIEFLY FAMOUS FOR THE DEATH OF 'STONEWALL' JACKSON, WHOSE LOSS WAS BITTERLY FELT.

WHY DID IT HAPPEN?

WHO The Union Army of the Potomac under Major-General Joseph Hooker (1814–79), numbering about 130,000, opposed by the Confederate Army of Northern Virginia under General Robert E Lee (1807–70), numbering about 100,000.

WHAT Although outnumbered, Lee split his force and launched a flanking action, manoeuvring to bring his smaller force to bear at the critical point.

WHERE To the west of Fredericksburg, Virginia.

WHEN 1–5 May 1863.

WHY Newly appointed Union army commander 'Fighting Joe' Hooker launched an operation against Lee, hoping to destroy the Army of Northern Virginia. Although his aim was offensive, his battle plan was entirely defensive.

OUTCOME Lee's outnumbered army inflicted a defeat on the Union force and caused it to retreat. This opened the way for Lee's Second Invasion of the North.

M uch has been made of the apparent incompetence and ineptitude shown by both sides at times during the Civil War, but the truth is that mistakes were inevitable. The Civil War was fought by armies that had to be created more or less from scratch, with very small numbers of regulars to provide guidance. It was fought with weapons whose capabilities had not been fully explored.

Moreover, political considerations meant that commanders were sometimes chosen as much for their connections and the support they would garner in their home states as for their military abilities. The necessity of political support, without which the war was lost before a shot was fired, sometimes placed individuals in positions that they

were not trained or experienced enough to cope with. Some rose to the occasion; others tried and failed.

The armies and commanders on both sides were essentially learning their trade on the job, so to speak, and new ideas had to be tried. These were not always successful. One such was the system of 'Grand Divisions' in the Union Army, in which divisions were grouped into corps, and those then into Grand Divisions. The result was cumbersome and after the defeat at Fredericksburg the Union Army of the Potomac discarded the idea.

The Army of the Potomac also gained a new commander at this time, with Joseph Hooker replacing Major-General Ambrose Burnside (1824–81) in overall command.

'Jeb' Stuart (left) was a daring and aggressive cavalry commander who liked to be given scope to use his initiative. General Lee made good use of this factor at Chancellorsville, but at Gettysburg the partnership broke down with disastrous consequences.

Hooker reorganized the army, creating an independent cavalry corps, and worked at improving morale before setting out on an operation that would result in the destruction of Lee's Army of Northern Virginia and open the way for a triumphant march into Richmond.

The plan was sound enough, but the Confederacy was fortunate indeed to have gained the services of Robert E Lee and Lieutenant-General Thomas J Jackson (1824–63), better known as 'Stonewall' Jackson.

HOOKER'S PLANS
Hooker's idea was to launch a cavalry raid on Lee's supply line and cut his link to Richmond, forcing the Confederate army to leave its winter camp, where it still resided, and retreat. Hooker would then attack with overwhelming force and destroy the Army of Northern Virginia.

With this plan in mind, Hooker decided to cross the Rappahannock River, which separated the two armies, north of Fredericksburg. The cavalry, over 11,000 men and 22 guns under Major-General George Stoneman (1822–94), was sent off to cross the river and get into Lee's rear. However, Stoneman's crossing was delayed by bad weather for a fortnight, so Hooker decided to force the issue. He sent 60,000 men in three corps (which would previously have constituted a Grand Division) across the Rappahannock.

There were three practicable fords for the crossing. Two of these – Bank's Ford and United States Ford – were guarded, but the force was able to get across at Kelly's Ford, advancing to cross the Rapidan as well. With an additional corps and the cavalry across the rivers, Hooker's plan was beginning to come together.

LEE REACTS
Suspicious already that the Federals were up to something, Lee reacted quickly when word came that Union troops were across the Rappahannock River. He pulled in

1ST SHARPSHOOTERS
While several Union regiments were raised with fanciful titles like Guards, Irrepressibles and Sharpshooters, the 1st Sharpshooters was a deliberate attempt to create a formation composed entirely of excellent shots. The standard infantry rifle was accurate out to a good distance in the hands of a well-trained man, but once the regiment received Sharps breech-loading rifles they became a deadly instrument that inflicted heavy losses on the enemy. Indeed, the regiment gained a reputation as the unit that had inflicted the most casualties on the enemy.

The Sharpshooters fought with distinction at Chancellorsville, Gettysburg, the Wilderness and many other major actions. With their fast-firing rifles they were constantly pushed to the front of the line and consequently suffered heavy casualties – of 2570 men who served with the regiment, some 1300 were killed or wounded in the course of the war.

Lieutenant-General James Longstreet (1821–1904), who was detached to besiege Suffolk, and sent off units to prepare defensive positions. Critically, two brigades of Major-General Richard H Anderson's (1821–79) division were sent towards Chancellorsville to prepare positions there.

Leaving slightly over 10,000 men under Brigadier-General Jubal Early (1816–94) in defensive positions at Fredericksburg, Lee began concentrating his main force to counter the new threat. He now had a good idea where the Union forces were, and in what numbers. Lee was outnumbered but that was nothing new. There was certainly no question that the Army of Northern Virginia would retreat as Hooker hoped.

THE FIRST DAY (1 MAY)
Marching westwards, the three divisions of the Confederate Second Corps under

LOCATION
Chancellorsville ✝✝ • Washington
Fredericksburg • Washington

The eastern theatre of war was critical for both sides as the capitals of both the Union and the Confederacy were located there, and close together. Thus several major actions took place in a relatively small space.

CHANCELLORSVILLE

The four Union corps that were supposed to be operating in Lee's rear, and trying to force a retreat, pulled back to Chancellorsville and established positions in the early hours of the morning. Hooker was now hoping that Lee would attack him and smash his army to pieces on the Federal forces in the process, and even proclaimed that the Army of Northern Virginia was now the property of the Army of the Potomac. This was an odd thing to say, having just handed the initiative to Lee, who was not known for acting in accordance with his enemy's wishes.

THE SECOND DAY (2 MAY)

While Lee and Jackson were planning their next move on the evening of 1 May, Lee's cavalry informed him that the Union right flank was 'in the air', in other words, not properly covered or anchored by defensive terrain. The plan they came up with was audacious. Leaving just 15,000 men with Lee (the divisions of Anderson and McLaws), Jackson would take his 30,000 off on a wide flank march and fall on the enemy's rear. Meanwhile, Hooker was ordering up another corps from Fredericksburg to Chancellorsville, which would bring the Union force to 90,000.

At about 9:00 a.m. on 2 May, Hooker received news that Confederate forces had been spotted moving south, and concluded that Lee was retreating. Stoneman's cavalry was in position to attack their likely route, and everything seemed to be going well. Hooker ordered Major-General John Sedgwick (1813–64), who was still in front of Fredericksburg, to attack if the chances seemed good, and later modified this to an order to attack with his entire force.

At 2:00 p.m. or so, Jackson's force became aware of Federal troops ahead of them, and after a careful deployment, Jackson put in a very aggressive attack that began just after 5:00 p.m. Two divisions of

A sergeant from the Confederate 1st Virginia Cavalry. As a rule the Confederate cavalry was better than its Union counterpart, being recruited from country-bred men who could already ride and shoot. The carbine was the most effective of cavalry weapons in the Civil War, though Confederate cavalry still liked to attack with sabre and revolver.

Lieutenant-General 'Stonewall' Jackson and a division under Major-General Lafayette McLaws (1821–97) arrived on the flank of Anderson's brigades. Jackson was in overall command and had orders from Lee

to halt the Union advance. Lee's command style was loose, allowing his subordinates to act as they thought best, and as usual Jackson thought it best to attack.

Thus, as elements of Major-General George G Meade's (1815–72) corps came down the Orange Turnpike near Chancellorsville, they ran into a skirmish line from Anderson's division. Breaking through, they were confronted by five divisions of Rebel troops and faced flanking if reinforcements did not come up. They were on their way when Hooker's order to fall back to Chancellorsville came through.

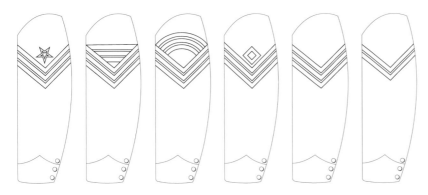

US Army non-commissioned chevrons. From left to right: ordnance sergeant, quartermaster sergeant, sergeant-major, first sergeant, sergeant and corporal.

Union troops were scattered and routed, and confusion spread throughout the Union force. Union Major-General Daniel Sickles (1819–1914) decided to pull his command back as it was in danger of being crushed between Lee and Jackson.

The retreat turned into disaster as Sickles' force became totally disorganized. One division became lost and wandered towards Lee's entrenched force. The other became involved in a three-way running fight and was cut up badly before reaching safety by midnight.

As night fell the Federals were able to regain some control of the situation and established positions facing the new threat. Jackson wanted to launch a night assault against the hasty Union redeployment and take advantage of the confusion that reigned. It was whilst reconnoitring for this attack that he was fired on by his own side's pickets and seriously wounded.

Jackson had been hit three times and was evacuated to a field hospital. His left arm was amputated, but he died several days later of pneumonia. His loss was keenly felt in the Confederate Army. Not only was he a brilliant commander in his own right, but he also worked well as a team with Lee. The rapport and mutual trust they had established was one of the keys to Confederate success, and without it the Army of Northern Virginia was more prone to delays and mistakes than before.

Meanwhile, command passed to Major-General JEB 'Jeb' Stuart (1833–64), the Confederate cavalry commander. While he was establishing control, the Union army managed to re-form somewhat, though Major-General Oliver O Howard's (1830–1909) corps in particular was in a bad way.

THE THIRD DAY (3 MAY)

Lee now decided to recombine his force and inflict a deathblow on Hooker's army. He led his command towards Chancellorsville to meet up with Stuart, who was pressing the Federals. Stuart had placed more than

Sabres drawn, the Federal 8th Pennsylvania Cavalry engage with Confederate forces at Chancellorsville. Cavalry rarely used sabres in the Civil War: revolvers and carbines proved more effective skirmishing weapons.

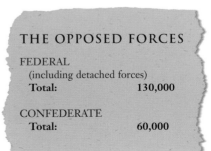

THE OPPOSED FORCES

FEDERAL
  (including detached forces)
  Total: 130,000

CONFEDERATE
  Total: 60,000

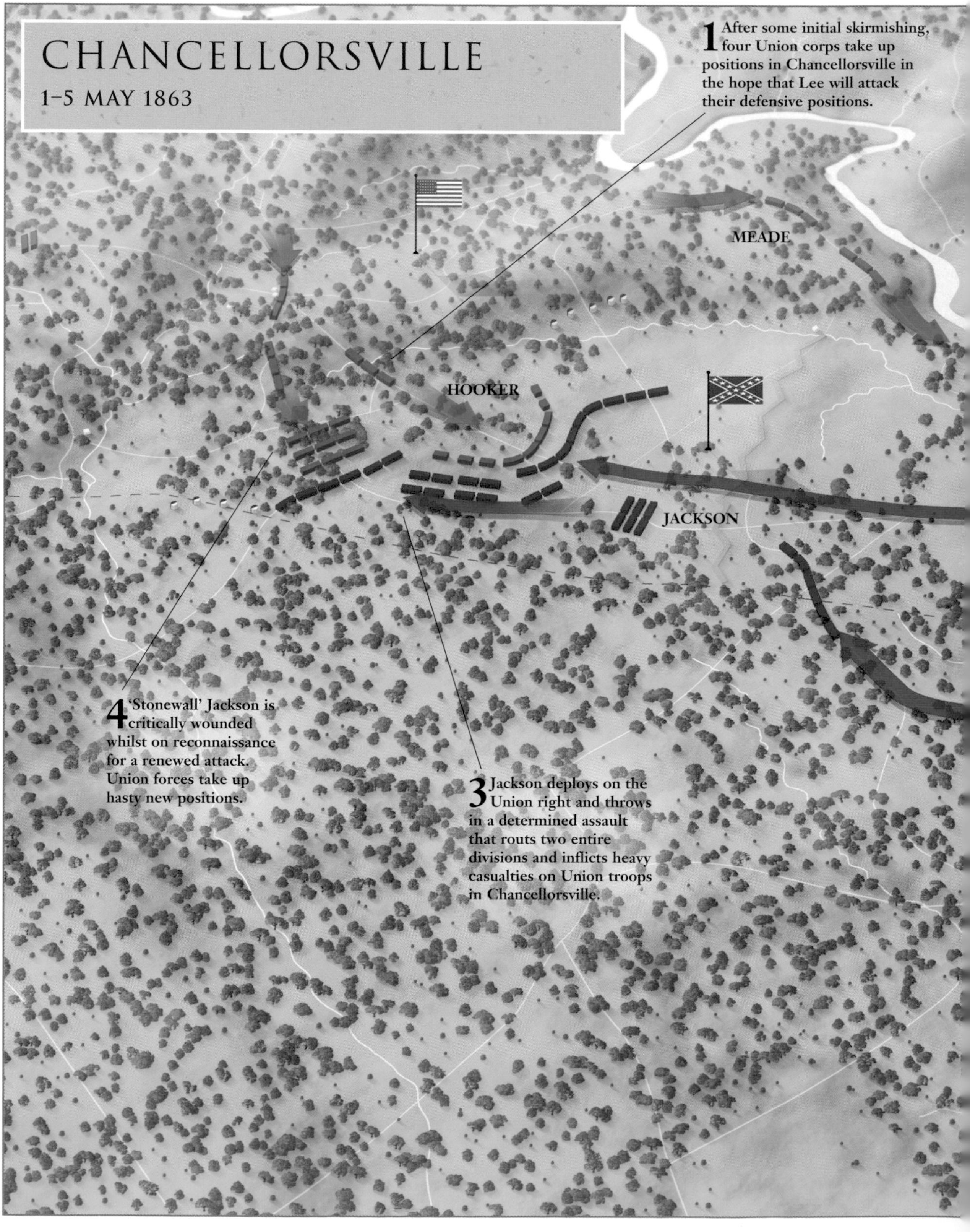

CHANCELLORSVILLE
1–5 MAY 1863

1 After some initial skirmishing, four Union corps take up positions in Chancellorsville in the hope that Lee will attack their defensive positions.

MEADE

HOOKER

JACKSON

4 'Stonewall' Jackson is critically wounded whilst on reconnaissance for a renewed attack. Union forces take up hasty new positions.

3 Jackson deploys on the Union right and throws in a determined assault that routs two entire divisions and inflicts heavy casualties on Union troops in Chancellorsville.

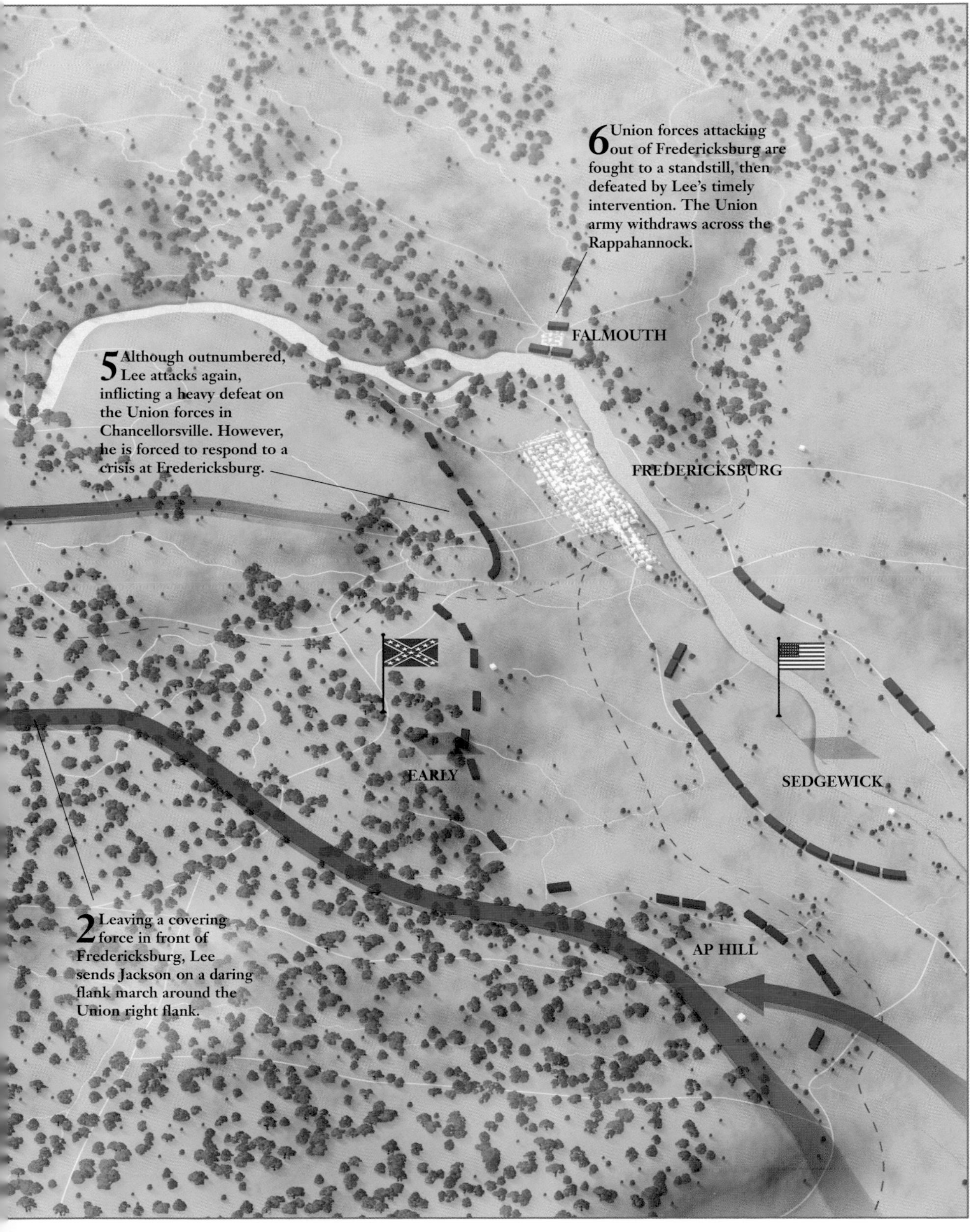

6 Union forces attacking out of Fredericksburg are fought to a standstill, then defeated by Lee's timely intervention. The Union army withdraws across the Rappahannock.

FALMOUTH

5 Although outnumbered, Lee attacks again, inflicting a heavy defeat on the Union forces in Chancellorsville. However, he is forced to respond to a crisis at Fredericksburg.

FREDERICKSBURG

EARLY

SEDGEWICK

2 Leaving a covering force in front of Fredericksburg, Lee sends Jackson on a daring flank march around the Union right flank.

AP HILL

CHANCELLORSVILLE

100 guns to fire into the Union force. This included 70 atop Hazel's Grove, which Sickles abandoned at Hooker's order. Their fire was more than the Federals could stand, and in the face of attacks by Lee and Stuart the Union troops began to break.

The fighting was extremely bloody but victory was nearing when Lee received word from Early, who was in trouble to the east. Sedgwick's assault had broken through his thinned lines and he was being pushed westwards. He had started with about 10,000 men and was outnumbered four to one at least.

Again, Lee reacted decisively. Reasoning that the Union force in front of him was unlikely to take the offensive, Lee sent off McLaws with his division to stop Sedgwick. They arrived just in time; Early's command had been pushed to the south and out of the way of the advancing Union corps. Sedgwick would have been clear to advance into Lee's rear but for the arrival of McLaws at about 4:30 p.m. Despite the disparity in numbers, McLaws was able to stall the Union advance, and Sedgwick set up defensive positions to protect his force in the coming night.

THE FOURTH DAY (4 MAY)

Depending on the observer's point of view, Lee was ether stuck between Sedgwick's hammer and Hooker's anvil, or he had the advantage of a central position between two forces of rather hesitant enemies. Lee took the latter view. Although 'Jeb' Stuart commanded only about 25,000 men to contain Hooker's 80,000 or so around Chancellorsville, Lee correctly gambled that the Union force would not come out to fight. In the event, Hooker was busy setting up defences around United States Ford to ensure he had an escape route; hardly the action of a commander determined to go on the attack.

The combined forces of Generals Anderson, McLaws and Early, under Lee's

Opposite: Confederate troops killed at the Battle of Chancellorsville lie in a shallow trench behind the stone wall on Mary's Heights, Fredricksburg. This photograph was taken by Union officer Captain Andrew J Russell.

Left: 'Fighting Joe' Hooker got his nickname accidentally from a newspaper headline which was supposed to read 'Fighting – Joe Hooker' and led into a story about a minor battle. Instead a misprint trumpeted 'Fighting Joe Hooker' across the nation.

Below: James Ewell Brown ('Jeb') Stuart was an able and aggressive cavalry commander who had already distinguished himself as a junior officer when war broke out. He was mortally wounded in action against cavalry under Philip H Sheridan (1831–88), his Union counterpart.

overall guidance, got into position to attack Sedgwick from three sides, with Early's men retaking positions around Fredericksburg that Sedgwick had not garrisoned. The Confederate attack did not go in until 6:00 p.m., and Sedgwick fought a hard defensive battle before pulling back across the Rappahannock River at Bank's Ford during the night.

THE LAST DAY (5 MAY)

Chancellorsville ended with Hooker accepting that he could not win, although in truth the Union general had been defeated for some time before that, at least in his own mind. He lost his chance to force a victory when he allowed his army to be bottled up in defensive positions by a vastly inferior force. When asked why he allowed this to happen, Hooker confessed to having had a loss of confidence.

Once Sedgwick had withdrawn, Hooker decided that nothing further could be done

and began to pull back across the Rappahannock, completing the move by 6 May. He had hoped Sedgwick would be able to hold Bank's Ford and thus allow Hooker's army to pull back across the river, regroup and renew the offensive, but the order was miscommunicated like several others, and the opportunity was lost.

UNION CAVALRY FAILS

The large body of Union cavalry sent out at the very outset of the campaign by Hooker achieved very little. It might have been some use if the Confederate army really had come its way or had retreated as Hooker had hoped. When this did not come to pass, Stoneman's foray proved fruitless. During the week of 1–7 May Stoneman's force did carry out some minor raids but these did not affect the outcome of the campaign in any way. By 7 May, Stoneman had rejoined the main Union army and at this point, with the last of the

This colour illustration depicts the death of Jackson at Chancellorsville. Hearing that Jackson was wounded and in hospital, Lee remarked that Jackson had lost his left arm – but Lee had just lost his right. As subsequent events would show, he was not far wrong.

AFTERMATH

Hooker's plan may have been basically sound, but it did not take sufficient account of the fact that Robert E Lee was an aggressive and innovative general. Giving him the initiative was unwise, even when Lee was outnumbered. 'Fighting Joe' Hooker displayed a very passive mindset once the fighting started, even though his initial manoeuvring was good. The resulting Union defeat might have been avoided by even the hint that Hooker might come out of his positions around Chancellorsville and attack.

Chancellorsville was important to the course of the war in many ways. The people of the Union were shocked by the defeat of Hooker's army, which had repercussions for the re-election chances of Abraham Lincoln (1809–65). Hooker himself was sacked as army commander a little later, paving the way for Meade to take command just in time to defeat Lee at Gettysburg.

However, the news was not all bad for the Federals. They had taken 17,000 casualties compared to the 13,000 or so taken by the Confederates, not counting the thousands of prisoners taken in the chaos of the second day. However, the Union troops had demonstrated a fighting ability that had previously been somewhat lacking. Up to this point the Rebels could rely on being able to outfight even a superior Union force, but at Chancellorsville many Federal units gave as good as they got. This trend was repeated at Gettysburg.

More seriously, the Confederacy's losses represented nearly 25 per cent of the committed force and could not be replaced as readily as those on the Union side. With the Confederacy having a smaller population base and less industry than the North, casualties had a more serious effect on the Southern side, and even a victory in the field might lead to eventual strategic defeat if the price were too high. At Chancellorsville the Union began to exact that price.

One casualty in particular was keenly felt. The death of 'Stonewall' Jackson was not merely a blow to morale, especially with

the tragic circumstances in which it occurred, but it ended the team that had been so effective for Lee up to that point. Hooker's campaign at Chancellorsville suffered from misunderstandings and subordinates not doing what the commander wanted. Up to now, Lee had not had to contend with this problem to a great extent. That had changed, as would be apparent at Gettysburg.

However, on balance, things looked good for Lee and the Army of Northern Virginia after Chancellorsville. A vastly superior force had been sent packing, and Jackson's last great attack had been an enormous success. The way was now open for a new invasion of the North and the prospect of bringing the war to a successful end.

Several monuments to 'Stonewall' Jackson exist, as is only fitting. He is buried in the Stonewall Jackson Memorial Cemetery at Lexington, Virginia.

CHAMPION HILL
16 MAY 1863

CHAMPION HILL, ONE OF FIVE LAND BATTLES OF THE VICKSBURG CAMPAIGN FOUGHT IN 1863 IN CENTRAL MISSISSIPPI, VIRTUALLY SEALED THE FATE OF THE CONFEDERATE ARMY OF VICKSBURG, AND SUBSEQUENTLY ENSURED NORTHERN CONTROL OF THE LOWER MISSISSIPPI RIVER VALLEY. THAT CONTROL WAS VITAL TO UNION STRATEGY AND, JUST AS IMPORTANTLY, WAS A POLITICAL NECESSITY FOR A BELEAGUERED PRESIDENT LINCOLN.

WHY DID IT HAPPEN?

WHO The Union army commanded by Major-General Ulysses S Grant (1822–85), in order to capture the citadel of Vicksburg, Mississippi, and achieve total control of the Lower Mississippi River Valley, invaded Mississippi and attacked Confederate Lieutenant-General John C Pemberton's (1814–81) divided forces.

WHAT Grant's seven swiftly marching infantry divisions of 32,000 men outmanoeuvred Pemberton's three infantry divisions, totalling 23,000 soldiers, crashing into them on three axes of advance.

WHERE In central Mississippi, between the railroad towns of Edwards and Bolton, along the wooded ridge known as Champion Hill.

WHEN 16 May 1863.

WHY Grant's rapid offensive and multiple axes of advance surprised Pemberton, who was attempting to avoid a general engagement by moving to destroy Grant's line of communications.

OUTCOME Pemberton's army was driven back into the trenches surrounding the port city of Vicksburg and was penned in by Grant's army and Rear-Admiral David Dixon Porter's (1813–91) fleet, compelling the Confederates to surrender after a 47-day siege.

Just after dusk on 28 January 1863, the steamer *Magnolia* skirted up to the muddy western bank of the Mississippi River at Young's Point, Louisiana. On board was Major-General Ulysses S Grant, who, without fanfare, had journeyed the 759km (410 river miles) south from Memphis to assume field command of his army. That night he wrote to his wife Julia by the lamplight in his cabin and advised her that he would 'not learn anything of the situation of affairs until morning'. The words were tempered with caution as he suggested that he may not return to her until 'the reduction of Vicksburg is attempted'. Five months later, on 1 July, Grant's letter to his wife reflected confidence rather than caution as he wrote: 'You remain where you are … until you know I am in Vicksburg.' On 4 July, Grant triumphantly rode into Vicksburg at the head of his army.

MUD AND MARCHING

In the 156 days since his virtually unnoticed arrival at Young's Point, Grant and his men had slogged and marched over 322km (200 miles), first in fetid swamps and later in choking dust. Their destination had been Vicksburg, a goal that was ironically perched on a bluff across the Mississippi River just 11km (7 miles) to the east of Young's Point. Those momentous days and difficult miles witnessed the transformation

Grant asked Rear-Admiral Porter to run the fleet past the batteries of the Fortress City. Pictured are seven gunboats, a tug, a captured Confederate ram, three transport ships, and coal barges that ran the gauntlet of 37 guns on the night of 16 April 1863.

CHAMPION HILL

of Ulysses Grant from a much-criticized general to one of the great figures of military history. In that five-month period Grant prosecuted 'the most brilliant campaign ever fought on American soil', and delivered to the people and the government of the United States a victory that very possibly saved both a presidency and the Union.

When Grant arrived in Louisiana he found his army immersed in a sea of mud and ooze, with a vast and bridgeless Mississippi River between him and his ultimate objective. The army had been deposited there one month earlier when Grant's subordinate, Major-General William Tecumseh Sherman (1820–91), had been ordered to embark on transports at Memphis and steam south to capture Vicksburg in a bold amphibious thrust. Simultaneously, Grant was to march overland to the south from Oxford, Mississippi, towards the capital city of Jackson, 72km (45 miles) east of Vicksburg. Between Grant and Jackson was Confederate Lieutenant-General John C Pemberton's army, which had dug in on the south bank of the Yalobusha River at

Greenwood, Mississippi, to await Grant's attack. The plan seemed simple enough, and if all went well, Sherman would slink in through the back door at Vicksburg while Grant pounded on the front door at Greenwood. But, as Clausewitz wrote, 'in war the simplest thing is difficult'.

REARGUARD ACTION

On 20 December, the same day that Sherman's amphibious force steamed out of Memphis, Pemberton's ad hoc cavalry division, 3500 troopers strong and commanded by the fearless Major-General Earl Van Dorn (1820–63), galloped into Grant's rear echelon and destroyed the Federal supply depot at Holly Springs, Mississippi. While the flames of Van Dorn's men consumed Grant's precious food and ammunition, the Confederate cavalry of

ubiquitous Brigadier-General Nathan Bedford Forrest (1821–77) boldly destroyed Grant's railroad line and supplies in western Tennessee at Jackson, Humboldt, Trenton and Union City, thus ending any hope of replenishment of the Holly Springs depot. With his line of communications in flames, Grant had to bring his landward thrust to an ignominious end. The threat to his front gone, Pemberton quickly transported his men along the railroad to Jackson, then Vicksburg, to confront Sherman.

Sherman's unsuspecting and unlucky soldiers disembarked on the Yazoo River 8km (5 miles) north of Vicksburg and attacked, unsupported, through the bitterly cold swamps of Chickasaw Bayou, only to suffer a bitter repulse on 29 December. The badly mauled Union soldiers then limped back onto the transports to be shipped to the relative safety, if not comfort, of Louisiana. Sherman's acerbic after-action report of 5 January 1863 told the story: 'I reached Vicksburg at the time appointed, landed, assaulted, and failed.'

ACHIEVABLE OBJECTIVES

When Grant arrived at Sherman's miserable Louisiana campground three weeks later, he was acutely aware of the problems that he faced, not only militarily, but also politically. The North had suffered dramatic military losses from mid-December 1862 to early

LOCATION

• Memphis

Vicksburg •┿• Champion Hill

• New Orleans

The Mississippi was vital to both North and South. By 1863 Union forces had wrested control of the Lower Mississippi Valley from Cairo IL to Vicksburg and from New Orleans to Port Hudson LA.

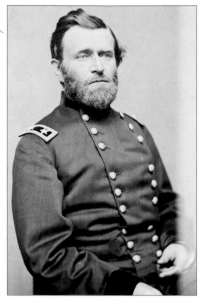

*Ulysses S Grant, pictured here during the Civil War,
reflected in an 1879 interview: 'I don't think there is
one of my campaigns with which I have not some fault
to find, and which, as I see now, I could not have
improved, except perhaps Vicksburg.'*

January 1863. Preceding these losses were major political losses in October 1862. The mid-term state elections had been disastrous for President Lincoln (1809–65) and his Republican Party, and five key states that had supported Lincoln in 1860 had abandoned the Republicans and sent Democratic majorities to Congress. The war had dragged on, the losses had dramatically escalated, and the voters had expressed their displeasure with the Lincoln administration.

In the midst of the dire situation for the Northern war effort, Grant, with his army mired in the Louisiana swamps during a rain-filled winter, knew that the correct military move would have been to recall his troops to the dry ground of Memphis and prepare for a springtime offensive – precisely what those closest to him advised. However, Grant correctly sensed that a retrograde action at that time would be viewed as another defeat to a discouraged and angry Northern populace. He recalled that 'There was nothing left to be done but to go forward to a decisive victory.'

As any commander worth his salt would do, Grant immediately established an achievable objective: 'The problem was to secure a footing upon dry ground on the east side of the river from which the troops could operate against Vicksburg.' Thus his men would spend the next three months working to achieve that objective. February, March and April were exacerbating months in which Grant faced opposition not only from the Confederates but also from the Northern press, from members of Congress and from some of his own generals. He was accused of stupidity and drunkenness, and one attempt after another failed to get his army onto dry ground. To make matters worse, Grant was physically plagued by a nasty case of boils and an accidentally discarded set of false teeth.

GRAND GULF

Grant's situation did not improve until his troops were finally ferried across the Mississippi to Bruinsburg, Mississippi, on 29–30 April. The hardships and stress of this period in Louisiana are reflected in Grant's missive to his superior officer, Major-General Henry Halleck (1815–72), written just as Grant's army was crossing the

Mississippi: 'I feel that the battle is more than half won,' he scrawled. One must wonder if Halleck, far away in Washington, truly understood these words.

Fittingly, once across the Mississippi, Grant immediately established a new objective: 'Capture Grand Gulf to use as a base.' On 1 May, at Port Gibson, Grant defeated a much smaller Confederate force that had been belatedly sent to prevent his army from establishing a beachhead. Then, on 3 May, he flanked and captured Grand Gulf on the Mississippi River. Thus, in two days Grant achieved his second objective.

The capture of Grand Gulf provided Grant with a much-needed base from which to operate and, with the help of Rear-Admiral Porter's Navy, by 8 May Grant's logistics officer had gathered two million rations at Grand Gulf. As the Federal columns moved inland, they were followed by ammunition, coffee, hardtack and salt piled into confiscated buggies and wagons.

On the same day that Grand Gulf was captured, Grant's rapidly moving forces seized a critical Confederate boat bridge at Hankinson's Ferry across the Big Black River – the last major water barrier between Grand Gulf and Vicksburg. The road north to Vicksburg seemed to be open. Grant arrived at Hankinson's in the pre-dawn hours on 4 May, and on 5 May he sent a one-day reconnaissance patrol north towards Vicksburg.

The report from this expedition convinced Grant that the road to Vicksburg was not quite as open as it seemed, because Pemberton had dug in on Redbone Ridge – the high ground between the Big Black River and Vicksburg – to await an attack. Grant then surprised everyone, from Pemberton to his bosses in Washington, by refusing to do the obvious.

After evaluating the reconnaissance report at Hankinson's Ferry, Grant established his next objective. He decided to feign an attack across the captured bridge, but would actually swing to the northeast, using the Big Black to protect his left flank. He would then manoeuvre his army into position to sever Pemberton's railroad line of communications connecting Vicksburg to Jackson. Grant had learned a valuable lesson at Holly Springs the previous December –

the vulnerability of a railroad – and he would use this lesson against John Pemberton, the very man who had taught it to him.

THREE-PRONGED ATTACK

By 12 May, Grant had manoeuvred his army into three attacking columns with plans to attack the railroad at three points: Edwards Station, 24km (15 miles) east of Vicksburg; Midway Station, 5km (3 miles) east of Edwards; and Bolton, 5km (3 miles) east of Midway. Meanwhile, Pemberton somehow divined Grant's intentions and eventually sent 23,000 men to dig in on a commanding ridge 3.2km (2 miles) south of Edwards at Mount Moriah. Just as he had done at Yalobusha and Redbone, Pemberton planned to fight a defensive battle on commanding terrain.

Realizing that the left of Grant's army was bounded by the Big Black River, Pemberton decided to send a lone brigade out of Jackson to scout and harass the Federal right flank. Pemberton wrote his orders poorly, however, and his cavalry, which was intended to ride from Jackson to the town of Raymond to scout for this 3000-man brigade, galloped instead to Edwards. Meanwhile, Grant's right column of almost 12,000 men marched towards Raymond, which was on their route to Bolton. At Raymond, 10km (6 miles) southeast of Bolton, an aggressive Confederate brigade commander, with no cavalry and with vague orders from Pemberton, decided to attack on the morning of 12 May. He mistakenly perceived the 12,000-soldier corps on the Union right flank to be a 1500-man brigade. The resulting Battle of Raymond lasted several hours, ending with the greatly outnumbered Confederates retreating back to Jackson.

At his campsite on Dillon's Farm, 10km (6 miles) to the west of Raymond, Grant

heard the reverberations of the guns. He knew then that there were enemy forces on his right flank. He was also cognizant of Pemberton's forces to his front at Mount Moriah, and due to his excellent intelligence-gathering, he knew that General Joseph E Johnston (1807–91) was en route to Jackson with more forces. Grant realized that, despite his successful manoeuvring to strike the railroad, the situation had changed and he must change with it. That night, he ordered a feint on Mount Moriah to hold the Confederate forces there in place while he swung the rest of his army northeast and eastwards to Jackson, to drive Johnston out of the capital city. Major-General John McClernand's (1812–1900) 13th Corps would conduct the

Major-General John A McClernand's 13th Corps led the way through the Louisiana wetlands; provided the vanguard across the Mississippi; fought the battles of Port Gibson and Champion Hill; and penetrated the defences of Vicksburg. Yet, due to his turbulent relationship with Grant, the aggressive McClernand has been unfairly labelled as an incompetent general.

THE OPPOSED FORCES

FEDERAL
Infantry 30,000
Artillery 100 guns
Total: 32,000

CONFEDERATE
Infantry 22,000
Artillery 66 guns
Total: 23,000

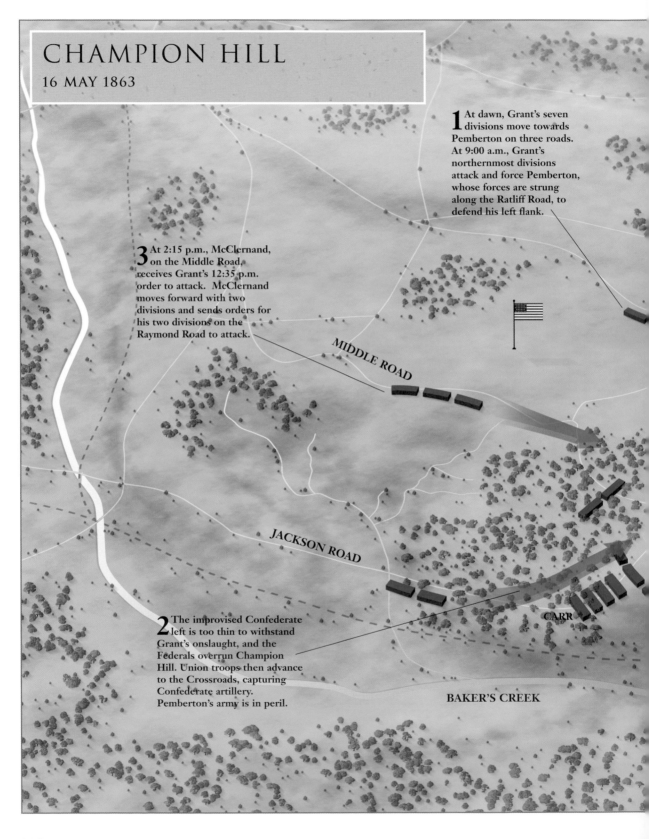

CHAMPION HILL
16 MAY 1863

1 At dawn, Grant's seven divisions move towards Pemberton on three roads. At 9:00 a.m., Grant's northernmost divisions attack and force Pemberton, whose forces are strung along the Ratliff Road, to defend his left flank.

3 At 2:15 p.m., McClernand, on the Middle Road, receives Grant's 12:35 p.m. order to attack. McClernand moves forward with two divisions and sends orders for his two divisions on the Raymond Road to attack.

MIDDLE ROAD

JACKSON ROAD

2 The improvised Confederate left is too thin to withstand Grant's onslaught, and the Federals overrun Champion Hill. Union troops then advance to the Crossroads, capturing Confederate artillery. Pemberton's army is in peril.

CARR

BAKER'S CREEK

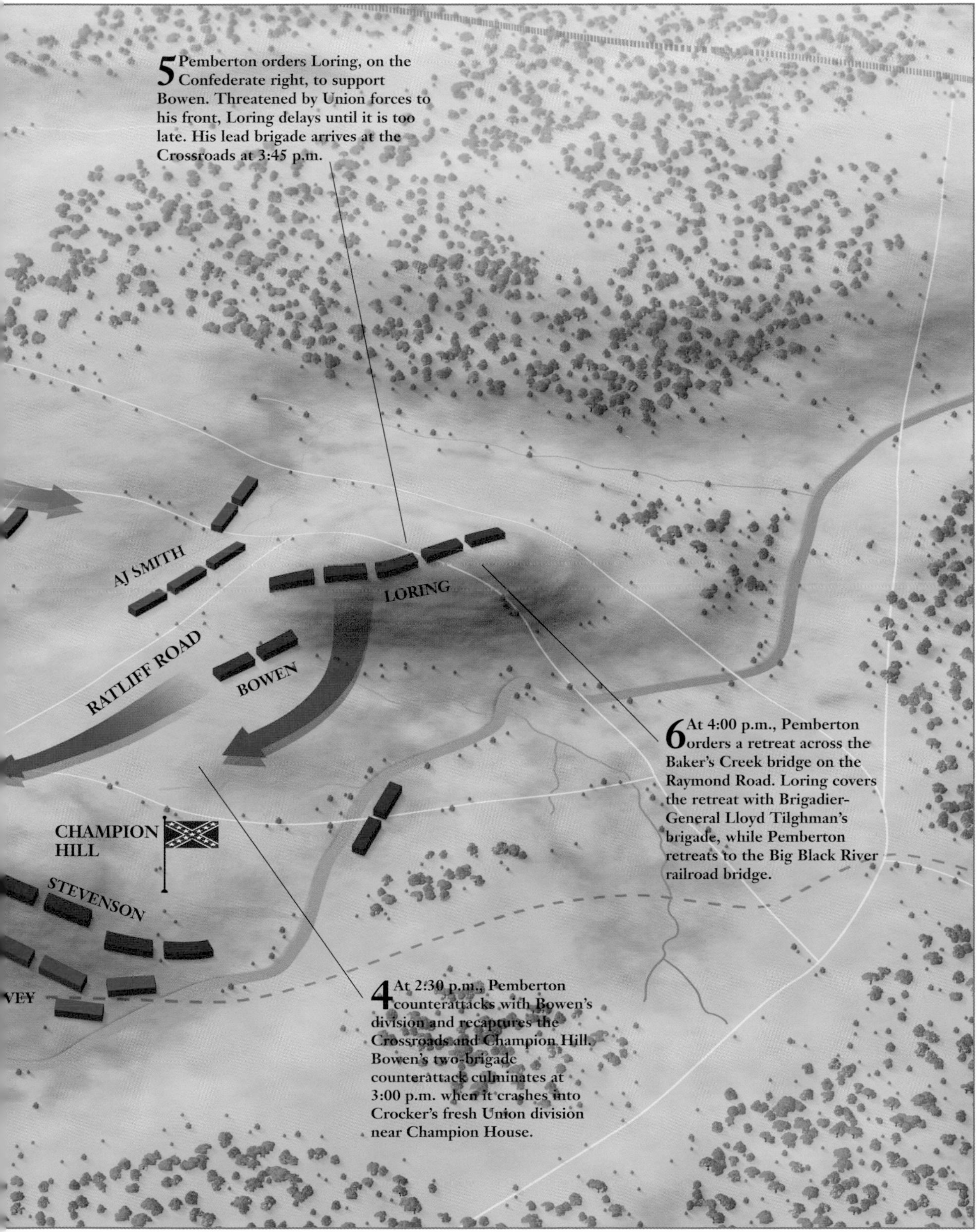

5 Pemberton orders Loring, on the Confederate right, to support Bowen. Threatened by Union forces to his front, Loring delays until it is too late. His lead brigade arrives at the Crossroads at 3:45 p.m.

AJ SMITH

LORING

RATLIFF ROAD

BOWEN

6 At 4:00 p.m., Pemberton orders a retreat across the Baker's Creek bridge on the Raymond Road. Loring covers the retreat with Brigadier-General Lloyd Tilghman's brigade, while Pemberton retreats to the Big Black River railroad bridge.

CHAMPION HILL

STEVENSON

VEY

4 At 2:30 p.m., Pemberton counterattacks with Bowen's division and recaptures the Crossroads and Champion Hill. Bowen's two-brigade counterattack culminates at 3:00 p.m. when it crashes into Crocker's fresh Union division near Champion House.

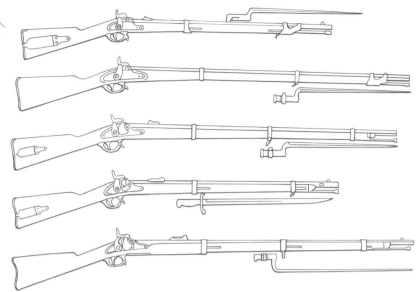

A selection of Civil War muskets. From top to bottom: an M1841 'Mississippi' rifle; an M1861 rifle musket; a P1858 British-made file musket, commonly used by Confederate forces; an M1863 rifle musket; and a Whitneyville rifle made under US Navy contract.

feint and remain behind to protect the rear of the army. Meanwhile, Major-General James McPherson's (1828–64) victorious 17th Corps at Raymond would march 13km (8 miles) northeast to Clinton and destroy the railroad at that point. Sherman's 15th Corps would march from Dillon's through Raymond to Mississippi Springs, and then move to attack Jackson in concert with McPherson's force.

Arriving on 13 May at Clinton, McPherson's men destroyed the railroad and telegraph lines that were vital to the Confederates, thus accomplishing Grant's third objective. On 14 May, both he and Sherman marched eastwards on two separate roads and drove Johnston's soldiers out of Jackson. With Johnston retreating to the northeast and Pemberton now virtually isolated to the west, Grant went to his fourth objective – the destruction of Pemberton's army.

On 15 May, Grant ordered McPherson and McClernand to march westwards to strike Pemberton, while Sherman remained in Jackson with two of his three divisions to destroy the railroads and military facilities

there. As Sherman's men burned Jackson on 15 May, McPherson's two divisions tramped westwards, following the railroad through Clinton to Bolton, where they encamped before dark. Awaiting McPherson at Bolton was one of McClernand's divisions, which Grant had ordered to Clinton to reinforce McPherson's smaller corps.

McClernand's other three divisions were supplemented by one division of Sherman's corps, which had lately arrived at Raymond after successfully completing its mission of

In December 1862 Grant learned a hard lesson about the vulnerability of a railroad when the Confederate cavalry destroyed his rail line of communications and doomed his first attempt on Vicksburg.

guarding Grant's supply trains from Grand Gulf. McClernand's four divisions spent the night of 15 May encamped just west of Raymond, and the politician-turned-general astutely placed these divisions along two axes of advance: two on the Raymond–Edwards Road, or the direct road to Edwards; and two on the Middle Road, which paralleled the Raymond–Edwards Road just 3.2km (2 miles) to the north. Just 3.2km (2 miles) further north, on the road that ran from Bolton to Edwards, were McPherson's three divisions. Through expert manoeuvring, Grant's army now occupied a 6.5km (4-mile) front, with seven Union divisions poised to attack along three axes of advance.

While Grant's men were rapidly closing on Pemberton's army on 15 May, Pemberton was himself moving his forces, albeit with much less success. After a contentious council of war at Mount Moriah on 14 May, in which Pemberton's general officers had literally voted on several courses of action, Pemberton compromised and ordered his army to

march the next day in a single column in an attempt to attack Grant's supply line at Dillon's. However, in the hours of 14 May, while the council deliberated, Grant's supply wagons were safely passing through Dillon's on their way to Raymond. So, Pemberton's odyssey of 15 May, in which his men marched, detoured or stood in place the entire day and much of the ensuing night, was a fool's errand accentuated by poor staff preparation and non-existent route reconnaissance.

THE BATTLE

The fateful morning of 16 May 1863 found Pemberton's tired army strung along a dirt farm road after having marched most of the night, with their commanding general facing south to an objective – the enemy supply line – that no longer existed. To make matters worse, Grant's well-rested seven divisions broke camp barely 10km

(6 miles) to the east, marched westwards and attacked the Confederate forces on three separate roads. Pemberton was surprised by Grant's triple-axis attack and, to all intents and purposes, the battle had already been decided.

One of McPherson's three divisions moved around the Confederate left flank, forcing the Southerners to reform their line to form the top of a crude figure '7'. But the grey line was too thin, and Major-General John Alexander Logan's (1826–86) Federals broke through.

To close this gap, Pemberton ordered a counterattack, and the Missourians and Arkansans of Brigadier-General John Bowen's (1830–63) division let loose a Rebel yell and drove the Federals back until the tired Southerners ran out of ammunition. Bowen's men then crashed into massed Federal artillery and were simultaneously struck by a fresh Union division. Exhausted,

In this highly dramatized 1887 chromolithograph, Major-General John Logan (left of centre with hat in hand) leads his 3rd Division of the XVII Corps at Champion Hill to attack the Confederate left flank at 10:30 a.m., 16 May 1863. The railroad connecting Vicksburg to Jackson is in the background. As Logan's division crashed into two brigades from Alabama and Georgia, General Grant, at the nearby Champion House, instructed a staff officer to 'Go down to Logan and tell him he is making history today.'

Opposite: The Eagle of the Eighth. Carrying their live Bald Eagle mascot into battle, the men of the 8th Wisconsin Volunteers lead the assault on Vicksburg, Mississippi.

Siege of Vicksburg. On 18 May 1863 General Sherman's XV Corps drove Confederate sharpshooters from Mrs. Martha Edwards' farmhouse (centre right). The encircled Vicksburg garrison eventually surrendered on 4 July 1863.

outnumbered and bulletless, Bowen's soldiers had no choice but to retire.

Grant had manoeuvred well, and his men not only outnumbered the Confederates but, due to his choice of approach routes, the Northern troops were also in the right places at the right times. Eventually, Pemberton had no choice but to order a retreat towards Vicksburg and, in the process of retreating, Major-General William Loring's (1818-86) Confederate division became separated from the rest of the army.

Loring's discouraged men retreated south, abandoned their artillery in the dark of night, and then trudged eastwards around Grant's army eventually to join General Johnston's forces.

Disgruntled over the way the battle had been managed, Loring did not send Pemberton a message to advise his commander that the division was going away from, not towards, the rest of the army. Consequently, on 17 May, a bewildered Pemberton placed a blocking force at the Big Black River to hold the planked-over railroad bridge so that the errant Loring could cross and rejoin the army. Grant's advancing forces struck this luckless 5000-man force and quickly captured more than 1700 of them, along with 18 cannon.

AFTERMATH: VICKSBURG

The remainder of Pemberton's army fell back into the trenches of Vicksburg, only to be surrounded by Grant's army on land and Porter's fleet on water. It was a foregone conclusion that Pemberton must surrender, which he did on 4 July 1863.

On that day, Grant achieved his fourth and final objective of the Vicksburg Campaign and, blessed with the Union victory at Gettysburg the previous day, President Lincoln could breathe a sigh of relief. Both his war to save the Union and his 1864 re-election campaign were infused with new life. And as Grant later wrote: 'The fate of the Confederacy was sealed when Vicksburg fell.'

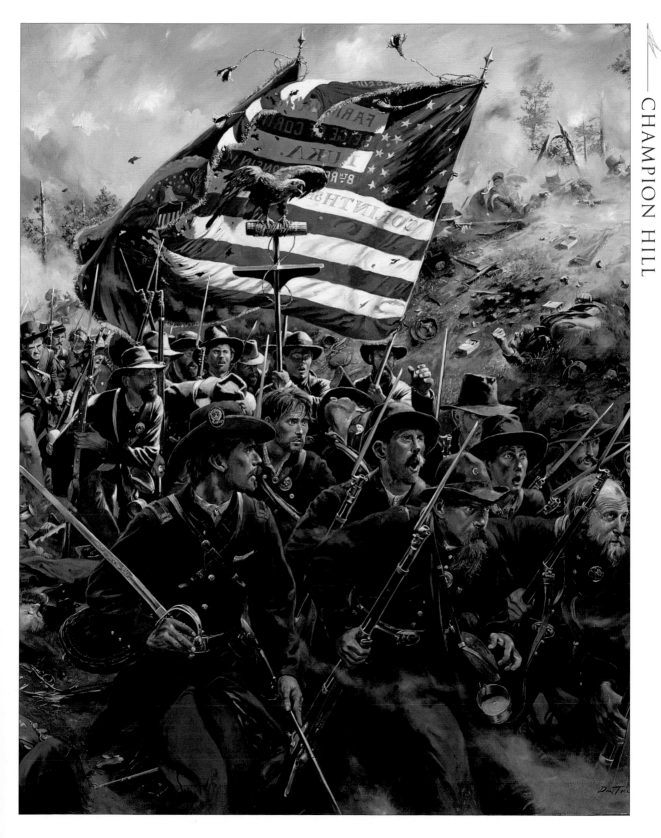

GETTYSBURG
1–3 JULY 1863

GETTYSBURG IS OFTEN THOUGHT OF AS THE TURNING POINT OF THE CIVIL WAR, BUT IT WAS NOT IMMEDIATELY DECISIVE. HOWEVER, THE SOUTH NEEDED A MAJOR VICTORY MORE THAN THE NORTH, AND FAILURE TO WIN ONE TIPPED THE BALANCE IN FAVOUR OF THE UNION. IT WAS IN SOME WAYS A BATTLE DECIDED BY MISTAKES, AND, IN THE END, THE UNION ARMY MADE FEWER OF THEM THAN ITS OPPONENTS.

WHY DID IT HAPPEN?

WHO The Union Army of the Potomac under the command of Major-General George G Meade (1815–72) numbering about 95,000, opposed by General Robert E Lee's (1807–70) Confederate Army of Northern Virginia, about 75,000 strong.

WHAT A 'meeting engagement' gradually drew in both armies, developing into a major battle in which the Confederate army generally attacked and the Union force fought from defensive positions atop Cemetery Ridge.

WHERE Gettysburg, Pennsylvania.

WHEN 1–3 July 1863.

WHY The Confederate army was operating in Union territory during Lee's Second Invasion of the North and was foraging for supplies. The location was a matter of chance, though it was inevitable that a clash would occur.

OUTCOME Lee's army was unable to defeat the Union force opposing it, and took casualties that it could not afford. Although the battle was indecisive in immediate military terms it was important politically and strategically.

In the summer of 1863, both sides were facing their own crises. In the North, with presidential elections looming, there was a real danger that a pro-peace president might be elected, who would be willing to let the secession states go in return for an end to the war. In the South, it was becoming increasingly difficult to find supplies, weapons and manpower to maintain the war effort. With Vicksburg under siege, there was a real possibility that the Confederacy might lose the use of the vital Mississippi waterway.

General Robert E Lee's advance into the North was critical for both sides. He might even take Washington and dictate the terms of peace in Napoleonic style, but his mere presence on Union soil was an affront to the prestige of President Lincoln (1809–65), who needed public confidence if he was to win the coming election. Just by having an army 'in being' in enemy territory, Lee was a threat to the Union. But he was also exposing his irreplaceable Army of Northern Virginia to defeat.

The Union Army of the Potomac was shadowing Lee's force, trying to prevent it from moving against Washington. It, too, could not risk defeat or the capital would be open to attack. During this tense period, Lee's army was sending out units to forage across the countryside in search of vital

Arriving during the battle, Meade positioned his headquarters in this farmhouse, sufficiently close to the action that stray artillery rounds narrowly missed the general and his staff during the battle.

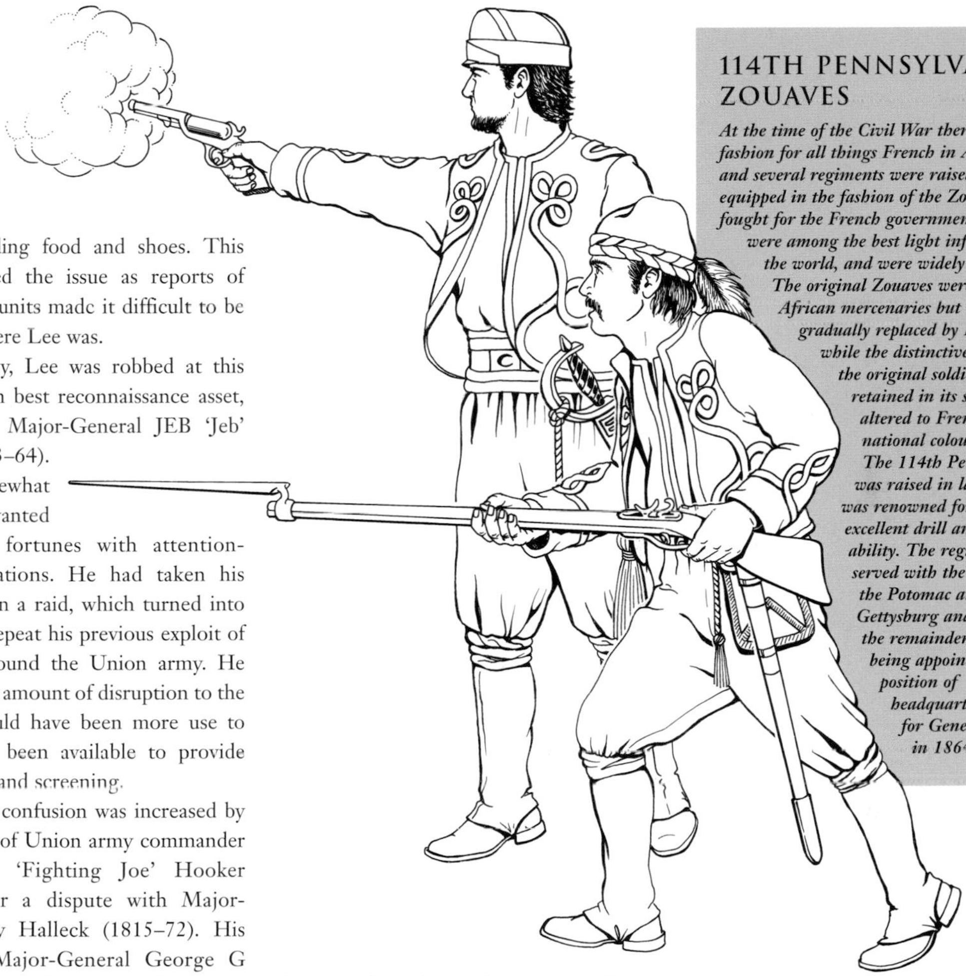

supplies, including food and shoes. This further confused the issue as reports of these detached units made it difficult to be sure exactly where Lee was.

Unfortunately, Lee was robbed at this time of his own best reconnaissance asset, the cavalry of Major-General JEB 'Jeb' Stuart (1833–64). Stuart was somewhat in eclipse and wanted to renew his fortunes with attention-grabbing operations. He had taken his command off on a raid, which turned into an attempt to repeat his previous exploit of riding right around the Union army. He caused a certain amount of disruption to the enemy but would have been more use to Lee if he had been available to provide reconnaissance and screening.

The general confusion was increased by the resignation of Union army commander Major-General 'Fighting Joe' Hooker (1814–79) after a dispute with Major-General Henry Halleck (1815–72). His replacement, Major-General George G Meade, would need time to familiarize himself with the situation and his new command, but time was not to be had; events precipitated a major battle whether or not anyone was ready for it.

COLLISION AT GETTYSBURG

The town of Gettysburg, Pennsylvania, was an important road junction and was said to contain a warehouse with large supplies of shoes, something the Confederate army badly needed. A brigade under Brigadier-General James Pettigrew (1828–63) was sent into the town to forage, and was encountered there by a Union cavalry force under Brigadier-General John Buford (1826–63). Buford's cavalry were trained as mobile infantry, fighting in a dismounted skirmish line.

Buford's force was something of an experiment, and among the ideas on trial was the use of repeating rifles. So, when Pettigrew's brigade began to advance against them, Buford's outnumbered men were able to hold their ground on McPherson Ridge for a time, though they were hard-pressed. The arrival of elements of the Union First Corps turned the tide, and now the Confederate force was pushed back. Other units were coming up as quickly as possible, and the fight began to spread out as units fell in on the flanks of those already engaged.

The situation was chaotic, with units arriving unexpectedly and rushing straight into action. Sometimes, this led to dramatic success and sometimes to disaster. Occasionally, both occurred in rapid succession, as when Brigadier-General James Archer's (1817–64) Confederate brigade made a dramatic attack on McPherson's Woods and captured the area, only to be outflanked by the Union Iron Brigade and captured – almost to a man.

114TH PENNSYLVANIA ZOUAVES

At the time of the Civil War there was a fashion for all things French in America, and several regiments were raised and equipped in the fashion of the Zouaves who fought for the French government. They were among the best light infantry in the world, and were widely copied. The original Zouaves were North African mercenaries but were gradually replaced by Frenchmen, while the distinctive clothing of the original soldiers was retained in its style but altered to French national colours.

The 114th Pennsylvania was raised in late 1862. It was renowned for its excellent drill and fighting ability. The regiment served with the Army of the Potomac at Gettysburg and through the remainder of the war, being appointed to the position of headquarters guard for General Meade in 1864.

LOCATION

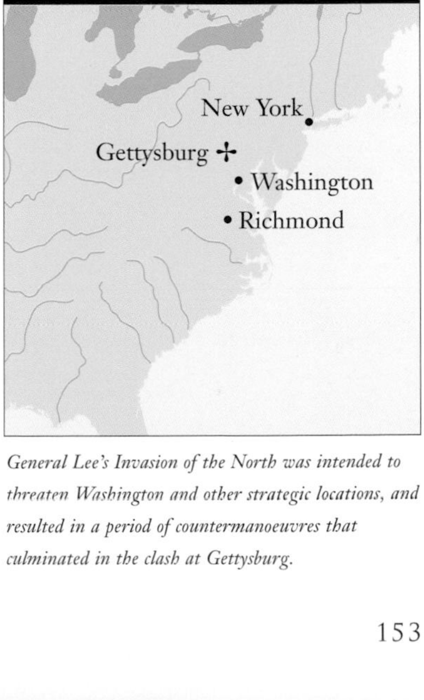

General Lee's Invasion of the North was intended to threaten Washington and other strategic locations, and resulted in a period of countermanoeuvres that culminated in the clash at Gettysburg.

It was during the fight for McPherson's Woods that Major-General John Fulton Reynolds (1820–63), at that point the senior Union officer on the field, was killed. It was also the point at which the true situation began to become clear. Seeing the black hats of the Iron Brigade advancing, a voice in the Confederate ranks was heard to call out: 'Hell, that ain't no milishy, that's the Army of the Potomac!'

The advantage swung one way, then the other. At one point the Rebels outnumbered the Federal troops on the field but were forced to attack across a railroad cut and took heavy casualties. The cut was bitterly contested for hours, and gradually two semi-coherent battle lines began to emerge from the chaos.

The Confederates were getting the better of it, and the Federal troops were gradually pushed back into, and through, Gettysburg. Thousands were taken prisoner and whole units were broken, with the survivors rallying on or behind Cemetery Ridge. They were covered by a determined rearguard action fought by the Union First Corps, which reached the ridge battered but in fairly good order.

Meanwhile, a succession of increasingly senior Union officers were reaching the field and assuming command, as each had a right to do. This created more confusion but gradually order asserted itself, with units being sent to defensive positions on the ridge.

This was the best chance Lee had of winning the battle, with the Union army shaken and disorganized. Lee gave orders to the effect that the Confederate army was to advance and push the enemy off the heights, but the attack was delayed too long and the moment passed.

By nightfall on the first day, the Union army was formed in a 'fish-hook' shape along Cemetery Ridge, with the Confederate army in a similar shape along Seminary Ridge and curving around the top of the fish-hook to the north. This gave the Union force the advantage of a shorter line, allowing reinforcements to be moved quickly from one point to another. Lee did have control of the Chambersburg and Hagerstown roads, however, and thus good communications to his rear.

THE SECOND DAY DAWNS

Both the Union and the Confederate armies spent the morning of the second day improving their position and their situation, slotting newly arrived units into their corps and divisional positions, and sorting out the chaos of the previous day's hurried deployments. Skirmishers exchanged fire but there was little major activity.

However, it was obvious that a battle was going to be fought here. Meade knew he had a strong position and was determined to defend it. Lee had the initiative and was equally determined to attack. Lee moved his forces into position and, as noon approached, began to mass troops opposite the southern end of the Union line. Lee had

John Fulton Reynolds was a career soldier from a military family, who had served with great distinction in the Mexican War. He was one of the best Federal corps commanders and a severe loss to the Union cause.

in fact ordered an attack to be launched at daybreak, but it was delayed, a problem that beset the Confederate army.

Detecting the movement opposite his command, Union Major-General Daniel Sickles (1819–1914) moved his Third Corps forward into a better position to meet the coming attack, occupying a peach orchard and the surrounding terrain. He had already asked for (and not been given) permission to do so, and now acted on his own initiative, leaving a dangerous gap in the Union line.

LEE ATTACKS ON THE LEFT

Lee was becoming increasingly impatient with Lieutenant-General James Longstreet (1821–1904), who was still stalling instead of attacking as ordered. Longstreet was short of one of his divisions, commanded by Major-General George Pickett (1825–75), which was still on the road. He did not want

to 'fight with one boot off', but was finally pushed into action by Lee.

The attack opened with a massive artillery bombardment of the Union troops occupying the Peach Orchard. Then Longstreet's assault finally went in. As a result of his earlier stalling, Longstreet's attack was disjointed but, despite hard resistance from Sickles' Third Corps, the Union forces were pushed back.

During the next four hours, the Union left flank was in severe danger. Six times the Confederates captured the Wheat Field but were driven off, and skirmishers hunted one another through the tumbled rocks of the Devil's Den. First one side, then the other, gained the advantage, but eventually Sickles' corps was pushed back. One Rebel brigade, under Brigadier-General Ambrose R Wright (1826–72), gained Cemetery Ridge but was pushed off again.

The confusion that reigned during the first day of the Battle of Gettysburg prevented either side from realizing the importance of the hill of Little Round Top. The subsequent defence of the hill was one of the decisive moments of the Civil War.

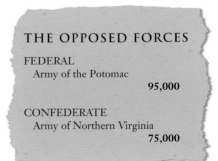

THE OPPOSED FORCES

FEDERAL
   Army of the Potomac
                                    95,000

CONFEDERATE
   Army of Northern Virginia
                                    75,000

A Confederate infantryman of the 1st Texas Brigade lunges forward with his bayonet-tipped musket. Troops of the 1st Texas were heavily engaged in the capture of Devil's Den on 2 July 1863, at Gettysburg.

As the Union line was broken, crisis loomed. On the Union right were two hills: Round Top and Little Round Top. The former was too steep and rocky to be much use. Little Round Top, however, could be used as a position for artillery to enfilade the Union line along Cemetery Ridge, and it was entirely undefended other than by a signals detachment.

FIGHT FOR ROUND TOPS

Meade reacted decisively and quickly to the news that Sickles was in trouble, committing most of his army reserve, and weakening his right flank, to send reinforcements to the embattled left. This was a courageous move: the Union centre

and right were also under attack, but Meade correctly decided that the most serious threat was to his left.

However, they could not have reached the Round Tops in time to prevent them being occupied in strength. Meade needed time, and that time was bought for him on the personal initiative of the Chief Engineer of the Union Army, Brigadier-General Gouverneur K Warren (1830–82).

Realizing the importance of Little Round Top, Warren rushed to the nearest troops – Brigadier-General James Barnes's (1801–69) division of Fifth Corps – and borrowed a brigade under the command of Colonel Strong Vincent (1837–63). These troops reached the crest of Little Round Top just as Confederate troops – elements of Major-General John Bell Hood's (1831–79) division, which had already taken Round Top – were coming up the other side.

For a while the fate of Little Round Top was undecided but, despite being badly outnumbered, Vincent's brigade was able to cling on and then even counterattacked downhill at bayonet point. Although there was still heavy fighting going on, the successful defence of Little Round Top meant that the crisis had passed for the Union army. Reinforcements arrived and the situation was gradually restored.

LEE ATTACKS ON THE RIGHT

Meanwhile, another Confederate attack was going in against the northern end of the fish-hook, with the aim of dislodging the Union army from Culp's Hill and turning its right flank. After an artillery preparation that was met by overwhelming counterfire

from Cemetery Hill, Lieutenant-General Richard S Ewell's (1817–72) corps finally moved forward with Major-General Edward 'Allegheny' Johnson's (1816–73) division in the lead.

Exploiting the weakened Union position (caused by sending brigades south to assist Sickles), Johnson's division was able to take the southern slopes of Culp's Hill and to advance almost as far as the Baltimore Pike. It was chiefly opposed by a single brigade under Brigadier-General George S Greene, (1801–99) which held out long enough to receive reinforcements. Meanwhile, Brigadier-General Jubal Early's (1816–94) command made an attempt on Cemetery Hill but the expected support did not materialize and the attack was beaten off.

As night fell, the Confederates were in possession of important terrain at the right of the Union line, and were within a few hundred metres of the Union supply wagons. However, darkness concealed the situation and the fighting died down.

THE THIRD DAY OPENS

The Union army was still in danger as the third day began. Although there had been no big successes on the Confederate part, they held part of Culp's Hill and some territory around the bases of the Round Tops. They had exerted serious pressure and, arguably, had only failed to win a victory due to lack of coordination.

On the Union side, more reinforcements had arrived in the form of Major-General John Sedgwick's (1813–64) 15,000-strong corps, but the Confederate army had also been reinforced by late arrivals, including that of Stuart's cavalry. On balance, however, it would appear that Lee had missed his chance. He did not have an objective viewpoint, and things probably looked more favourable from where he stood. He still believed that he could win.

Having attacked heavily on the right and left, and only weakly in the centre, Lee reasoned that the Union centre must have been weakened to meet his thrusts on the second day. Meade correctly predicted this move and reinforced his centre with infantry plus an artillery redeployment to allow massed fire down the hill.

Equally importantly, Meade bolstered the centre psychologically by informing Brigadier-General John Gibbon (1827–96) of Lee's intentions and his preparations to meet them, saying that Gibbon's command would be where the blow was to fall – and be repulsed. Seeing their commander proven correct must have been good for morale among the defending troops.

One other thing was necessary to remedy the Union position: Culp's Hill must be retaken. Twelfth Corps was given the task,

and reinforced accordingly. Some of the troops involved in the assault had an affront to avenge – they had been sent off to reinforce Sickles and had returned to find their positions in enemy hands. This deprived them of food and, they told themselves, a more comfortable night than the one they had just spent in the open.

Johnson's Confederate division wished to widen the penetration it had made into the Union line, and the Federal force wanted to see it off. Johnson's men came out to attack and fighting rapidly spread until about 10:00 a.m., when the Federals finally dislodged Johnson's division from its captured positions. Forced to retreat to the main Confederate line, Johnson's division was shot up badly by Union artillery on the way.

LEE PLANS A DECISIVE BLOW

Although his scouts (and General Longstreet) informed him that it would be possible to manoeuvre around Meade's

This was the terrain so bitterly fought over; hilly and liberally sprinkled with obstacles to break up an infantry advance. The same obstructions provided cover for sharpshooters on both sides.

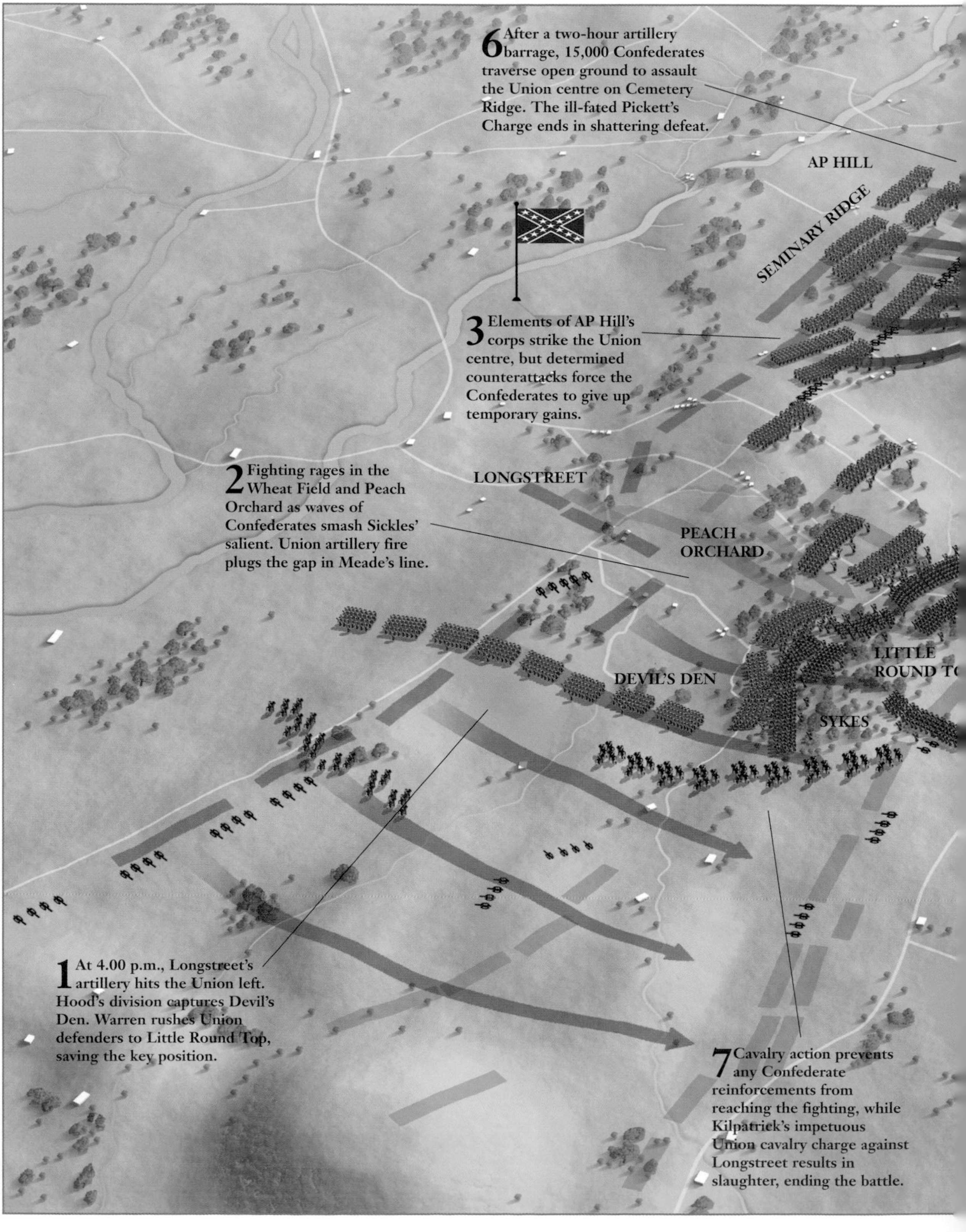

6 After a two-hour artillery barrage, 15,000 Confederates traverse open ground to assault the Union centre on Cemetery Ridge. The ill-fated Pickett's Charge ends in shattering defeat.

AP HILL

SEMINARY RIDGE

3 Elements of AP Hill's corps strike the Union centre, but determined counterattacks force the Confederates to give up temporary gains.

2 Fighting rages in the Wheat Field and Peach Orchard as waves of Confederates smash Sickles' salient. Union artillery fire plugs the gap in Meade's line.

LONGSTREET

PEACH ORCHARD

LITTLE ROUND TO

DEVIL'S DEN

SYKES

1 At 4.00 p.m., Longstreet's artillery hits the Union left. Hood's division captures Devil's Den. Warren rushes Union defenders to Little Round Top, saving the key position.

7 Cavalry action prevents any Confederate reinforcements from reaching the fighting, while Kilpatrick's impetuous Union cavalry charge against Longstreet results in slaughter, ending the battle.

GETTYSBURG

CEMETERY HILL

CULP'S HILL

HOWARD

JOHNSON

NEWTON

ROCK CREEK

4 In gathering darkness, Ewell fails to capture Culp's Hill, while Early gains the summit of Cemetery Hill but, without reinforcements, is compelled to abandon the effort.

5 Ewell vainly renews the assault at Culp's Hill and Spangler's Spring, and Union counterattacks end the threat to the heights on Meade's right.

GETTYSBURG
1–3 JULY 1863

army and perhaps force it to attack on ground of his choosing, Lee was determined to end this matter here and now. Pointing to Cemetery Ridge, he stated that 'the enemy is there and I am going to strike him'.

Lee's strike would take the form of 15,000 men advancing en masse to break through the Union centre. Many of his troops had been only peripherally involved the previous day and Lee believed that they were fresh enough and sufficiently determined to carry Cemetery Ridge. Longstreet disagreed, suggesting that 'no fifteen thousand men ever arrayed for battle can take that position'. But Lee was in command, not Longstreet, and the only concession to the latter was some compromise over details of the plan.

PICKETT'S CHARGE

Preparations were made, troops were shifted and the hour approached. Longstreet's misgivings grew, but at about

1:00 p.m., the artillery preparation began. This was not as effective as Lee had hoped for, partly due to lack of ammunition, and partly because the guns were firing upwards and tended to shoot over the ridge rather into the forces arrayed along its crest. A tremendous storm of fire came from the massed Federal artillery in reply.

Finally, Pickett, who had been detailed to lead the assault, asked Longstreet if he should advance. Longstreet was unable to give him an answer but nodded, and Pickett's Charge began. This was one of the great military undertakings of the period – a full 15,000 men advancing with their colours, almost as if on parade. There was a brief lull in the firing, during which the Rebel lines crossed about half the distance to the base of the ridge. Then, the Federal artillery began firing.

The massed Union guns fired ceaselessly as the Confederate infantry struggled forward and began to ascend the hill. Gunners changed from roundshot to shell and finally canister as Pickett's Charge came towards them, but the Rebels just closed ranks and kept coming. More artillery (including some guns positioned, ironically enough, on Little Round Top) enfiladed the lines, and as the range dropped, rifle fire broke out along the crest line.

Gaps were opening up between Confederate units, but the advance continued. However, Union Major-General Winfield Scott Hancock (1824–86) pushed a brigade into the gap and began firing into the flank of the advancing enemy units. They broke up two brigades on the Confederate right and sent the survivors back towards their own lines.

By now the leading elements of the Confederate force were approaching the main Union line. Pickett positioned himself, an inviting target on his black horse, to direct units coming up and remained there within range of enemy

A cavalryman from Rush's Lancers, 6th Pennsylvania Cavalry. The lance was going out of fashion in the 1860s, though some units still carried it. The Union cavalry made better use of their firearms than hand weapons. Note that the revolver is worn in 'reverse cavalry' position.

A section of the Gettysburg Cyclorama, painted in 1883 by French artist Paul Phillippoteaux (1845–1923), depicting Pickett's Charge on the final day of the battle. In many ways this was the last hurrah for the Confederacy. Afterwards, the tide had fully turned in favour of the North.

sharpshooters. He fed in units as they arrived, trying to maintain some kind of organization to the assault.

On the left, Pettigrew's division came under murderous flanking fire and broke up. With both flanks stalled and falling back, the only chance for success lay with Pickett's central units. They came forward, pausing only to shoot, and were within 100 metres (110 yards) of the stone wall behind which Gibbon's men waited with loaded weapons. Just as Meade had predicted, the main thrust was coming straight at Gibbon.

Gibbon gave the command to fire, and within five minutes the determined assault was shot to pieces. A scant 150 Confederate

soldiers reached the stone wall and clambered over it, led by Brigadier-General Lewis Armistead (1817–63). A Union brigade under Brigadier-General AS Webb (1835–1911) broke and ran, and nearby gunners were chased off or shot down.

This was the high watermark, the point where Pickett's Charge crested and began to ebb. Rallied Union troops, assisted by artillery firing point-blank, blasted the intrepid general and his tiny force off the hill. The assault began to thin out and break up as the Union defenders returned to their positions and continued firing. Soon, Confederate regiments began to break and scatter back down the ridge. The charge was over, and Lee's chance of winning the battle was gone with it. Estimates of Southern dead and wounded in the assault range from 7000 to more than 10,000.

ENDGAME

Longstreet did what he could to rally the shattered survivors and form some kind of

battle line in case of a counterattack. It did not come, however. The reason might have been that Meade was thinking defensively and was unable to switch to aggressive operations. It might have been that the Union army was exhausted, and there is also the possibility that Meade did not know that the Confederates were beaten. He may have been expecting another assault from his highly determined enemies.

Lee knew he was beaten, though. Despondently telling Pickett that he and his men had done all that could possibly be asked of them, he accepted the blame for the failure with the simple words: 'This was all my fault.'

The Rebel army was perhaps less despondent. Once out of immediate danger most of the survivors of the charge returned to their units at a walk rather than fleeing into the distance. They knew they had been dealt a beating, but defeat was a new experience for them and, rather than breaking their spirit, it provoked a desire for revenge. It is perhaps as well for the Army of the Potomac that Meade did not choose to counterattack, given the mood in the Confederate lines at that point.

CAVALRY SKIRMISHES

As Pickett's Charge was going in, a cavalry fight broke out at the southern end of the battlefield. This was an inconclusive but violent business, and went on for some time. Meanwhile, to the north, a rather more serious cavalry action took place. Four Confederate brigades under the legendary 'Jeb' Stuart fought it out with three Union brigades. The prize was control of the roads in the Union army's rear. Lee had hoped that the sudden appearance of Stuart's cavalry in the Union rear would be a factor in breaking the Army of the Potomac, coinciding with Pickett's Charge. In the event the fight, though hard, did not materially affect the result of the battle.

The cavalry fight involved dismounted men fighting as skirmishers and several

batteries of artillery as well as the more traditional running fight. In general, the Union cavalry was inferior to that of the Confederacy in terms of horsemanship and dash. As a result, the Rebels liked to get stuck in with sabres and revolvers, while the Union cavalry tended to come off worse in such engagements. However, one brigade on the Union side was only too willing to meet the Confederate *beau sabreurs* on their own terms – headlong at the point of the sword. This brigade was commanded by a man who had been a captain on the staff a few days earlier and had been promoted, with two others, to general rank for lunatic bravery. His name was George Armstrong Custer (1839–76).

Custer's brigade clashed with the advancing Rebels in a violent mutual charge that became a classic cavalry mêlée of charge and countercharge, while a firefight around Rummell House drew in ever-larger numbers of dismounted men. The fight went on for some time before winding

Entitled 'Come on you wolverines!', this modern painting depicts General George Armstrong Custer leading the Michigan Brigade in a charge at the Battle of Gettysburg, 3 July 1863.

Photographer Timothy O'Sullivan (c1840–82) recorded this grisly scene of Union dead in a meadow near the Peach Orchard. These soldiers were probably killed on 2 July 1863, defending the advanced positions of the Union Third Corps.

down somewhat inconclusively. The Confederate cavalry withdrew into the gathering darkness.

One other cavalry action took place that day. While Confederate General James Longstreet was trying to rebuild the battle line, the Union cavalry commander Major-General Hugh Judson Kilpatrick (1836–81) decided to make a cavalry attack. It is possible that he believed that Meade might be about to counterattack and was trying to assist. Whatever the reason, he ordered one of his regiments forward.

Led by the newly promoted Brigadier-General John F Farnsworth (1820–97), 300 Union cavalrymen charged. They punched through the Confederate line and into the rear, then broke through and came back without their commander, who was killed.

LEE RETREATS

As darkness fell on the third day of Gettysburg, there was a real possibility that the fighting would be resumed on 4 July. However, after waiting for a Union attack

and choosing not to launch one of his own, Lee began a withdrawal.

It seems that Meade was not entirely sure that Lee was withdrawing until 5 July, at which point he sent orders to some of his detached troops to impede and harass the retreat. The most effective action against the retreating Confederates was a cavalry attack made at night, which caused a fair amount of damage.

Union cavalry intermittently harassed the withdrawing Army of Northern Virginia and were driven off at times by walking

wounded who had retained their rifles. However, there was no serious attempt at a close pursuit. Heavy rains, which had flooded the Potomac, hampered the retreat and made the going difficult.

However, Meade was reluctant to press the pursuit and, once the river had subsided, Lee was able to get his army across and out of danger.

AFTERMATH

Gettysburg was, in truth, an inconclusive affair, but the Union could afford to fight a struggle of attrition and the Confederacy simply could not. There was a point when Lee might have broken the Army of the Potomac and perhaps even taken the Federal capital of Washington, but that moment had now passed. The odds against the Confederacy were growing ever longer, especially with a victory to shore up Lincoln's bid for re-election.

Gettysburg was, therefore, the point at which the Confederacy lost its best chance to win to war, and from then onwards it was on the road to defeat.

In one of the few photographs taken during the dedication of the Gettysburg National Cemetery on 19 November 1863, President Abraham Lincoln is barely visible seated at the left on the crowded speakers' platform. Lincoln's Gettysburg Address, consisting of slightly more than 200 words, remains one of the principal documents of American freedom.

CHICKAMAUGA
18–20 SEPTEMBER 1863

CHICKAMAUGA WAS ONE OF THE FEW OCCASIONS THAT THE CONFEDERATES ACTUALLY OUTNUMBERED THEIR OPPONENTS. IT WAS THE MOST SERIOUS DEFEAT SUFFERED BY THE UNION IN THE WESTERN THEATRE OF WAR, AND MARKED THE END OF WHAT HAD BEEN UP TO THEN A SUCCESSFUL CAMPAIGN BY GENERAL ROSECRANS.

WHY DID IT HAPPEN?

WHO Union Army of the Cumberland (62,000 men) under Major-General William S Rosecrans (1819–98) opposed by the Confederate Army of Tennessee (65,000 men) under General Braxton Bragg (1817–76).

WHAT The battle was something of a 'meeting engagement', which developed into an all-out brawl in very difficult terrain. Confederate forces were able to exploit a gap in the Union line.

WHERE Near Fort Oglethorpe near Chattanooga, Georgia.

WHEN 18–20 September 1863.

WHY Bragg's objective was to regain control of Chattanooga, an important railroad junction.

OUTCOME Most of the Union army collapsed and scattered, forcing Rosecrans to retreat into Chattanooga. Bragg's army then laid siege to the town.

After his defence of Cincinnati during the Confederate invasion of Kentucky, Rosecrans was given command of the Union armies in the western theatre, replacing the hesitant Brigadier-General Don Carlos Buell (1818–98). He embarked on a successful advance through Tennessee, pushing Bragg's army southwards.

Rosecrans' superiors and President Lincoln (1809–65) were determined that he should capture Chattanooga as soon as possible. The city was critical as it controlled a vital rail junction whose loss would reduce the Confederates' ability to move supplies and troops about, weakening their whole war effort. It would also serve as a base to attack Atlanta and to launch operations into the Deep South.

The Confederates knew how vital the city was, and were prepared to defend it

heavily, so Rosecrans decided to dislodge them by manoeuvre rather than assault. His plan was to position his army to the south of the city and cut off its supply lines, and in mid-August, he set out to do just that.

To cover Rosecrans' crossing of the Tennessee River, he ordered diversionary attacks to be made. These included a bombardment of the city's defences. In fact, the bombardment was made by a single battery of light artillery covered by just one brigade of troops, but it reinforced Bragg's preconceived ideas about what Rosecrans would do and so occupied his full attention. Rosecrans was therefore able to carry out the first part of his flanking march more or less unopposed.

Meanwhile, the Confederacy was taking steps to ensure that Chattanooga was properly defended and so pulled in forces

The American Civil War was one of the first conflicts in which large-scale movements of troops and supplies by rail played an important part. Control of rail junctions such as the one at Chattanooga was a vital strategic factor.

from other regions, including a corps of the Army of Northern Virginia under the command of Lieutenant-General James Longstreet (1821–1904).

Rosecrans was moving through difficult terrain and was obliged to divide his force. His three corps each moved by a different road and became widely separated on the march. Once Bragg learned of the situation, he realized that he had been handed an opportunity to move against each corps in turn and defeat the Union army in detail.

Bragg pulled out of Chattanooga on 8 September and began his move. Rosecrans duly learned of it and decided that Bragg was retreating, perhaps intending to fall back on Atlanta. In part, this belief was due to a successful deception operation on Bragg's part.

Deserters have always been a useful source of information to their opponents, and Bragg made sure that Rosecrans captured some. These men were in fact volunteers carrying false information, deliberately fostering the impression that Bragg was in retreat. In fact, he was encamped at La Fayette, and was ready and willing to fight.

Sending cavalry to cut a railroad supplying Bragg's force, Rosecrans also sent a corps to capture Chattanooga while the rest of the army advanced after Bragg's supposedly retiring force. The 14th Corps, under Major-General George H Thomas (1816–70), was heading for La Fayette, when the lead division ran into resistance. The resulting action became known as the Battle of Davis' Cross Roads or the Battle of Dug Gap.

A Confederate division under Major-General Thomas C Hindman (1828–68) was detailed to attack the lead division of Thomas' corps – commanded by Major-General James S Negley (1826–1901) – in the flank as it moved through Dug Gap, at which point Major-General Patrick Ronayne Cleburne's (1828–64) division would assault it from the front. The plan involved reinforcements that did not arrive in time, so the attack was postponed until

CONFEDERATE RIFLEMAN

Drawn from a smaller population and with less industry available to support them, the armies of the Confederacy were less uniform in appearance than the Federal forces and tended to be equipped with whatever was available. The Confederacy made more use of irregular units than the North, and in this it had an advantage in that a large segment of its population was composed of resourceful backwoodsmen already skilled in fieldcraft and shooting.

This individual is armed with an early sniper rifle. The long optical sight is primitive but under the right conditions his weapon could kill a specific individual – say an officer or a colour-bearer – from a great distance.

the next day, by which time Negley, too, had been reinforced.

The Confederate attack went in against two divisions, whose commanding officers conducted a skilled fighting withdrawal, leapfrogging back to Stevens' Gap to await reinforcement by the rest of the corps. This was accomplished in spite of constant harassment and determined attacks by the Confederate forces.

Perhaps Bragg realized that he had lost his opportunity to defeat Thomas' corps, or perhaps he just changed his mind as he was very prone to do, but in any case he decided to move north and attack 21st Corps under Major-General Thomas Leonidas Crittenden (1819–93) instead.

Bragg ordered Lieutenant-General Leonidas Polk (1806–64) to move with his command against Crittenden's corps. Polk advanced but, finding that Crittenden's division had concentrated, decided not to make the attack. Rosecrans was by now concentrating his three dispersed corps and was no longer vulnerable to defeat in detail.

THE FIRST DAY

Bragg's army began the operation on 18 September, marching northwards back up the La Fayette road. Crittenden's corps was on the northern, left, flank of the Union army, and to get at it the Confederates had

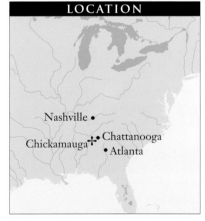

The Battle of Chickamauga was fought close to the critical rail junction of Chattanooga. The actual location was coincidental – the decisive clash could have occurred at a number of other points.

Whenever they halted for any length of time, the troops on both sides would make themselves as comfortable as possible. This peaceful scene is a stark contrast to the savage short-range fighting that would soon erupt.

to cross the Chickamauga Creek. The attempt ran into determined resistance from Union cavalry and mounted infantry.

One of the defending officers, Colonel John T Wilder (1830–1917), had been forced to surrender a river crossing the previous year when badly outnumbered. There was to be no repeat of that incident in 1863. Wilder's cavalry put up a spirited fight, their lack of numbers partially offset by the fact that some of them carried repeating rifles. Wilder's troops inflicted considerable casualties on Brigadier-General St John R Liddell's (1815–70) division and were able to destroy the bridge that the Confederates wanted to use.

Meanwhile, cavalry under Colonel R Minty were eventually pushed back from Reed's Bridge, and the Confederates were able to cross in force. Finally getting into position to attack Crittenden, Polk was to have assaulted frontally after a flanking force consisting of the corps under Major-General Simon B Buckner (1823–1914), Major-General WHT Walker (1816–64) and Brigadier-General Nathan B Forrest (1821–77) moved into position. However, the delay imposed by crossing the creek prevented the flanking operation from taking place and the attack did not develop.

The situation was confused on both sides. Neither Bragg nor Rosecrans knew exactly where his enemy was, nor how many men he commanded. During the night of the 18/19 September, reconnaissance patrols from both forces probed the enemy positions, and as each one reported back, the respective commanders moved units accordingly.

Rosecrans' thinking was defensive at this point. Bragg planned to attack. Each army occupied about 10km (6 miles) of front, in terrain that was entirely unsuitable for a major battle. Dense woods covered most of the ground and it was not possible to see more than 50m (55 yards) or so. Artillery would be no use at all in the coming battle, except in the fields that had been cleared between the stands of trees. Nevertheless, Bragg was determined to fight.

THE SECOND DAY

At dawn on 19 September, Crittenden's corps was no longer the northern flank of the Union position. Thomas' corps was now on its flank. Bragg was unaware of this and still thought Crittenden's corps represented the end of the Union line.

Thomas ordered Brigadier-General John Milton Brannan's (1819–92) division to reconnoitre towards Chickamauga Creek and find out what the Confederates were up to. Brannan ran into Forrest's cavalry, which was dismounted, and launched an attack that drove the cavalry back. The fighting drew in nearby Confederate infantry and gradually spread until a major engagement was under way.

First Buckner's corps and Major-General BF Cheatham's (1820–86) division joined the action, and Bragg fed in more troops as the scale of the fighting became apparent. By the end of the day all but two of his divisions had been in action and on the Union side the whole of 14th, 20th and 21st corps were engaged.

Bragg launched several assaults, but all were beaten back, and by nightfall no real gains had been made by either side. The fighting had been ferocious, often at very close quarters in difficult terrain. Hand-to-hand combat had occurred in several places, with no overall guidance by senior officers. Chickamauga had turned into a soldier's battle, one that would be decided by the resolve and raw fighting power of the men on both sides.

FURTHER REDEPLOYMENTS

Nevertheless, the two commanders did what they could to influence the outcome, shifting units around during the night of 19/20 September. Bragg may not have known just how severe the fighting had been. He referred to the day's action as 'heavy skirmishing' that had taken place while his command was trying to get into line of battle. However, he did make one very good decision.

Realizing that it was going to be impossible to re-form the army according to its original command structure, Bragg reorganized according to where each unit was at the time, placing Polk in command of the right wing, containing Lieutenant-General DH Hill's (1821–89) corps and the reserve corps, and Longstreet in command of the left wing, which contained Buckner's corps and the one Longstreet himself had brought from Virginia. Out-of-position units were assigned to the nearest high command structure, rather than moved across a wooded battlefield in the dark.

THE OPPOSED FORCES

FEDERAL
Army of the Cumberland (mostly infantry) — 62,000

CONFEDERATE
Army of Tennessee (mostly infantry) — 65,000

Confederate Major-General Patrick Cleburne rallies his troops at the battle of Chickamauga. Cleburne's division was involved in the assault on Thomas' Corps.

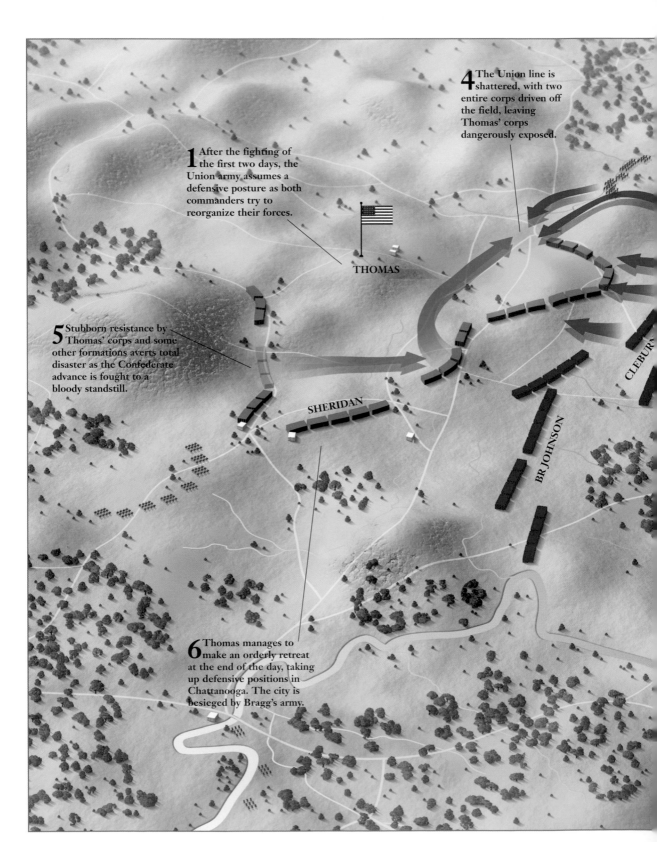

1 After the fighting of the first two days, the Union army assumes a defensive posture as both commanders try to reorganize their forces.

4 The Union line is shattered, with two entire corps driven off the field, leaving Thomas' corps dangerously exposed.

THOMAS

5 Stubborn resistance by Thomas' corps and some other formations averts total disaster as the Confederate advance is fought to a bloody standstill.

SHERIDAN

CLEBURN

BR JOHNSON

6 Thomas manages to make an orderly retreat at the end of the day, taking up defensive positions in Chattanooga. The city is besieged by Bragg's army.

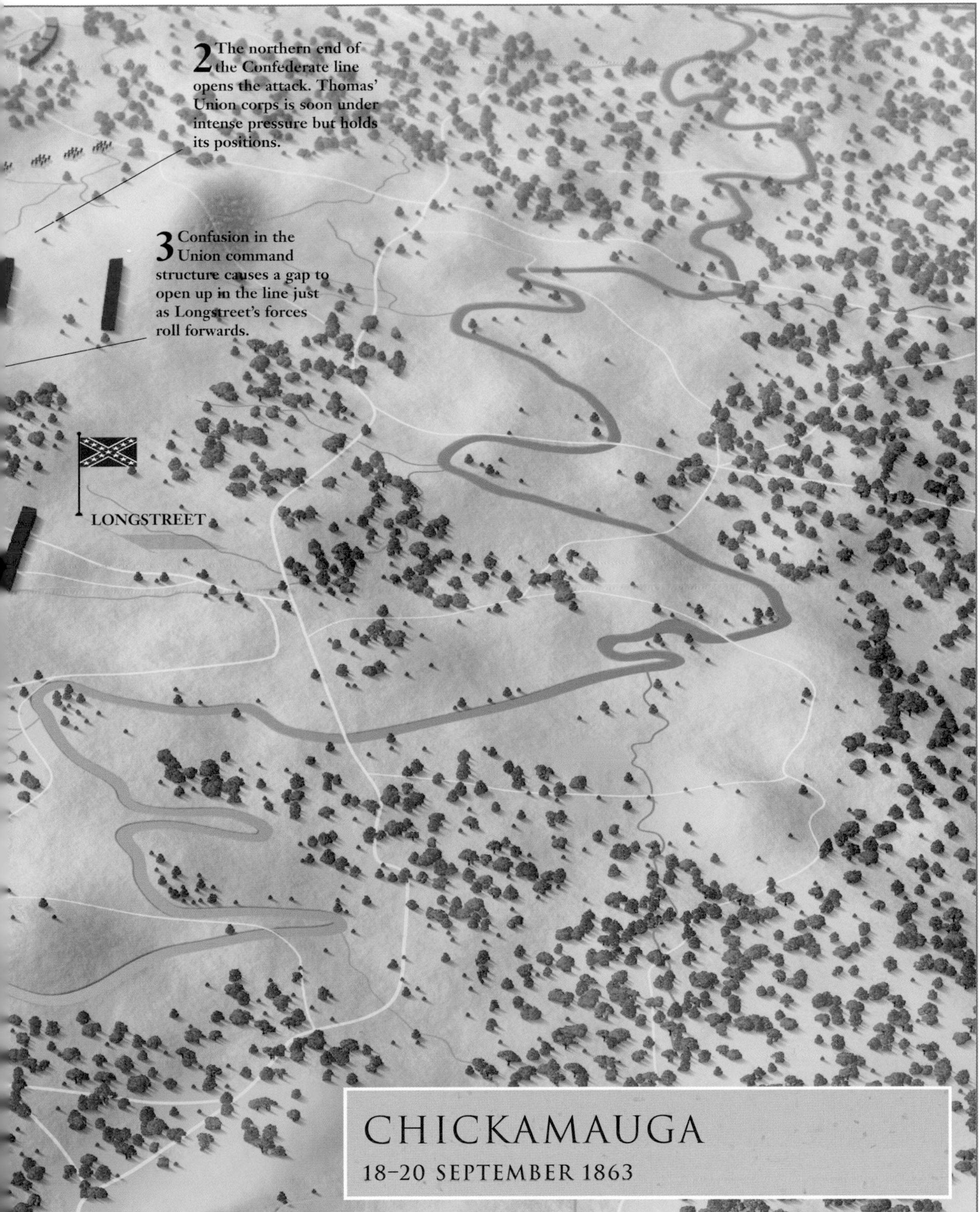

2 The northern end of the Confederate line opens the attack. Thomas' Union corps is soon under intense pressure but holds its positions.

3 Confusion in the Union command structure causes a gap to open up in the line just as Longstreet's forces roll forwards.

LONGSTREET

CHICKAMAUGA
18-20 SEPTEMBER 1863

Leonidas Polk was a West Point graduate and an ordained bishop. He was a friend of Jefferson Davis (1808–89), who appointed him a major-general in the Confederate Army. He was not a successful commander but was well liked by his troops.

Meanwhile, the Union Army was on the defensive again, chopping down trees to make breastworks in order to strengthen its positions. This was probably the right decision, as Bragg was planning an assault for the next morning. His plan was to roll forwards in succession from north to south across the entire battlefield. At 9:00 a.m. the following morning, the attack began.

THE FINAL DAY

Major-General John C Breckinridge's (1821–75) division opened the Confederate attack, engaging Thomas' corps. Under serious pressure, Thomas called up Negley's division, which had been placed in reserve – or so the Union commanders thought. In fact, Negley's division was in the line, but he was still able to send troops to help Thomas once Brigadier-General Thomas Wood (18923–1906), whose division was in reserve instead of Negley's, came up to relieve him.

Up to about 11:00 a.m., Thomas' corps was able to fend off the Confederate assault. However, the mismanaged deployment was to have serious consequences for Rosecrans. Misapprehending the location of Wood's

division, Rosecrans ordered Wood to close up and support Major-General Joseph J Reynolds (1822–99). This would have been appropriate if Wood was where Rosecrans thought he was, but in the event the order required Wood to pull back out of the line, move behind Brannan's division and finally close up with Reynolds' right flank, where Rosecrans had thought he was all along.

This unfortunate movement left a gap in the Union line, which Major-General Philip Henry Sheridan (1831–88) and Brigadier-General Jefferson C Davis (1828–79) began moving their divisions to cover. However, they were a little too late. At about 11:30 a.m., Longstreet's wing was rolling forward and hit the Union line while the gap was open. Sheridan's and Davis' divisions were overwhelmed and scattered, and the Union line was compromised.

Thinking that a general collapse was occurring, Rosecrans precipitated one. Along with Major-General Alexander McCook (1831–1903), commanding 20th Corps, and Crittenden (21st Corps commander), he panicked and fled the field, along with most of the units of the two affected corps.

Not everyone fled, and total disaster was averted by the initiative and determination of several Union commanders. As the corps around them disintegrated, Wilder's cavalry again distinguished themselves, advancing to counterattack with their repeating rifles.

Although terribly hard-pressed, Wilder's men were able to slow Longstreet down long enough to save many of the fleeing men, and also bought time for the sole remaining corps commander on the field to realize what was happening and act.

Thomas remained in the field, and with him his corps. He pulled back some of his units to anchor his flanks, but otherwise stayed where he was, determined to make a fight of it. In this, he was nobly assisted by two brigades under Major-General Gordon Granger (1822–76). Granger was supposed to be in the rear, in reserve to cover the rear and flank. Correctly deciding that there were more important tasks at hand, Granger led his force forward and offered his units to Thomas. They were just in time to prevent Thomas' flank being enveloped.

Two factors prevented he total collapse of the Union army. One was the stubborn fight put up by Thomas, who became known as the 'Rock of Chickamauga'. The other was that Bragg had not allowed for a general pursuit and was not able to make the most of his unexpected victory.

Beating off more attacks on his thin line, Thomas was able to hold out for the rest of

This illustration tries to give an impression of the close-quarters fighting that took place all along the line. It is somewhat unlikely that formed units fired into one another from quite such close range, however.

the day and was then able to retire into the defences of Chattanooga, where Rosecrans had taken refuge. The Confederate army then laid siege to the city.

AFTERMATH

Chickamauga was a major defeat for the Union, although it came at great cost to the Confederacy. Around 16,000 Union soldiers were killed or wounded, while the Rebels lost 18,500 or so. Although Bragg won a tactical victory, he was not able to make much of it, due partly to the difficult terrain, partly to Thomas' defiance and partly to his own decision not to create an army reserve capable of conducting a vigorous pursuit.

Rosecrans' career was finished, though Thomas was rightly elevated to high command, and Granger's timely initiative was also rewarded. One other individual distinguished himself: James A Garfield (1831–81), Rosecrans' chief of staff. After accompanying his commander off the field

of battle, Garfield went back to see what help he could be while the general in command of the army fled to Chattanooga. Garfield was eventually elected President of the United States.

On the Confederate side, General Bragg relieved three of his commanders for 'misconduct' during the battle, though his own abrasive nature had played its part in the friction that had beset the command structure of the army.

Bragg did not retake Chattanooga. He besieged the city until November, when a relief force under Major-General William Tecumseh Sherman (1820–91) and Major-General Ulysses S Grant (1822–85) arrived to break the siege. Some months before, President Lincoln (1809–65) had suggested that whoever controlled Chattanooga would win the war. He had said much the same thing about the state of Kentucky, and now the Union had both. Although its army had been beaten in the field, the Union was still winning the war.

After their defeat at Chickamauga, the Union forces were besieged in Chattanooga with the Confederates cutting off their supply lines. A Union offensive to reopen the lines resulted in the Battle of Lookout Mountain on 24 November 1864.

THE WILDERNESS/ SPOTSYLVANIA COURTHOUSE

5–20 MAY 1864

WHEN LIEUTENANT-GENERAL ULYSSES S GRANT BECAME GENERAL-IN-CHIEF ON 12 MARCH 1864, HE BROUGHT A NEW PERSPECTIVE TO THE FEDERAL WAR EFFORT. FOR THE FIRST TIME THE FEDERALS WOULD TREAT THE WAR AS A WHOLE, PRESSING THE CONFEDERATES ON ALL SIDES SIMULTANEOUSLY, RATHER THAN ALLOWING THEM TO REINFORCE FIRST ONE THREATENED AREA, AND THEN ANOTHER.

WHY DID IT HAPPEN?

WHO Federal forces under Lieutenant-General Ulysses S Grant (1822–85) attacked Confederates under General Robert E Lee (1807–70) in the opening battles of what proved to be the war's decisive campaign in Virginia.

WHAT Lee defeated Grant by thwarting the Federal turning movements, but Grant relentlessly maintained the pressure.

WHERE The Wilderness and Spotsylvania Courthouse, Virginia.

WHEN 5–7 May 1864 (The Wilderness) and 7–20 May 1864 (Spotsylvania Courthouse).

WHY At the Wilderness, Lee used restrictive terrain to offset Grant's superior numbers. At Spotsylvania Courthouse, Lee used excellent analysis of intelligence reports to ascertain Grant's intentions and then beat Grant in a race to Spotsylvania Courthouse.

OUTCOME At the Wilderness, Grant sustained 17,000 casualties compared to 10,000 for Lee. At Spotsylvania Courthouse, Grant suffered 18,000 more compared to just 12,000 for Lee. However, at this point in the war Grant knew that he could replace his losses while Lee could not.

Grant devised a cohesive strategy for 1864 to attack the Confederates from all directions. Major-General Franz Sigel (1824–1902) would advance up the Shenandoah Valley. Major-General Benjamin Butler (1818–93) would conduct an amphibious operation against the Richmond-Petersburg area. Major-General Nathaniel Banks (1816–94) would march on Mobile, Alabama, and shut down the Confederacy's last major port on the Gulf of Mexico. Major-General William Tecumseh Sherman (1820–91) would attack the Confederate war-making ability in the Deep South. Major-General George G Meade (1815–72) would focus on Confederate General Robert E Lee. 'Lee's army is your objective point,' Grant told Meade. 'Wherever Lee goes, there you will go also.'

While Meade would command the Army of the Potomac, Grant would accompany it in the field. All these operations were designed to jump off simultaneously in May, and on 4 May Grant crossed the Rapidan River into an area of Virginia appropriately called the Wilderness. It was the beginning

Grant brought a new attitude to the Army of the Potomac, telling one subordinate, 'Oh, I am heartily tired of hearing what Lee is going to do. Some of you always seem to think he is suddenly going to turn a double somersault and land in our rear.... Go back to your command and try to think what we are going to do ourselves, instead of what Lee is going to do.'

of the campaign that would ultimately lead to Lee's surrender at Appomattox on 9 April 1865. Only Grant's persistence and grand strategic vision made this outcome possible, because in the beginning, Lee would use terrain and entrenchments to thwart the Federal forces at the Wilderness and Spotsylvania Courthouse.

DISPOSITIONS

As both sides readied for battle, the odds appeared to favour the Federals. Including his cavalry, Grant had a force of more than 118,000 men while Lee could muster fewer than 62,000. One Federal general on the scene figured that if Grant's force could have been deployed properly, it would have covered a front of 34 km (21 miles), two ranks deep, with one-third of its strength held in reserve. Under the same conditions, Lee could cover a total of only 18km (12 miles). More important than mere size was the composition of the force. In the key areas of firepower and manoeuvrability, Grant had 274 guns manned by 9945 artillerymen as well as Major-General Philip H Sheridan's (1831–88) crack command of 11,839 cavalrymen.

On the other hand, Lee had only 224 guns manned by roughly 4800 artillerymen and Major-General JEB 'Jeb' Stuart's (1833–64) cavalry of some 8000 men. In order to be successful, Lee would have to overcome this discrepancy. He would do this by selecting a battlefield on which restrictive terrain would mitigate his small numbers and negate Grant's firepower advantage.

The virgin timber of the Wilderness had been cut down many years before, and a tangled second growth of stunted pines, vines, scrub brush and creepers had engulfed the region. The few roads in existence often led to dead ends in the middle of nowhere and were inaccurately mapped. The ground itself was broken by irregular ridges and crisscrossed by numerous streams that cut shallow ravines. In many places these streams followed serpentine routes that resulted in brush-covered swamps. Civil War correspondent William Swinton

(1833–92) wrote that it was 'impossible to conceive a field worse adapted to the movements of a grand army'. Historian Bruce Catton (1899–1978) would agree, calling the Wilderness 'the last place on earth for armies to fight'.

Such a place, however, was just what Lee needed. The thick vegetation neutralized the mobility of the Federal cavalry and made observed artillery fire nearly impossible. The dense woods would prevent Grant from massing his superior numbers, and would make command and control difficult. By picking his ground carefully, Lee was able to make the otherwise indifferent terrain work to the advantage of his smaller and lighter force.

SHERIDAN'S CAVALRY

The cavalry served as the commander's eyes and ears in the Civil War. However, instead of providing Grant with much-needed reconnaissance at Spotsylvania Courthouse, Major-General Phil Sheridan had convinced Grant to dispatch him on a raid towards Richmond. The raid was less successful than Sheridan and Grant had hoped, but it did lead to the death of Major-General 'Jeb' Stuart, Lee's trusted cavalry commander, at Yellow Tavern.

Battlefield communications were a major challenge for Civil War commanders. Line-of-sight systems such as guidons offered communications capability at the tactical level, as did couriers, which were used to deliver messages around the battlefield.

LOCATION

Spotsylvania Courthouse   Washington   Fredericksburg

The area of the Wilderness and Spotsylvania Courthouse was familiar to both armies. It was the same general area that Lee and Hooker had fought over a year earlier. The thickness of the Wilderness favoured the defender.

THE WILDERNESS

After crossing the Rapidan, Grant had hoped to clear the inhospitable Wilderness with the least possible delay, but instead he had to wait for his supply train to catch up. The armies were in close proximity to each other, but neither side knew exactly where the other was. On 5 May, the Federals made contact with Lieutenant-General Richard S Ewell's (1817–72) corps, mistakenly thinking it was a smaller element. At first the Federals drove back Ewell's lead division but then Brigadier-General John B Gordon (1832–1904) launched a counterattack that overwhelmed both flanks of the Federals' attempted frontal assault. Having halted the Federal advance, Ewell dug in and held his

Grant's 1864 campaign in Virginia began with two days of costly fighting in the Wilderness. Many wounded on both sides died horrible deaths when the trees and thick underbrush caught fire.

ground until the corps of Lieutenant-Generals AP Hill (1825–65) and James Longstreet (1821–1904) could arrive.

Both Grant and Lee had offensive plans for 6 May, and the fighting resumed at 5:00 a.m. Again the Federals gained the initial advantage, partially collapsing Hill's line. As the battle wore on, however, the restrictive terrain caused Grant's units to dissolve into smaller and smaller groups. Using an unfinished railroad cut that provided a covered approach to the Federal southern flank, Longstreet was able to stabilize the line with an attack that began at 11:00 a.m. Lee had prepared personally to lead the first counterattacking units, but passionate cries of 'Lee to the rear' dissuaded him. Then, just before dark, Gordon attacked the Federal right, gaining ground but not being able to sustain the advance. During the night, both sides dug new lines.

The heavy fighting during the day had ignited many brush fires in the thick undergrowth and at several points shooting had stopped by mutual consent as both sides worked together to rescue wounded soldiers from the flames. Cries for help and water pierced the battlefield. Nonetheless, during the night of 7/8 May, some 200 men suffocated or burned to death.

In the end, the Wilderness was a lopsided victory for the Confederates, with Grant suffering 17,000 casualties compared to 10,000 for Lee. But what was most important was what happened next. In the past, after taking such a beating, the Army of the Potomac would have retreated and licked its wounds. Grant, however, was a new type of commander. He chose to keep the pressure on Lee by simply disengaging and continuing the effort to get around Lee's flank. Late on 7 May, Grant rode at the head of his army and approached a road junction in the Wilderness. A left turn would mean the usual withdrawal toward the fords of the Rapidan and Rappahannock

Rivers. To the right was the road to Richmond via Spotsylvania Courthouse. As the blue columns approached, Grant pointed to the right. The soldiers cheered. They knew that things were different now. There would be no turning back. In that sense, the battle of the Wilderness marked the beginning of the end for Lee's Army of Northern Virginia.

THE NEXT MOVE

After the Wilderness, Lee understood Grant had two basic options: to advance or to retreat. Many, like Gordon, believed that after such a sound thrashing, Grant would opt to retreat, but Lee told Gordon, 'Grant is not going to retreat. He will move his army to Spotsylvania.' Surprised, Gordon asked Lee if there was any evidence that the Federals were moving in that direction. 'Not at all, not at all,' Lee said, 'But that is the next point at which the armies will meet. Spotsylvania is now General Grant's best strategic point.'

Lee based this conclusion on reports from Major-General Jubal Early (1816–94) on the extreme left of the Confederate line that the Union troops had abandoned their positions opposite his division and had done the same for part of Brigadier-General Edward 'Allegheny' Johnson's (1816–73) command. Likewise, Ewell had reported that the Federals were dismantling their pontoon bridges at Germanna. From these indicators, Lee concluded that Grant had severed his line of communications via Germanna and would not retreat back across the Rapidan River. With this course of action discounted, Lee had then to determine in which direction Grant would advance. He had two possibilities: either Grant would move eastwards towards Fredericksburg or southeastwards towards Spotsylvania Courthouse.

TERRAIN

As Lee examined these two possibilities in an effort to determine which was more likely, he discovered there was much more to recommend Spotsylvania Courthouse to Grant. First of all, if Grant intended an advance on Richmond, the direct road to Spotsylvania Courthouse was less than half as long as the Fredericksburg route.

Secondly, Spotsylvania Courthouse was key terrain for anyone desiring to control Hanover Junction, where two major railroads met, and if Grant wished to drive Lee back on Richmond by cutting off his supplies, Grant would almost certainly try to seize the junction.

Thus Lee's analysis seemed to recommend Spotsylvania Courthouse as Grant's objective, but reports from the field were conflicting. Cavalry scouts had reported heavy wagon traffic in the Fredericksburg direction, but Stuart was also reporting that a strong Federal force had occupied Todd's Tavern, midway between Grant's present position and Spotsylvania Courthouse.

Here, Lee took the counsel of his analysis and began hedging his bets towards Spotsylvania Courthouse. He sent Brigadier-General William Pendleton (1809–83) to cut a road southwards through the woods from the Plank Road to the highway running from Orange Courthouse to Spotsylvania. This precaution would give the Confederates an inner line in the eventuality of a race to Spotsylvania. Lee also advised Stuart to study the roads in the direction of Spotsylvania.

With these steps in motion, Lee continued his close monitoring of every intelligence report of Grant's probable movements. All day, the cumulative evidence supported a move toward

Although the Wilderness cost Grant 17,000 casualties compared to just 10,000 for Lee, Grant knew he could replace his losses while Lee could not. Rather than being a callous butcher Grant was actually a thoroughly modern general who understood that the only way to end the war was to keep unrelenting pressure on Lee.

THE OPPOSED FORCES

THE WILDERNESS

FEDERAL (excluding cavalry)	101,895
CONFEDERATE	61,025

SPOTSYLVANIA COURTHOUSE

FEDERAL	100,000
CONFEDERATE	52,000

SPOTSYLVANIA COURTHOUSE
7–20 MAY 1864

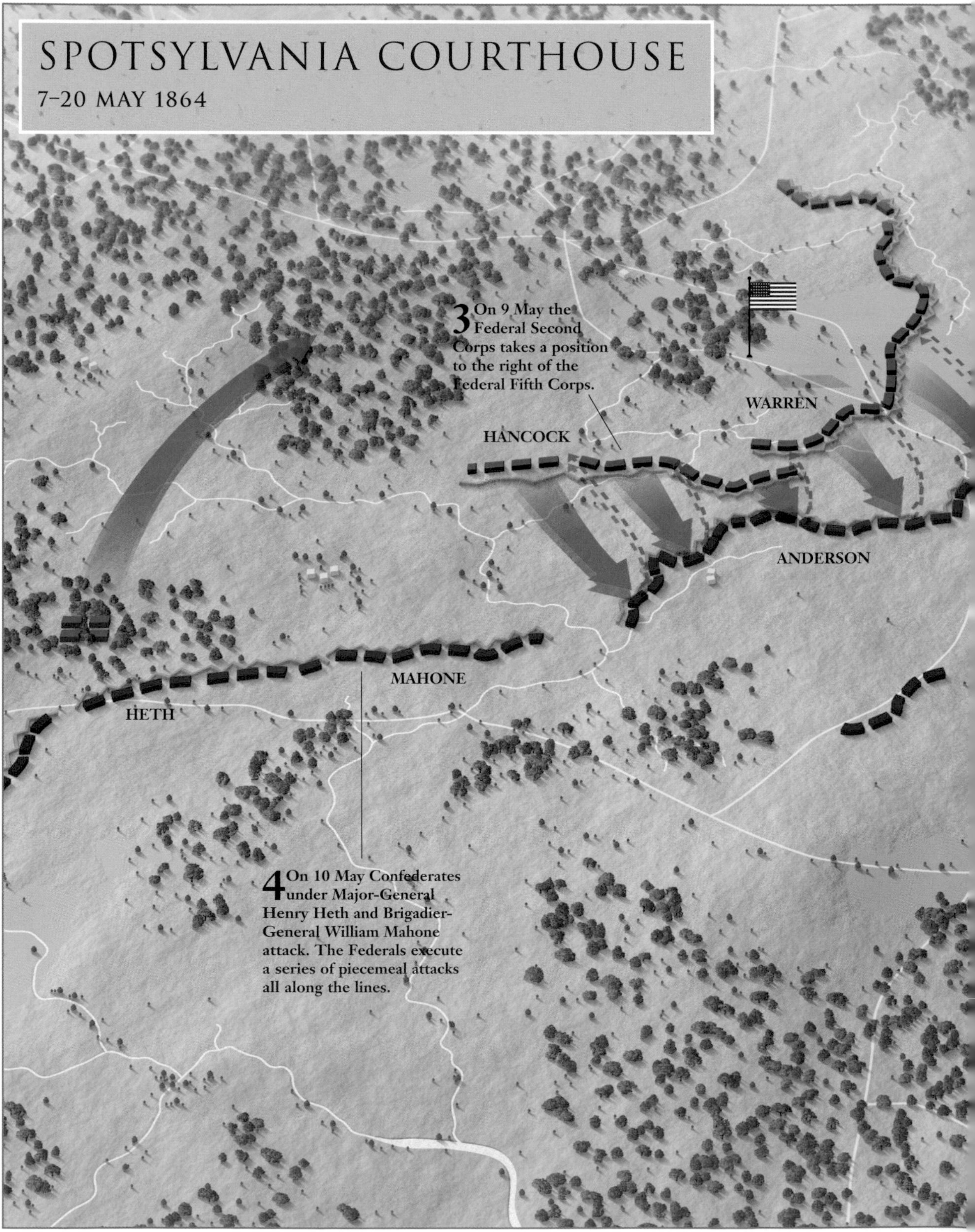

3 On 9 May the Federal Second Corps takes a position to the right of the Federal Fifth Corps.

WARREN

HANCOCK

ANDERSON

MAHONE

HETH

4 On 10 May Confederates under Major-General Henry Heth and Brigadier-General William Mahone attack. The Federals execute a series of piecemeal attacks all along the lines.

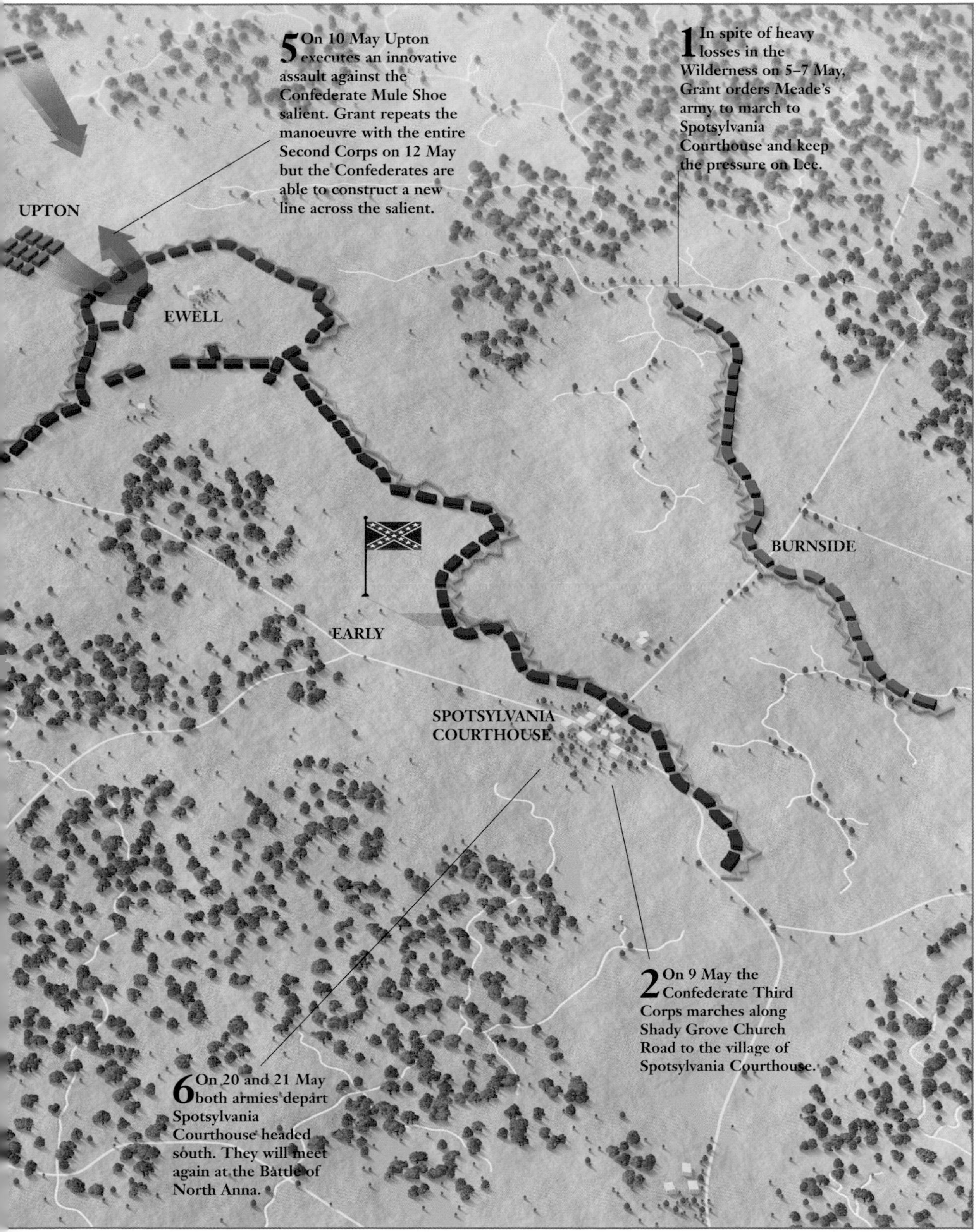

5 On 10 May Upton executes an innovative assault against the Confederate Mule Shoe salient. Grant repeats the manoeuvre with the entire Second Corps on 12 May but the Confederates are able to construct a new line across the salient.

1 In spite of heavy losses in the Wilderness on 5–7 May, Grant orders Meade's army to march to Spotsylvania Courthouse and keep the pressure on Lee.

UPTON

EWELL

BURNSIDE

EARLY

SPOTSYLVANIA COURTHOUSE

2 On 9 May the Confederate Third Corps marches along Shady Grove Church Road to the village of Spotsylvania Courthouse.

6 On 20 and 21 May both armies depart Spotsylvania Courthouse headed south. They will meet again at the Battle of North Anna.

Early in the Civil War, the Confederates had enjoyed a vast superiority over the Federals in terms of the quality of their cavalry. By this point, however, the Federal cavalry had developed into an effective arm of the Union Army.

Spotsylvania Courthouse, and in the afternoon came the decisive indicator. At 4:00 p.m., a staff officer came down from an observation post in the attic of the deserted house that served as the headquarters of Hill's Third Corps. The observer reported that, with the aid of a powerful marine glass, he had seen a number of heavy artillery pieces, which had previously been held in reserve, now being moved south down the Brock Road, towards the Confederate right and, ultimately, Spotsylvania.

No Federal infantry had yet begun to move, but the artillery indicator was all Lee needed to reach his conclusion and to dispatch his First Corps under Major-General Richard H Anderson (1821–79) along Pendleton's newly cut road. Lee dispatched two of his staff officers with all haste to instruct the cavalry to hold Spotsylvania Courthouse. As they rode, one said to the other, 'How in God's name does the old man know General Grant is moving to Spotsylvania Courthouse?' The answer lay in Lee's detailed and critical study of intelligence reports that both eliminated certain Federal courses and suggested the likelihood of others. The race to Spotsylvania Courthouse was on, and, thanks to Lee's analysis, the Confederates had a head start.

SPOTSYLVANIA COURTHOUSE

Throughout 8 May, the two armies flowed onto the battlefield and built corresponding lines of earthworks east and west of the Brock Road. The Confederate line ended up including a huge salient, or bulge, pointing north in the direction of the Federals. Its shape gave rise to the salient being dubbed the 'Mule Shoe'. Grant probed both of Lee's flanks on 9 and 10 May, to no avail. Unlike at the Wilderness, where Lee had counterattacked extensively, at Spotsylvania he fought almost entirely from behind entrenchments. Grant viewed this as a confession of weakness, but at the same time found it difficult to crack the Confederate line.

THE MULE SHOE

However, Grant saw a possibility in an imaginative attack on 10 May by just 12 regiments led by Colonel Emory Upton (1839–81). Upton was a visionary, though he was just 24 years old and less than three years out of West Point. Instead of undertaking a broad-front attack in line, Upton advanced in column formation. In order to keep up their momentum, the troops closed without firing en route – an eventuality Upton ensured by having all but his first rank advance with uncapped muskets. The attack enjoyed remarkable initial success. In just 60 seconds, Upton's men closed with a startled brigade of Georgians, seized four guns and a reserve line of works, and almost reached the McCoull House in the centre of the Mule Shoe. There Confederate artillery at the top of the salient halted the advance. Without additional support, Upton was unable to hold his gains and was forced to withdraw.

The new tactic impressed Grant, so he decided to try it again, this time by

This illustration shows Union Army officers' sleeve design. The greater the number of braids, the higher the rank. From left to right: first lieutenant, captain, major, lieutenant-colonel, colonel and general.

throwing Major-General Winfield Scott Hancock's (1824–86) entire Second Corps against the Mule Shoe. On 12 May at 4:30 a.m., a massed attack of 20,000 Federals advanced, and in just 15 minutes they were pouring through gaps in the Confederate lines. Hancock captured 4000 Confederate prisoners. The contested area became known as the 'Bloody Angle'.

In a desperate attempt to restore the breach, Lee counterattacked and succeeded in completing a new line of entrenchments across the base of the salient. For nearly 20 hours the fighting continued almost unabated in what may have been the most ferociously sustained combat in the entire war. The firing had been so intense that musket balls cut down an oak tree 56cm (22in) in diameter. There was more inconclusive fighting on 18 and 19 May, but the Confederate line held. Federal losses at Spotsylvania Courthouse included Major-General John Sedgwick (1813–64), the popular commander of Sixth Corps and, in a related battle at Yellow Tavern, the famed Confederate cavalryman Major-General JEB 'Jeb' Stuart was killed. Fighting mostly behind the protection of entrenchments, Lee suffered just 12,000 casualties compared to Grant's 18,000.

Having survived this close call, Lee withdrew on 20 May to a new position at Hanover Junction, thwarting another attempted turning movement by Grant.

In a pattern that would foreshadow World War I (1914–18), the defenders had proved able to repair a breach in a fortified line faster than the attackers could exploit it.

THE BIGGER PICTURE

Nonetheless, part of Grant's genius was an ability to look beyond individual battles and see the campaign as a whole. Although battles like the Wilderness and Spotsylvania Courthouse were costly, Grant could afford the losses while Lee and the Confederacy could not. On 11 May, Grant wired Major-General Henry Halleck (1815–72) in Washington that he intended 'to fight it out on this line if it takes all summer'. It would take even longer than that, but Grant had made his point. He would continue the relentless pressure of his Virginia Campaign at Hanover Junction, Cold Harbor and Petersburg, and ultimately lead the Army of the Potomac to victory.

Known as 'Hancock the Superb', Winfield Scott Hancock was one of Grant's most capable commanders. It was Hancock's corps that Grant selected to attack the Mule Shoe using Emory Upton's new tactics.

THE WILDERNESS/SPOTSYLVANIA COURTHOUSE

KENNESAW MOUNTAIN
27 JUNE 1864

GRANT'S COORDINATED STRATEGY FOR THE SPRING OF 1864 INVOLVED SIMULTANEOUS ADVANCES DESIGNED TO PRESS THE CONFEDERACY ON ALL FRONTS. THE TWO MOST IMPORTANT OFFENSIVES WERE GRANT'S OWN CAMPAIGN IN VIRGINIA, IN WHICH MEADE WOULD MAINTAIN CONSTANT PRESSURE ON LEE'S ARMY OF NORTHERN VIRGINIA, AND SHERMAN'S ATLANTA CAMPAIGN AGAINST JOHNSTON'S ARMY OF TENNESSEE. THE RESULTS WERE CATASTROPHIC FOR THE FEDERALS, BUT, UNDETERRED, SHERMAN TOOK POSSESSION OF ATLANTA ON 2 SEPTEMBER.

WHY DID IT HAPPEN?

WHO The Atlanta Campaign began with Major-General William T Sherman's (1820–91) Federals fighting Confederates commanded by General Joseph E Johnston (1807–91), who was ultimately replaced by Lieutenant-General John Bell Hood (1831–79).

WHAT Johnston fought a delaying action, withdrawing to successive entrenched positions to thwart Sherman's attempted turning movements. Only at Kennesaw Mountain did Sherman attack.

WHERE From Dalton to Atlanta, Georgia.

WHEN The Atlanta Campaign lasted from 1 May to 8 September 1864. The Battle of Kennesaw Mountain was fought on 27 June.

WHY Many argue that Johnston's defensive tactics were correct, but President Jefferson Davis (1808–89) grew frustrated by the steady withdrawals and replaced Johnston with Hood. Sherman relished the new opportunity to fight 'in open ground'.

OUTCOME Kennesaw Mountain was a resounding Confederate victory. Still Sherman was undeterred in his steady march to Atlanta. The Federal capture of Atlanta deprived the Confederacy of a critical industrial centre. More importantly, it gave the North a much-needed victory.

After his defeat in the Chattanooga Campaign, General Braxton Bragg (1817–76) retreated 40km (25 miles) south to Dalton, Georgia, and dug in his forces. By this time a public outcry had developed for Bragg's removal, and Bragg succumbed to the pressure and asked to be relieved. President Jefferson Davis replaced Bragg with General Joe Johnston, a man with whom Davis had had strained relations since the very beginning of the war. Johnston was a defensive fighter by nature and the fact that he began the campaign with only 62,000 men compared to Sherman's 100,000 reinforced this tendency.

Sherman, on the other, hand thrived on the offensive. By this point in the war he had developed an extremely close relationship with Grant (1822–85), and Sherman fully understood what the new General-in-Chief wanted him to do. Grant's instructions were 'to move against Johnston's army, to break it up, and to get into the interior of the enemy's country as far as you can, inflicting all the damage you can against their war resources'.

With the Confederates forced back into the defenses of Atlanta, Sherman could have used his artillery to mount a lengthy siege. Instead he launched attacks to try to cut Hood's open railroad to the south.

Grant and Sherman were thoroughly modern generals who understood manoeuvre, logistics and the support of the population. Atlanta was a vital supply, manufacturing and communications centre that was second only to Richmond in its industrial importance to the Confederacy. Thus far, it had escaped the ravages of war. By capturing Atlanta, Sherman would not only interrupt supplies that were helping keep General Robert E Lee's (1807–70) Army of Northern Virginia in the field, he would take the war to the Confederate people. But capturing Atlanta would not only dispirit the Confederate population, it would also silence those peace advocates in the North who considered Grant to be hopelessly deadlocked with Lee in Virginia, with no end to the fighting in sight. With President Lincoln (1809–65) facing a tough challenge in the 1864 election from a Democratic peace platform, capturing Atlanta would have as much political importance as it would military.

Sherman began his march on 7 May, just a few days after Lieutenant-General Ulysses S Grant and Major-General George G Meade (1815–72) began their offensive against Lee in Virginia. Sherman found Johnston's Dalton defences too strong, so he sent Major-General James McPherson's (1828–64) Army of the Tennessee to turn the Confederates from the west while Major-General George H Thomas' (1816–70) Army of the Cumberland advanced frontally along the Western & Atlantic Railroad. Fighting took place around Rocky Face Ridge on 5–9 May, but Johnston fell back without becoming decisively engaged.

Throughout the campaign, Johnston withdrew to positions that had previously been reconnoitred by his engineers. By this point in the war, his men had the breastwork construction process down to a science. First, trees were felled and trimmed, and the logs rolled in line to form

a revetment usually 1.2m (4ft) high. The logs were then banked with earth from a ditch dug to their front. The earth formed a sloping parapet about 2–3m (7–10ft) at the top and 1m (3ft) at ground level. On top of the revetment, skids supported a line of head logs interrupted by 8cm (3in) wide horizontal loopholes, through which the men could fire while still being protected. In front of these breastworks the men felled trees and bushes towards the enemy to form elaborate *chevaux-de-frise* and *abatis*. The defences went up so quickly that one Union soldier surmised that the Confederates must carry their breastworks with them. Sherman complained: 'The enemy can build parapets faster than we can march.'

Johnston received reinforcements in the form of Lieutenant-General Leonidas Polk's (1806–64) corps and took up strong defensive positions at Resaca, where fighting occurred on 13–16 May. As Sherman threatened an envelopment from the west, Johnston again withdrew. In this

CONFEDERATE 'BUTTERNUT' FIELD DRESS

The Confederate Quartermaster Department was seldom able to supply the Confederate soldier with all the required items of uniform. Instead soldiers wore whatever became available, and home-dyed butternut jackets and trousers became characteristic items rather than the traditional Confederate grey. One sketch in an 1861 Harper's Weekly shows 26 variations of the Confederate uniform. At times this lack of standardization caused confusion on the battlefield. At First Manassas, for example, the Federal 11th New York Infantry was dressed in grey and the opposing Confederate 33rd Virginia Infantry was still wearing civilian clothes.

LOCATION

Washington ●

Richmond ●

Kennesaw Mountain ✝ ● Atlanta

Kennesaw Mountain lay astride the Western & Atlantic Railroad and blocked Sherman's advance from Dalton to Atlanta, Georgia.

now relatively open country, Sherman chose to advance on a broad front. In the process, his forces were not in close supporting distance of each other. This situation gave the usually defensive-minded Johnston an opportunity to go on the offensive at Cassville. Major-General John Schofield's (1831–1906) small Army of the Ohio, augmented by Major-General Joe Hooker's (1814–79) corps, was on the road from Adairsville to Cassville while McPherson's army was marching about 8km (5 miles) west of Adairsville. Most of Thomas' army was on a road that went from Adairsville 16km (10 miles) south to Kingston before veering east to Cassville. Johnston had plans to concentrate his 74,000 men at Cassville and ambush the fewer than 35,000 Federals under Schofield and Hooker. Ideally, the other two Federal armies could then be defeated piecemeal as they rushed to Schofield's aid.

It was a promising opportunity but the normally aggressive Lieutenant-General John Bell Hood mistakenly assumed a small Federal cavalry detachment was a much larger force and faced east as a precaution, rather than west, as the attack plan called for. The ensuing delay foiled Johnston's initial plan and then, on 19 May, Hood and Polk convinced Johnston their lines were too vulnerable to enfilade fire, and Johnston again withdrew. Johnston occupied positions at Allatoona Pass, which Sherman considered too formidable to attack. Instead, Sherman rested his army for three days and then undertook another turning movement at Dallas. Fighting occurred there on 25–27 May, and Johnston retired to Kennesaw Mountain.

THE OPPOSED FORCES

FEDERAL
Army of the Tennessee
Army of the Cumberland
Army of the Ohio
Total: 100,000

CONFEDERATE

Army of Tennessee
Initially 62,000
After Polk's
reinforcements 74,000

KENNESAW MOUNTAIN

Johnston formed a 16km (10-mile) long defensive front that encompassed three mountains: Brush Mountain on the right, Pine Mountain in the middle and Lost Mountain on the left. Behind these three, at a distance of 3.2km (2 miles), stood Kennesaw Mountain, the strongest part of the Confederate line. The peak was nearly 305m (1000ft) above the surrounding landscape, and the Western & Atlantic Railroad skirted its base. Kennesaw Mountain blocked Sherman's approach to

the Chattahoochee, the last broad river north of Atlanta. General Sherman summed up the situation, writing to Washington DC: 'The whole countryside is one vast fort, and Johnston must have at least fifty miles of connected trenches with *abatis* and finished batteries.... Our lines are now in close contact and the fighting incessant, with a good deal of artillery. As fast as we gain one position the enemy has another all

ready.... Kennesaw ... is the key to the whole country.'

On 10 June, Sherman began probing Johnston's position but nearly two weeks of constant rains slowed progress. On 14 June, Polk was killed by an artillery round on Pine Mountain, and the next day, Johnston pulled his troops off of Pine Mountain to avoid being enveloped. On the night of 17/18 June, Johnston withdrew from Lost

Mountain and Brush Mountain because of another threatened envelopment and consolidated his position on Kennesaw.

In spite of the strength of the Confederate position, Sherman elected to deviate from his pattern of turning movements and instead attempted a frontal assault. There were a couple reasons behind Sherman's decision. First, he thought he had found a point where the Confederate

Entitled 'Thunder on Little Kennesaw', this modern painting shows Lumsdens' Alabama Battery defending Little Kennesaw Mountain against Sherman's attack, as incendiary devices stream overhead.

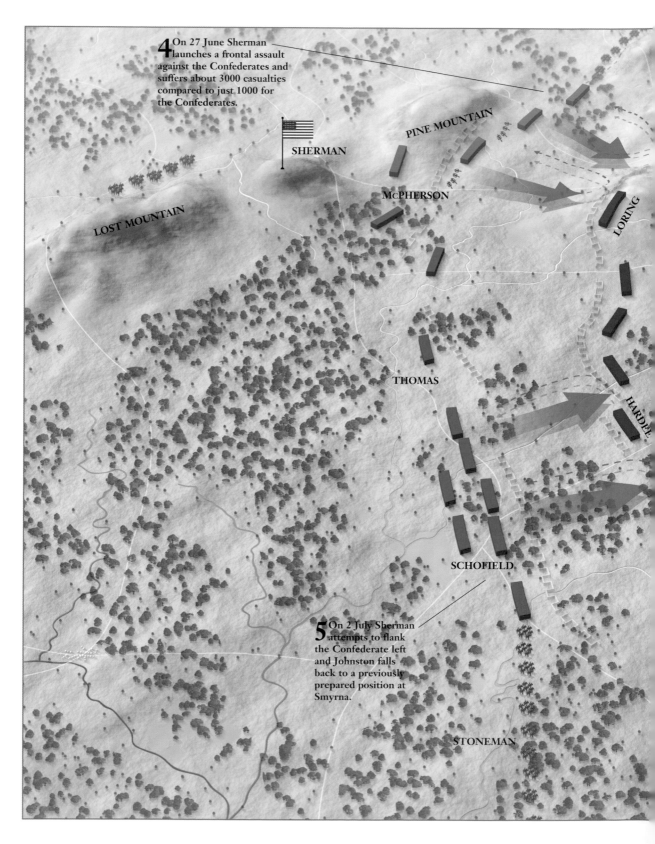

4 On 27 June Sherman launches a frontal assault against the Confederates and suffers about 3000 casualties compared to just 1000 for the Confederates.

SHERMAN

PINE MOUNTAIN

McPHERSON

LORING

LOST MOUNTAIN

THOMAS

HARDEE

SCHOFIELD

5 On 2 July Sherman attempts to flank the Confederate left and Johnston falls back to a previously prepared position at Smyrna.

STONEMAN

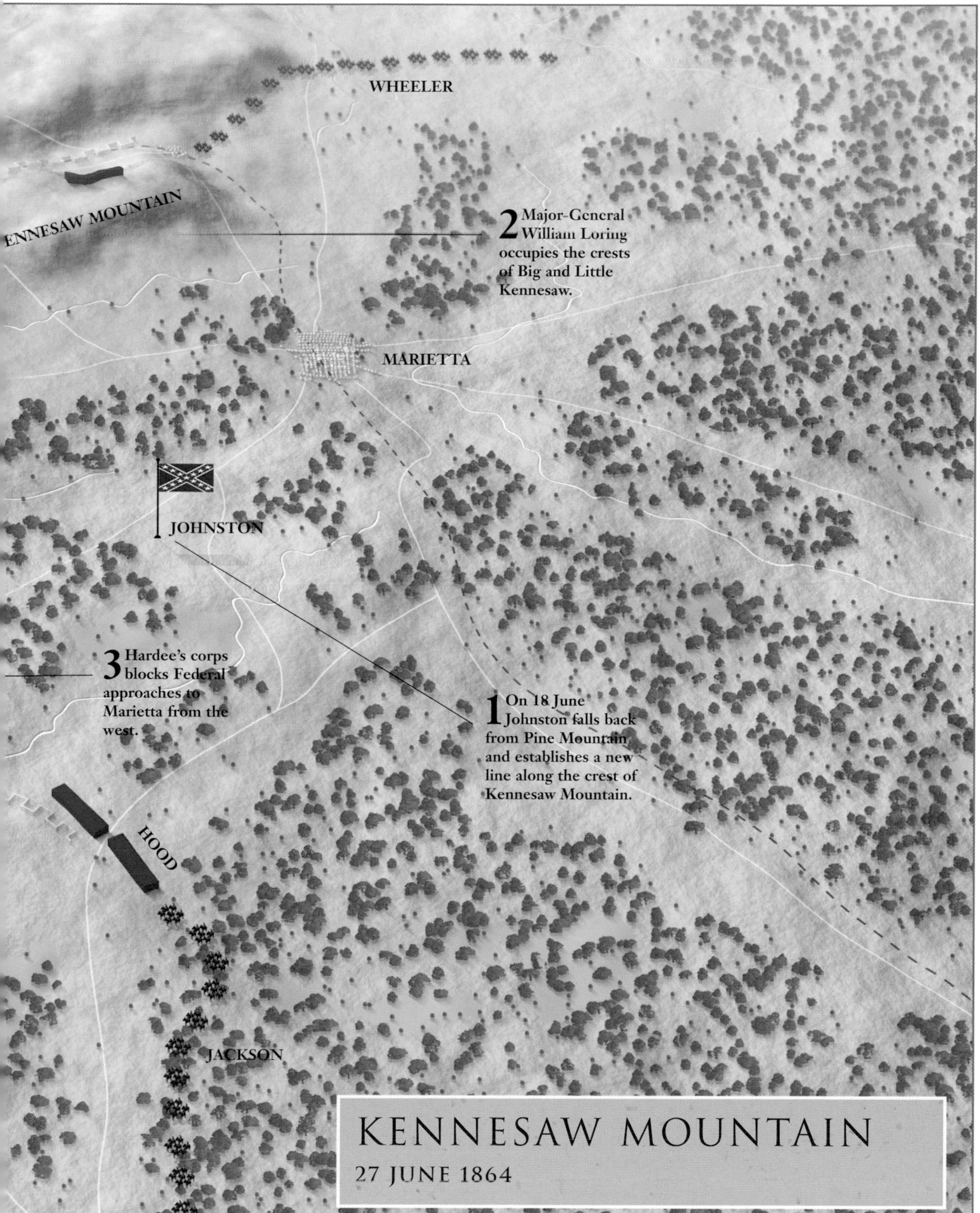

WHEELER

KENNESAW MOUNTAIN

2 Major-General William Loring occupies the crests of Big and Little Kennesaw.

MARIETTA

JOHNSTON

3 Hardee's corps blocks Federal approaches to Marietta from the west.

1 On 18 June Johnston falls back from Pine Mountain and establishes a new line along the crest of Kennesaw Mountain.

HOOD

JACKSON

KENNESAW MOUNTAIN
27 JUNE 1864

Three Federal assaults brought Sherman's men within 27m (90ft) of the Confederate lines at Kennesaw Mountain, but the defence held. His frontal attack thwarted, after Kennesaw Sherman resumed his turning movements.

line was weak and a breakthrough possible. Recent rains had reduced his mobility, adding to his frustration. The only alternative to attacking was to delay, an idea that was anathema to Sherman. Perhaps most importantly, Sherman thought an attack was important to maintaining the offensive spirit of his troops, who, he believed, 'had settled down to the belief that flanking alone was my game.... A fresh furrow in a ploughed field,' Sherman complained, 'will stop a whole column, and all begin to entrench.'

Sherman, therefore, ordered Schofield to extend his right in order to compel Johnston to lengthen and thin his lines. McPherson was instructed to make a feint on his extreme left with his cavalry and one

The seven-shot Spencer carbine was the most effective shoulder arm of the Civil War. A breech-loader rather than a more cumbersome muzzle-loader, the Spencer, it was said, 'could be loaded on Sunday and fired all week'. The shorter stock of the carbine and its rapid firepower made it a popular choice among Union cavalry troops.

division, but to make his main attack at a point southwest of Kennesaw. Thomas would assault the centre of the Confederate position. Schofield would exploit a toehold he had gained on 20 June in fighting south of Olley's Creek. Each column would try to penetrate the defences at a single point, consolidate in the Confederate rear, and be prepared to advance towards Marietta and the Western & Atlantic.

There was little finesse in the attack. At 8:00 a.m. on 27 June, Sherman initiated a

'furious cannonade' of about 200 guns. Some 5500 Federal soldiers advanced through the dense and rugged terrain. Their leaders had little specific information on the lie of the land or the nature of the Confederate positions. In some places the Federals had success against the Confederate outposts, but they could not get close to the main defences before encountering a murderous fire. 'The air seemed filled with bullets,' recalled one survivor. Three separate assaults got nowhere and for the next five days some Federals held their ground within 27m (90ft) of the Confederate positions, but there was no further fighting. The attack on 27 June had cost Sherman about 3000 men compared to less than 1000 for the Confederates. On 2 July, Sherman resumed his efforts to turn Johnston, who withdrew to a previously prepared position at Smyrna.

THE FALL OF ATLANTA

General Joe Johnston's new line was built along the Chattahoochee River, which

represented the last major obstacle between Sherman and Atlanta. In fighting on 4–9 July, Sherman again turned the Confederates and Johnston withdrew to Peach Tree Creek. By this time, President Davis was exasperated by Johnston's failure to make a stand. Davis replaced Johnston with Hood, a man with a marked reputation as a fighter. Many observers questioned the decision. Sherman wrote that by this act 'the Confederate Government rendered us most valuable service'.

Grant felt that replacing Johnston was a mistake, believing that 'Johnston [had] acted very wisely: he husbanded his men and saved as much of his territory as he could, without fighting decisive battles in which all might be lost.... I know that both Sherman and I were rejoiced when we heard of the change. Hood was unquestionably a brave, gallant soldier and not destitute of ability; but unfortunately his policy was to fight the enemy wherever he saw him, without thinking much of the consequences of defeat.' Even General Robert E Lee had

Confederate General Joe Johnston fought a skilful delay throughout the Atlanta Campaign. He would withdraw to successive defensive positions that were already reconnoitred and laid out by his engineers.

President Jefferson Davis placed Lieutenant-General John Bell Hood in command of the Confederate forces at Atlanta. The aggressive Hood launched a series of costly attacks, but ultimately was forced to withdraw.

advised Davis: 'Hood is a bold fighter. I am doubtful as to other qualities necessary.'

If Davis wanted offensive action, he was not to be disappointed. As Sherman closed in on Atlanta from the north and east, Hood ordered an attack to begin at 1:00 p.m. on 20 July. The target was Thomas' army, which had secured a shallow bridgehead across Peach Tree Creek and was now unsupported by Sherman's other armies. Thomas had earned the nickname the 'Rock of Chickamauga' for his ability to hold ground even when isolated and he would live up to this reputation at Peach Tree Creek. The Confederates launched a series of assaults until 6:00 p.m., but ultimately were forced to withdraw to the defences of Atlanta. Hood had suffered 2500 casualties, compared to about 1600 for the Federals.

As Hood withdrew, Sherman mistakenly thought the Confederates were abandoning Atlanta and sent Major-General McPherson in pursuit to the south and east. Hood sent his cavalry under Major-General Joseph Wheeler (1836–1906) and Lieutenant-General William J Hardee's (1815–73) corps on a night march to strike McPherson's southern flank. In the fighting on 22 July, the popular and capable McPherson was killed, but the Confederate attack was defeated. When Grant learned of McPherson's death, an observer said Grant's 'mouth twitched and his eyes shut … Then the tears came and one followed the other down his bronzed cheeks as he sat there without a word or comment.' In another lopsided battle, Hood's Confederates suffered 8500 casualties, compared to just 3700 among Sherman's Union forces.

By 25 July Sherman had invested Atlanta from the north and east. Hood still had an open railroad to the south, which Sherman tried unsuccessfully to sever with two raids between 26 and 31 July and the Battle of Ezra Church on 28 July. Hood finally evacuated Atlanta on 1 September and the Federal forces moved in to occupy the city the next morning.

MARCH TO THE SEA AND THE CAROLINAS CAMPAIGN

Having captured Atlanta, Sherman also gained a problem. Freed from having to defend Atlanta, Hood moved into northwest Georgia, where he had secure lines of communication into Alabama. Throughout October, Hood threatened Sherman's vulnerable Western & Atlantic Railroad supply line. Sherman was forced to devote much energy to this new menace from Hood.

To solve the problem, Sherman decided to cut loose from his railroad line of supply, abandon Atlanta, and strike out for a new base on the coast. In the process, Sherman proposed taking the war to a new level of totality. He wrote Grant that 'the utter destruction of [the Confederacy's rail] roads, houses, and people will cripple their military resources… I can make the march, and make Georgia howl!'

Dispatching Thomas to defend Tennessee and deal with Hood, Sherman abandoned Atlanta after destroying anything of value to the Confederate war effort. On November 15 he began a march against almost no opposition, cutting a sixty mile swath through Georgia. On 21 December Confederate Lieutenant General William Hardee abandoned Savannah on the Atlantic coast, and Sherman presented the city to President Lincoln as a Christmas gift. There Sherman received resupplies by sea and plotted his next move. Sherman wrote Chief of Staff Major General Henry Halleck, 'the whole United States, North and South, would rejoice to have this army turned loose on South Carolina to devastate the state in the manner we have done Georgia.' By 20 January, Sherman's army had entered South Carolina and began unleashing vengeful destruction against the very birthplace of secession.

As in Georgia, Confederate resistance was a mere token. As Sherman bore down on the South Carolina capital of Columbia, Confederate Lieutenant General Wade Hampton informed the mayor that resistance would be futile and on 17 February, the mayor approached Sherman with an offer to surrender.

What followed as Sherman's troops entered the city has become a matter of some debate. The end result was that the city was burned and destroyed. How much of the damage was malicious vengeance on the part of the Federals as opposed to an effort by the fleeing Confederates to destroy items of value to the enemy remains a subject of controversy. Whatever the genesis, high winds and inebriated soldiers only made matters worse. By the time Sherman marched out of Columbia on 20 February, he reported the city 'utterly ruined.' Sherman continued his march into North Carolina where Johnston had assembled a force of some 21,000 effectives to try to slow Sherman's 60,000-man juggernaut. Although Sherman was unable to completely destroy Johnston at the battle of Bentonville on 19 March, Johnston knew

the end was at hand. General Robert E. Lee had surrendered to Grant on 9 April. Johnston finally surrendered to Sherman on 26 April.

IMPACT

The combined effects of Sherman's Atlanta Campaign, March to the Sea, and Carolinas Campaign were profound. On September 3, Sherman had telegraphed Washington, 'So Atlanta is ours, and fairly won.' The news could not have come at a better time for President Lincoln, who was facing a stiff challenge from Major General George McClellan in the upcoming presidential election. War weariness had fallen upon the North and Lincoln had gone so far as to require his cabinet members to sign a statement saying, 'This morning, as for some days past, it seems exceedingly probable that this Administration will not be reelected. Then it will be my duty to so co-operate with the President elect, as to save the Union between the election and the inauguration...'

The capture of Atlanta, along with another Federal success at Mobile Bay, completely changed the picture. McClellan

began to distance himself from the Peace Democrats and Lincoln's reelection was assured. While Sherman had defeated a major Confederate army in the field and captured an important industrial city, the main impact of Atlanta was on the political front.

From there Sherman took the war to the Confederate people as his March to the Sea and Carolinas Campaign destroyed the Confederacy's infrastructure and morale. He proved himself to be a master of manoeuvre and logistics and completed the elevation of the Civil War from its limited war beginnings to its total war conclusion.

On 15 November 1864, Sherman destroyed the military resources of Atlanta and began his March to the Sea. On 21 December, Confederate Lieutenant General William Hardee evacuated Savannah and Sherman occupied it. On 17 February Sherman burned the secessionist capital of Columbia, SC. A month later, on 19 March, Sherman defeated Confederate General Joe Johnston at Bentonville, NC. Finally, on 26 April 1865, Johnston surrendered to Sherman at Raleigh.

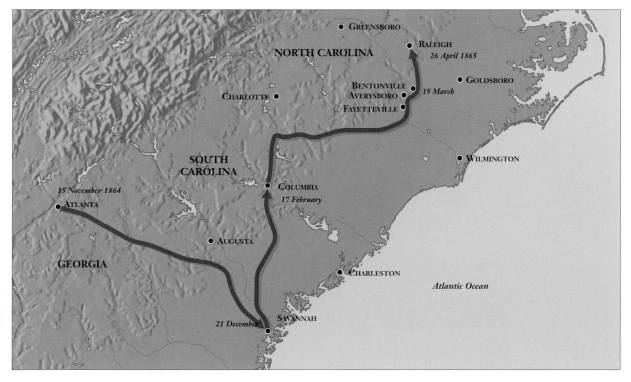

MOBILE BAY
5 AUGUST 1864

ON 5 AUGUST 1864, REAR-ADMIRAL DAVID GLASGOW FARRAGUT GAVE HIS IMMORTAL COMMAND, 'DAMN THE TORPEDOES! FULL SPEED AHEAD,' AND LED HIS FLEET INTO MOBILE BAY, ALABAMA. THE ENSUING FEDERAL VICTORY CLOSED THE CONFEDERACY'S LAST SIGNIFICANT PORT ON THE GULF OF MEXICO AND HELPED ENSURE ABRAHAM LINCOLN'S RE-ELECTION AS PRESIDENT.

WHY DID IT HAPPEN?

WHO Federal forces led by Rear-Admiral David Farragut (1801–70) attacked Confederate naval forces commanded by Admiral Franklin Buchanan (1800–74).

WHAT Farragut defeated Buchanan in a matter of hours, and the Confederate forts defending the bay surrendered shortly thereafter.

WHERE Mobile Bay, Alabama.

WHEN 5 August 1864.

WHY Farragut daringly commanded 'Damn the torpedoes! Full speed ahead,' as he led his fleet past the imposing Fort Morgan and the treacherous minefield in the bay.

OUTCOME The Federal victory closed the last major Confederate port on the Gulf of Mexico to blockade-running and, along with Sherman's capture of Atlanta, helped ensure Lincoln's re-election.

The last two holdouts among the Confederacy's major ports were Wilmington, North Carolina, and Mobile Bay. The Federals wanted to shut down both in order to halt the slow trickle of European supplies that was keeping General Robert E Lee's (1807–70) Army of Northern Virginia alive. Wilmington had survived because the Cape Fear River's two entrances made it difficult to blockade and because it was guarded by the mighty Fort Fisher. Mobile Bay, on the other hand, had been spared because of higher Federal priorities elsewhere. Vicksburg, Charleston and the Red River Campaign all had served to distract attention and resources from Mobile Bay.

In the meantime, blockading in the Gulf of Mexico had proven to be extremely difficult. There were some 966km (600 miles) between Pensacola and the Rio Grande, not counting the Mississippi River Delta. Behind the coast lay a complex network of inland waterways that allowed shallow draft schooners to find exits and inlets not covered by blockaders. Mobile was by far the most important Gulf port used by the Confederate blockade-runners. It was second only to New Orleans as the South's largest cotton-exporting port before the war, and the Federal capture of New Orleans on 25 April 1862 only increased Mobile's importance. During the war, blockade-runners plied their trade between there and Bermuda, Nassau and Havana.

Moreover, Mobile Bay and its port were vital to the Southern war effort. Alabama was second only to Richmond's Tredegar

Because Farragut was born near Knoxville, Tennessee, and had married a woman from Norfolk, Virginia, many people had concerns about his devotion to the Federal cause. In fact, Farragut proved to be a staunch Unionist.

MOBILE BAY

Iron Works as the Confederacy's centre for manufacturing iron and rolling heavy iron plate. About 209km (130 miles) north of Mobile along the Alabama River was Bassett's Yard in Selma. There, three ironclads were under construction. In all, eight were being built on the Alabama and Tombigbee rivers. Only one, the *Tennessee*, would be completed in time to see action, and the desire to halt further ironclad production made Mobile an even more important target for the Federals.

THE DEFENDERS
Mobile Bay would prove to be a difficult target because, although the bay stretched far inland, its entrance was only 5km (3 miles) wide. There, Fort Gaines guarded the western side from Dauphin Island. Stretching eastwards from the fort, the defenders had placed a series of sunken pilings that reduced the bay's entrance by over half. Beyond these obstructions, shallow water and 'torpedoes' – submerged mines fitted with percussion caps or fulminate of mercury fuses that were rigged to detonate upon contact with a ship's hull – further narrowed the channel. Brigadier-General Gabriel James Rains (1803–81), who had pioneered the use of land mines during the Peninsula Campaign, had been instrumental in laying out the system for Mobile. In all, 180 submerged torpedoes were arranged in three parallel rows. Most, however, had been in the water for some

time and many would prove defective.

On the eastern edge of the minefield was a thin opening stretching some 182m (200 yards) to Mobile Point that provided a passageway for blockade-runners. Mobile Point was a long neck of land that jutted out and controlled the entrance to the bay. There stood the powerful Fort Morgan, a massive pentagon-shaped, three-tiered structure with 47 guns. No ship could negotiate the opening in the minefield without passing underneath Fort Morgan's guns. Completing the defences, a much smaller Fort Powell blocked a narrow inter-coastal passage north of Dauphin Island via the Mississippi Sound. Brigadier-General Richard Page (1807–1901), a nephew of General Robert E Lee, was in charge of these outer defences. Page was well suited to understanding the requirements of a coastal defence. Before the Civil War he had served 37 years in the US Navy.

Behind these forts were the ironclad *Tennessee* and three wooden gunboats under the able command of Admiral Franklin Buchanan. Buchanan had commanded the *Virginia* (ex-*Merrimack*) and, like Farragut, was a seasoned and aggressive fighter. His gunboats were of little consequence, but the *Tennessee* was a force to be reckoned with. She had 15cm (6in) of armour on her casemate, 13cm (5in) on her sides and 5cm

(2in) on her deck. She had six Brooke Rifles, but she was inadequately powered for her weight and therefore hard to manoeuvre. Buchanan was pinning his hopes on the *Tennessee*, and Farragut knew it. He wrote to his son: 'Buchanan has a vessel which he says is superior to the *Merrimack* with which he intends to attack us…. So we are to have no child's play.'

THE FEDERAL NAVY
The Federals knew that the Confederates could mount a spirited defence against wooden vessels, so in January Assistant Secretary of the Navy Gustavas Fox

LOCATION

• Memphis

New Orleans • ✛ Mobile Bay

Mobile Bay was the last major port open to the Confederacy on the Gulf of Mexico. Blockade runners used it to provide the foreign commerce necessary for the Confederacy's survival.

An 86mm (3.5in) boat carriage gun. Before the Civil War, future Federal Rear-Admiral John A Dahlgren (1809–70) invented the Dahlgren gun, a rifled cannon, and boat howitzers with iron carriages. Dahlgren's boat howitzers were the finest guns of their time in the world and were used by both Federals and Confederates throughout the Civil War.

(15in) Dahlgren guns behind 28cm (11in) of turret armour. They were the most powerful warships then in existence. Complementing them were the *Chickasaw* and the *Winnebago*, twin-turret, quadruple-screwed river monitors with batteries of four 28cm (11in) guns. The *Tecumseh* was the last to arrive, reaching Farragut on 4 August, just in time for the battle. In addition, Farragut had 14 wooden ships and an initial Army contingent of 2000 troops.

THE BATTLE IS JOINED

On 3 August, Major-General Gordon Granger (1822–76) landed his brigade at the west end of Dauphin Island, in the rear of Fort Gaines. Farragut had hoped simultaneously to begin the naval engagement but the *Tecumseh*'s late arrival had made that impossible. As Granger moved to invest Fort Gaines the next day, Farragut retired to his cabin and wrote: 'I am going into Mobile in the morning if God is my leader, as I hope He is, and in Him I place my trust. If He thinks it is the place for me to die, I am ready to submit to His will.'

Farragut had good reason to be somewhat fatalistic. His plan was as dangerous as it was bold. The four monitors would take the lead, with their shallow

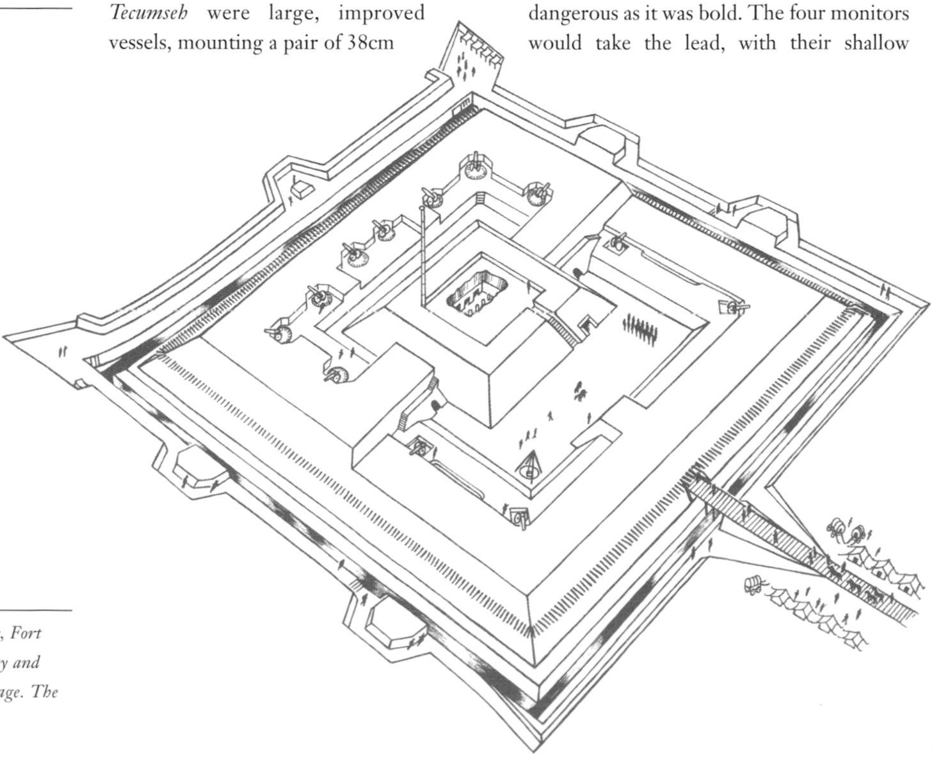

(1821–83) had asked Farragut how many ironclads he thought he would need to blast his way into Mobile Bay. 'Just as many as you can spare; two would answer me well, more would do better,' Farragut replied. By July the Navy had four monitors on the way to Farragut. The *Manhattan* and the *Tecumseh* were large, improved vessels, mounting a pair of 38cm

Armed with cannon and manned by infantry, Fort Morgan controlled the entrance to Mobile Bay and covered the minefield that narrowed the passage. The parapets of the fort were 4.3m (15ft) thick.

draught permitting them to hug the shore and avoid the mines, while their low profiles and armour plating would protect them from Fort Morgan's guns. The wooden ships would follow, echeloned slightly to the left of the monitors to use them as a shield.

As a further caution, Farragut would lash each of his smaller gunboats to the port side of one of his larger vessels. This measure would not only protect the smaller ships from Fort Morgan, but if the larger vessel's engines were disabled, the gunboat could also act as a tug to pull the damaged ship to safety. Once the pairs had passed out of range of Fort Morgan, the connecting cables would be cut and each vessel would operate independently.

Farragut was exactly the man for such a hazardous undertaking. He had already succeeded in a similarly daring manoeuvre to capture New Orleans. In terms of personality, Secretary of the Navy Gideon Welles (1802–78) considered Farragut to be 'better fitted to lead an expedition through danger and difficulty than to command an extensive blockade; [he] is a good officer in a great emergency, will more willingly take risks in order to obtain great results than any other officer in high position in either Navy or Army.'

Throughout the night of 4 August, the meticulous Farragut made his final preparations. Any unnecessary spars and rigging was removed to facilitate speed and manoeuvrability. As at New Orleans, chain garlands were hung over the ships' starboard sides and sandbags were piled 'from stem to stern, and from the berth to the spar deck' for added protection. At dawn on 5 August, the Federal fleet drew up in battle formation.

Farragut gave the order to get under way with the monitors leading and the wooden ships behind. A little after 6:30 a.m., the *Tecumseh* fired a ranging shot and the fleet pressed forward, closing its order as it advanced. Fort Morgan opened fire at 7:10 a.m., with the fleet 800m (880 yards) away. The *Brooklyn*, at the head of the Federal

wooden ships, returned fire. 'Soon after this,' Farragut deadpanned, 'the action became lively.'

Buchanan brought the *Tennessee* and the three small ships out from behind Mobile Point and lined them up just behind the minefield, executing the classic naval manoeuvre of crossing Farragut's 'T' and sending a raking fire down the long axis of the Federal line. By this time, the *Brooklyn*, with her superior speed, had drawn level with the rear of the monitors. At this rate, a wooden ship would end up leading the attack. Just then the *Brooklyn* spotted 'a row of suspicious looking buoys … directly

THE OPPOSED FORCES

FEDERAL
Navy:	4 ironclads
	14 wooden ships
Army:	5500

CONFEDERATE
Navy:	1 ironclad
	3 wooden gunboats
Army:	140 at Fort Powell
	600 at Fort Gaines
	400 at Fort Morgan

Gordon Granger had performed well at Chickamauga and Chattanooga and now commanded the Federal land forces at Mobile Bay.

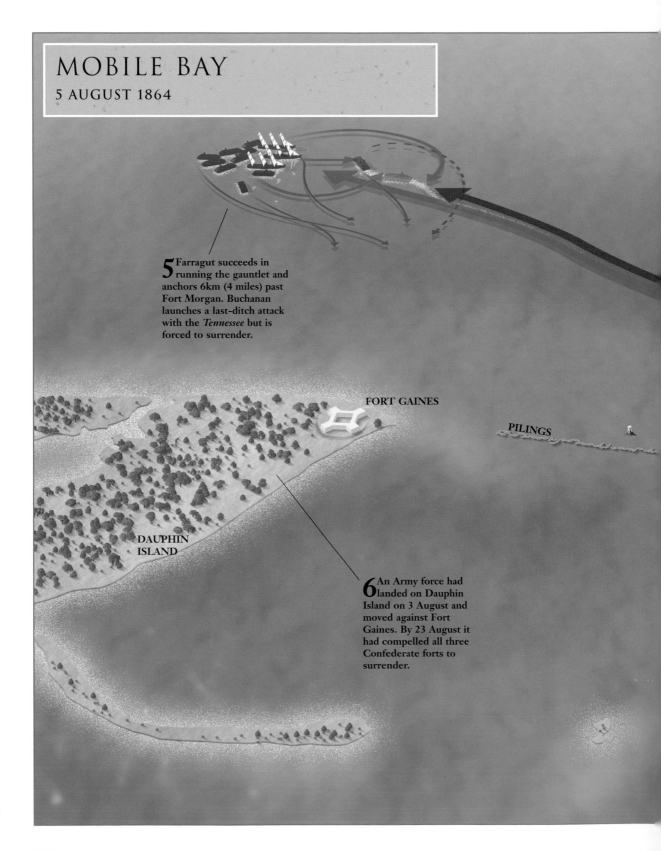

MOBILE BAY
5 AUGUST 1864

5 Farragut succeeds in running the gauntlet and anchors 6km (4 miles) past Fort Morgan. Buchanan launches a last-ditch attack with the *Tennessee* but is forced to surrender.

FORT GAINES

PILINGS

DAUPHIN ISLAND

6 An Army force had landed on Dauphin Island on 3 August and moved against Fort Gaines. By 23 August it had compelled all three Confederate forts to surrender.

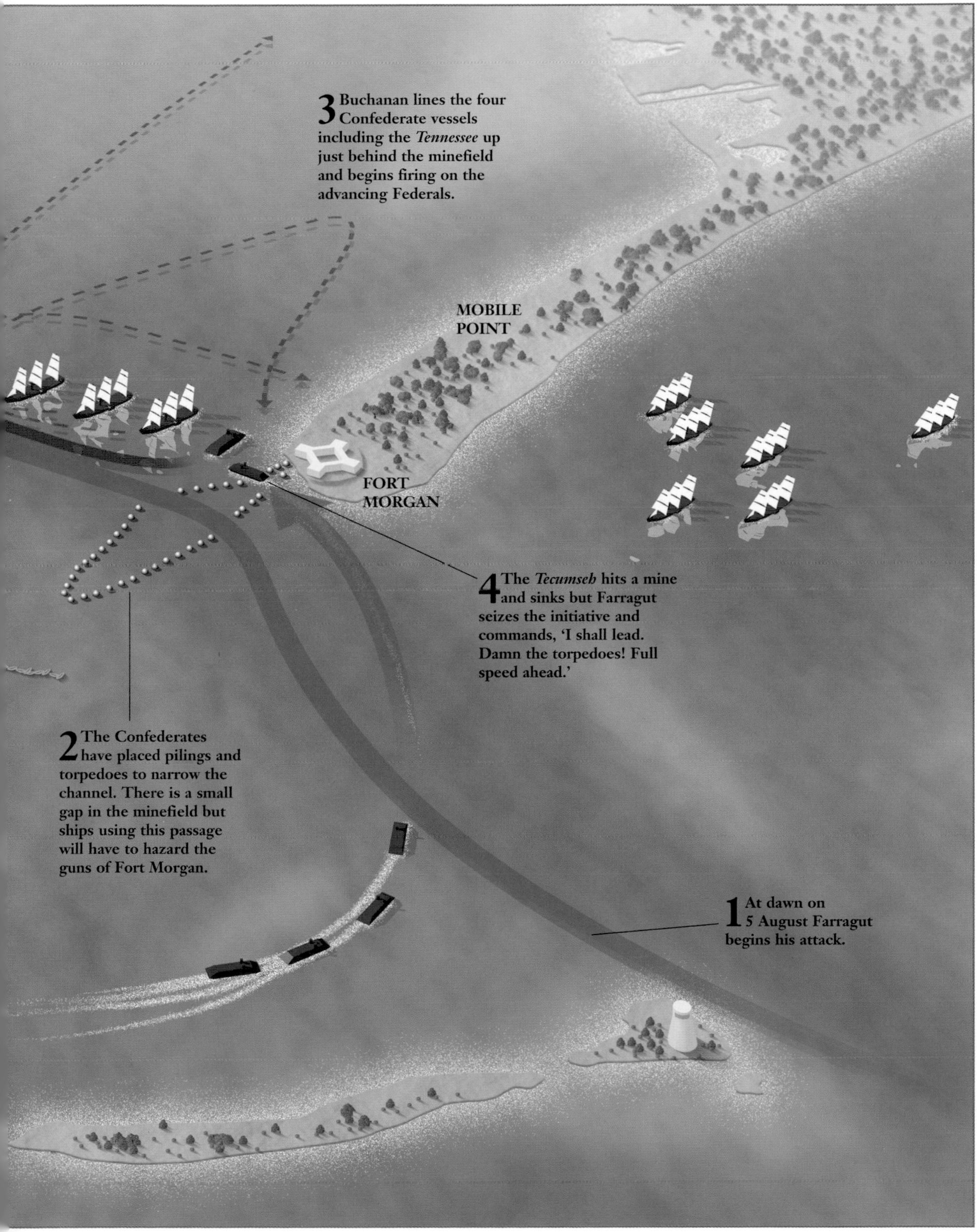

3 Buchanan lines the four Confederate vessels including the *Tennessee* up just behind the minefield and begins firing on the advancing Federals.

MOBILE POINT

FORT MORGAN

4 The *Tecumseh* hits a mine and sinks but Farragut seizes the initiative and commands, 'I shall lead. Damn the torpedoes! Full speed ahead.'

2 The Confederates have placed pilings and torpedoes to narrow the channel. There is a small gap in the minefield but ships using this passage will have to hazard the guns of Fort Morgan.

1 At dawn on 5 August Farragut begins his attack.

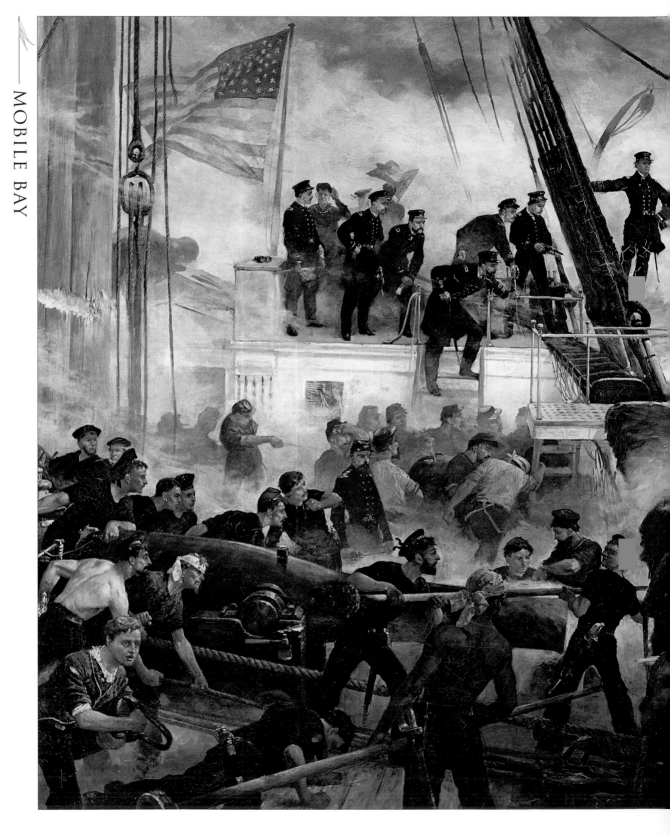

under our bows'. Unsure what to do, Captain James Alden (1810–77) ordered the ship to back engines to clear the hazard. Consequently, the manoeuvre compressed Farragut's entire fleet and exposed it to murderous fire from Fort Morgan. To make matters worse, the *Tecumseh*, at the head of the formation, struck a torpedo and went down swiftly. Remarkably spry for a 63-year-old, Farragut had climbed the rigging of his flagship *Hartford*'s mainmast to ascertain the situation. He knew the battle had reached its crisis point, and he knew what he had to do. 'I shall lead,' he said. 'Damn the torpedoes! Full speed ahead.'

With that, the *Hartford*, with the *Metacomet* lashed alongside, turned sharply to port and sped past the *Brooklyn* directly across the minefield into Mobile Bay. Buchanan continued his raking fire but, from the moment the Federal fleet made its turn, its starboard batteries unloaded on Fort Morgan, driving the Confederate gunners to shelter. However, once the stronger lead ships were past, Fort Morgan was able to return fire against the weaker ones in the rear. The last tandem, the *Oneida* and the *Galena*, were hit badly but limped on.

The main threat now was the *Tennessee*. The Federals delivered repeated broadsides that barely dented the ironclad. A mile into the bay, Farragut gave the order to cut loose the smaller ships and commanded 'Gunboats chase enemy gunboats'. The small Confederate ships were quickly neutralized, but Buchanan readied the *Tennessee* for one last run. With only six hours of coal left, Buchanan knew he had to act. He headed straight for the Federal fleet, which had anchored 6km (4 miles) beyond Fort Morgan and started eating breakfast. Farragut was in a state of disbelief. 'I did not think Old Buck was such a fool,' he said. 'Destroy the enemy's principal ship by ramming her.' The *Monongahela* obeyed the order and struck the *Tennessee* a glancing blow. The *Tennessee* stood its ground but was

The Battle of Mobile Bay *by William H Overend (1851–98). At the pivotal point of the battle, Admiral Farragut rose to the occasion and declared, 'I shall lead. Damn the torpedoes! Full speed ahead.'*

After the loss of Mobile Bay, Fort Fisher, North Carolina, remained one of the few important ports open to Confederate blockade-running.

soon swarmed by the *Manhattan* and then the *Lackawanna* and the *Hartford*. In the midst of the chaos the *Lackawanna*, a sloop-of-war, accidentally rammed the *Hartford*, momentarily endangering Farragut himself. By now the *Tennessee* was barely hanging on. The *Chickasaw* pulled into position and delivered a terrible fire. Buchanan, by now himself suffering from a compound fracture of his leg, turned to Commander James D Johnston (1817–96), captain of the *Tennessee*, and said, 'Well, Johnston, if you cannot do any further damage you had better surrender.' Johnston took one last look from the gun deck, saw the *Ossippe* fast approaching, and decided to lower the Confederate colours and hoist a white flag.

The naval battle had lasted but a couple of hours. Of the 3000 Federals engaged, there were 319 casualties, including 93 who drowned when the *Tecumseh* sank. The number of Confederate naval personnel lost was much higher: 312 out of 470 engaged.

The forts did not hold out much longer. First, the ironclad river monitor *Chickasaw* turned its four guns against the tiny Fort

Powell. The Confederates abandoned the fort on the night of 5 August, blowing it up as they departed. The 600-man garrison at Fort Gaines mustered a faint-hearted show of resistance and then surrendered early on 8 August. Granger took the Confederates prisoner and then moved his entire force of about 5500 against the 400 Confederates at Fort Morgan.

The Federals received a siege train from New Orleans on 17 August and began a heavy land and naval bombardment on 22 August. At the same time General Granger pushed his trenches to within assaulting distance of the fort. The Confederates raised a white flag the next morning and formally surrendered at 2:30 p.m. Losses on both sides were negligible. From all three forts, the Federals captured 1464 prisoners and 104 pieces of artillery.

RESULTS

Farragut considered Mobile Bay 'one of the hardest-earned victories of my life', and Secretary of the Navy Welles proclaimed that it 'sent a thrill of joy through all true

The CSS Tennessee *was one of the few ironclads available to the Confederate Navy. Her iron plate was 50x250mm (2x10in) and her armament included six Brooke Rifles (field artillery).*

hearts'. However, when Welles brought the news to President Abraham Lincoln (1809–65), he was disappointed by Lincoln's apparent lack of enthusiasm. After three years and four months of fighting, blockade-running on the Gulf of Mexico now virtually ceased altogether, and the only port that remained open to the Rebels was Wilmington. Welles considered this a magnificent accomplishment, but he lamented in his diary: 'It is not appreciated as it should be.'

Without access to the sea, the city of Mobile was of no strategic importance and

withered on the vine. It was finally occupied by Federal forces on 12 April 1865.

Like his president, General-in-Chief Lieutenant-General Ulysses S Grant (1822–85) found it hard to get too excited about the victory at Mobile Bay. He had planned for his spring 1864 campaign to include a drive against Mobile that would help support Major-General William T Sherman's (1820–91) Atlanta Campaign. Instead, however, Major-General Nathaniel Banks (1816–94) followed political motivations and marched up the cotton-rich but strategically unimportant Red River Valley. By early April, Banks's campaign was a failure and Grant's hope for a supporting operation in the rear of General Joseph E Johnston's (1807–91) Army of Tennessee was lost. When Mobile finally fell, Grant was unimpressed. In his *Memoirs* he

explained: 'I had tried for more than two years to have an expedition sent against Mobile when its possession by us would have been of great advantage. It finally cost lives to take it when its possession was of no importance....'

Perhaps the greatest significance of Farragut's success was political. When combined with Sherman's capture of Atlanta in September, Mobile Bay provided the Federals with twin victories that indicated the overall war effort was succeeding. Up to that point there was a real possibility that war weariness would cost Lincoln the 1864 election. Had that been the case, the Civil War would have likely ended in some negotiated settlement. Instead, the momentum gained by battlefield victories and the re-election of Lincoln as president ensured the ultimate defeat of the Confederacy.

The Federal fleet at Mobile Bay included four monitors and 14 wooden ships. Opposing them at sea the Confederates had the ironclad Tennessee *and a carefully placed minefield.*

FRANKLIN/NASHVILLE
24–30 NOVEMBER 1864

THE RACE TOWARDS NASHVILLE BETWEEN UNION AND CONFEDERATE FORCES IN THE NOVEMBER OF 1864 WAS CONFEDERATE GENERAL JOHN B HOOD'S LAST CHANCE TO DISTURB MAJOR-GENERAL WILLIAM SHERMAN'S BOLD 'MARCH TO THE SEA'. A SERIES OF CONFEDERATE TACTICAL ERRORS SAW THE UNION ARMY OF THE OHIO SLIP FROM HOOD'S GRASP.

WHY DID IT HAPPEN?

WHO The Union Army of the Ohio, commanded by Major-General John M Schofield (1831–1906), and General John Bell Hood's (1831–79) Confederate Army of Tennessee.

WHAT Schofield makes an advance through Tennessee towards Nashville, while Hood attempts to sever the advance by getting ahead of the Union troops, first at Columbia, then at Spring Hill.

WHERE The state of Tennessee, between Pulaski and Spring Hill.

WHEN 24–30 November 1864.

WHY Hood planned to destroy the Army of the Ohio and take Nashville, thus making Major-General William Tecumseh Sherman (1820–91) abandon his March to the Sea further east.

OUTCOME The Confederates allowed Schofield's forces to escape their trap, leading to major Confederate losses at the subsequent Battle of Franklin and a defeat at the Battle of Nashville.

On 1 September 1864, the Union forces of Major-General William Tecumseh Sherman took the city of Atlanta, Georgia – a cruel body blow for the Confederate strategists. The Confederate Army of Tennessee was unable to hold the city, despite a change of command from the cautious General Joseph E Johnston (1807–91) to the impetuous General John Bell Hood, and Sherman now planned his next move.

What Sherman conceived was his now-famous March to the Sea. He would take four corps of troops (around 60,000 men) and make a two-wing advance from Atlanta through Georgia to the Atlantic coast (aiming for Savannah, to the south of Charleston), crushing the Confederates' Georgian defence and, ultimately, opening the way for a swing northwards into the Carolinas. The plan was high-risk for two principal reasons. First, the march would be conducted through the very centre of hostile territory, with the accompanying danger that constant low-level actions, as well as set-piece battles, would steadily lead to the collapse of the march before it reached its objective. The second concern was Hood. His 40,000 Rebels remained to Sherman's rear, so could drag his march to a halt by making the Union forces fight constant rearguard and flanking actions.

A scene at the earthwork Fort McAllister, Georgia. The fort fell to Sherman on 13 December 1864 as Union forces invested Savannah. With the fort gone, the Union took control of the river and Savannah was doomed to fall.

Sherman was confident that his men could handle the former concern, and on 21 September the problem of Hood partially resolved itself. Hood transferred his army west to Palmetto, with the intention of attacking the Union supply lines into Atlanta. Sherman had to take this threat seriously, as he correctly deduced that Hood's ultimate goal might be to take Nashville. (Nashville was an extremely important supply hub for the Union Army, delivering thousands of horses, wagons and items of uniform to Sherman's men.) For the next month, Hood and Sherman played out a cat-and-mouse series of battles. Hood managed to destroy many supply depots, but also suffered heavy losses at Allatoona Pass on 5 October. It soon became apparent to Hood's men that they did not have the strength to crush Sherman. Sherman recognized this also, and decided to turn his back on Hood and focus once more on his March to the Sea, for which Lieutenant-General Ulysses S Grant (1822–85) gave his approval on 7 November.

To ensure Nashville's safety, Sherman sent Fourth Corps under Major-General David S Stanley (1828–1902), 23rd Corps under Major-General John M Schofield, who was in overall command of the two corps, and a large force of cavalry under Major-General James H Wilson (1837–1925) to reinforce the troops of Major-General George H Thomas (1816–70) that were garrisoning Nashville. Also earmarked for the city's defence was 26th Corps, under Major-General Andrew J Smith (1815–97), which would not arrive in Nashville until the end of November. The journey of these Union forces – collectively known as the Army of the Ohio – through Tennessee set the scene for a frantic race and a series of bloody engagements.

IN PURSUIT

The Union and Confederate forces in Tennessee ranked roughly equal in crude terms of manpower. The Fourth and 23rd corps together totalled around 30,000 men, with the cavalry, the Post of Nashville and other units making the Union numbers up to around 46,000. The Confederate Army of Tennessee had some 40,000 men, having lost 15,000 troops in the Atlanta Campaign

after Hood took over. The Rebel forces were divided into three corps, under the command of Lieutenant-General Stephen D Lee (1833–1908), Major-General Benjamin F Cheatham (1820–86) and Lieutenant-General Alexander P Stewart (1821–1908). In addition, Hood could rely on the 6000 elite horsemen under the great cavalry commander Major-General Nathan Bedford Forrest (1821–77).

The big difference between the two sides lay most acutely in the issue of morale. By this stage in the conflict, the Federal soldiers were motivated and confident, and had much belief in hard, intelligent

LOCATION

Nashville •   Raleigh •
✚ Franklin
Atlanta •   • Savannah

Had Hood succeeded in his offensive towards Nashville, Sherman might have been forced to break off his March to the Sea from Atlanta to Savannah.

UNION HUSSAR

This Union soldier mixes old and modern traditions in his dress. While many cavalry wore the black felt campaign hat, with one side turned up, this soldier wears a less ostentatious Union cap, featuring crossed swords. The jacket harks back to Hungarian hussar uniform, with ornate cord loop fastenings rather than normal buttonholes. A cavalry sabre with ornamental tassel hangs from the left side of his belt, but the soldier also has a musket set in a holster. The type of gun is unclear, but it is likely a carbine, of which some 50 different varieties were manufactured during the Civil War. With its shorter length, the carbine offered greater ease of use from horseback and easier storage. The soldier also has a pistol holster on his belt.

THE OPPOSED FORCES

FEDERAL
Army of the Ohio
Total: 46,000

CONFEDERATE
Three corps of the
Army of Tennessee
Total: 40,000

commanders such as Sherman. The Army of Tennessee, by contrast, had suffered a string of withering defeats, and morale was uncertain. For example, when Hood redeployed his troops to La Fayette after the Battle of Allatoona Pass, he discovered that not a single corps commander believed that they could defeat Sherman in open battle. In addition, the Army of Tennessee's previous commander, Joe Johnston, had been known for his caution with his men's lives, whereas Hood had a tendency to launch into bloody battles with sketchy advanced planning.

The consequent bloodshed did not inspire in the Confederate ranks great confidence in their leadership. Morale was

just kept afloat, however, by some of the victories in Georgia, and the fact that by moving into Tennessee many of the men were much closer to home.

Despite the doubts of his subordinates and superiors, Hood had a plan. Sherman had begun his March to the Sea, but Hood hoped that if he could destroy the Union's Tennessee formations one by one, and then take Nashville, the reversal of Union fortunes could force Sherman to make a costly about-turn and cancel his campaign. The ultimate goal – and also an unrealistic one – was for Hood to move into the North and join with the forces of General Robert E Lee (1807–70) to make a war-winning combination. Hood's first priority, however,

Sherman frequently exercised a policy of destruction towards the civilian infrastructure on his March to the Sea, wrecking telegraph lines, uprooting railroad tracks and scavenging heavily from the land. This policy subdued civilian resistance to his campaign.

Cox (1828–1900), managed to reach Columbia and set up an ad hoc defence only minutes before the Confederate cavalry arrived. The cavalry were fought off in a small engagement, and there was little they could do further to threaten Columbia, as Hood's infantry were still more than a day's march away. The bulk of Schofield's force now began to arrive in Columbia, and more substantial defensive lines were constructed.

NIGHT ESCAPE

Schofield could not keep his forces at Columbia indefinitely. He decided to pull the majority of his troops over to the north bank of the Duck River, leaving two divisions as a rearguard in the town. However, bad weather meant the operation was slowly executed, and many of the Union troops remained in Columbia through to 27 November. Once all were across the Duck River, however, the bridges were destroyed and Schofield entrenched his men on the north bank. Here was Hood's chance. He aimed to bypass Schofield's position and cross the Duck River to the north of Columbia, cutting the Union troops off from Nashville at Spring Hill. However, Hood would leave two divisions and a large artillery contingent, under the command of Lieutenant-General Stephen D Lee, around Columbia in an attempt to convince Schofield that the Confederates intended to do battle there.

Schofield initially took the bait, and stayed put. Hood's troops around Columbia even delivered an artillery barrage on 28 November to confirm the impression of an impending battle. Yet, that very morning, Schofield began to receive ominous reports from some of his advance cavalry that Confederate troops had been seen traversing the Duck at the Lewisburg crossing above them. Skirmishing between the cavalry also continued throughout the day. Critically, Schofield actually dismissed these initial reports. Only on 29 November

was to take on Schofield's two corps. Rather than let them reinforce their destination, Hood planned to cut ahead of their line of advance and crush them well before Nashville at the town of Columbia (at that point garrisoned by around 800 Union soldiers). Such an objective would require rapid movement to get ahead of Schofield, but Hood at first showed little urgency. In fact, Hood's decision to wait for Forrest's cavalry to join him (it had been out at Johnsonville on a raiding mission) resulted in a three-week delay before the Rebels finally moved out on 21 November. When they did move, however, they moved fast, and made 18km (12 miles) in the first day, the cavalry moving ahead of the three

corps-strength columns to provide reconnaissance and screening. By 23 November, the Confederates had travelled up to Mount Pleasant, just 76km (47 miles) south of Columbia.

The Union troops, stationed in Pulaski, had become aware of the potential trap they were falling into. On 22 November, Schofield gave orders for his troops to leave Pulaski and head for Columbia, where they could make an effective stand against Hood's advance. The move began the next day, but on 24 November Forrest's cavalry began fighting with Union cavalry as both raced for Columbia. A sharp, mobile battle began, in which the Union Third Division, 23rd Corps, under Major-General Jacob D

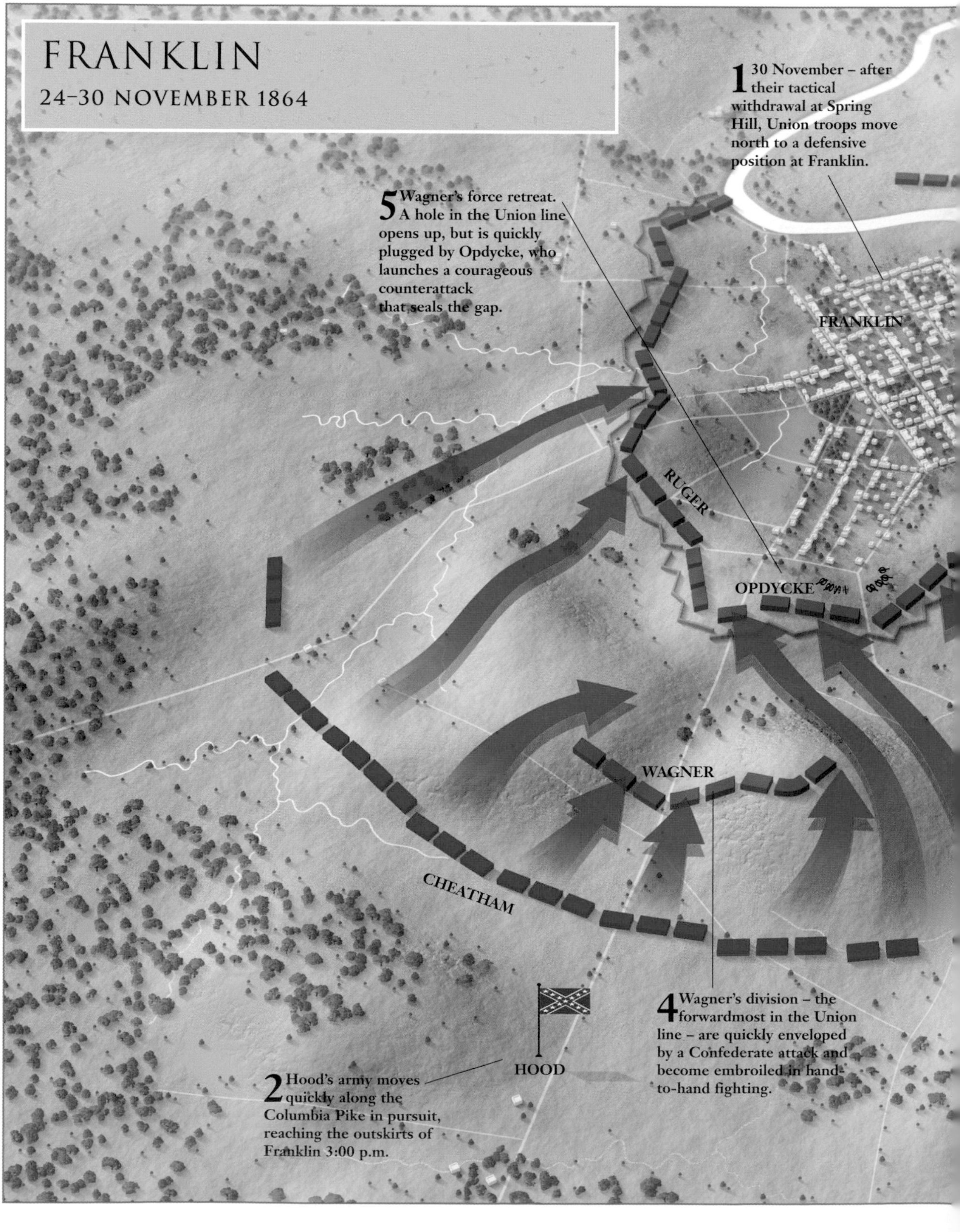

FRANKLIN
24–30 NOVEMBER 1864

1 30 November – after their tactical withdrawal at Spring Hill, Union troops move north to a defensive position at Franklin.

5 Wagner's force retreat. A hole in the Union line opens up, but is quickly plugged by Opdycke, who launches a courageous counterattack that seals the gap.

FRANKLIN

RUGER

OPDYCKE

WAGNER

CHEATHAM

HOOD

2 Hood's army moves quickly along the Columbia Pike in pursuit, reaching the outskirts of Franklin 3:00 p.m.

4 Wagner's division – the forwardmost in the Union line – are quickly enveloped by a Confederate attack and become embroiled in hand-to-hand fighting.

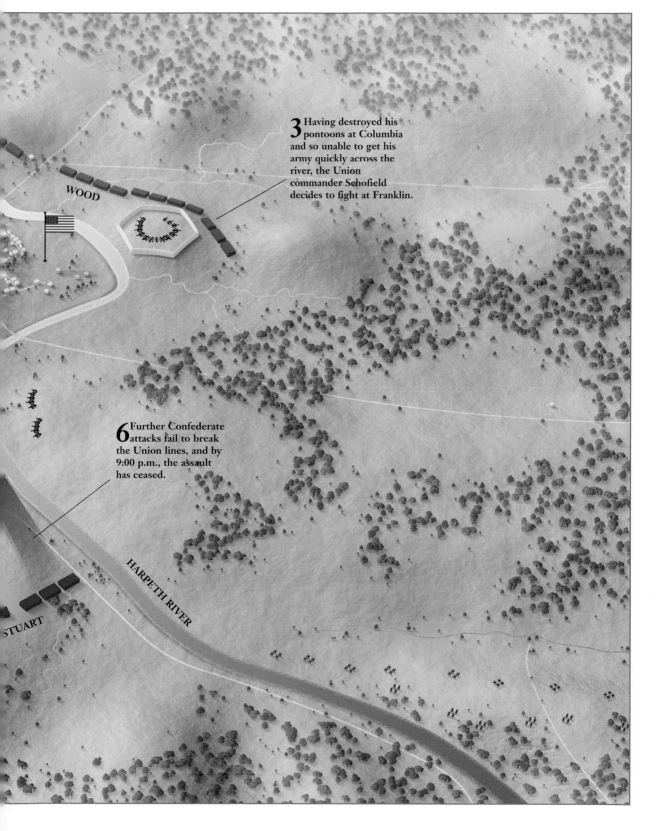

WOOD

3 Having destroyed his pontoons at Columbia and so unable to get his army quickly across the river, the Union commander Schofield decides to fight at Franklin.

6 Further Confederate attacks fail to break the Union lines, and by 9:00 p.m., the assault has ceased.

HARPETH RIVER

STUART

FRANKLIN/NASHVILLE

The Battle of Allatoona Pass (5 October 1864) was another defeat for Hood in Georgia. A Union brigade successfully defended the pass against a Confederate division. Both sides suffered 700–800 casualties.

General John Bell Hood (1831–79) was known for a fighting spirit that bordered on recklessness. Hood took command of the Army of Tennessee in July 1864, but his promotion brought little but defeat.

did he start to act, and then seemingly without conviction. Major-General Stanley was ordered to take two divisions – led by Brigadier-General Nathan Kimball (1822–98), and Brigadier-General George D Wagner (1829–69) – northwards. One was to secure Spring Hill, the other was to emplace itself halfway between Spring Hill and Columbia. These Union divisions would be racing against Forrest's cavalry, which was surging towards Spring Hill on the Mount Carmel Road.

It was a race only just won by the Union. Once Stanley's troops became aware of the threat running parallel to them, they drove hard up the Columbia Turnpike and, with little time to spare, lodged the First Brigade, Second Division, Fourth Corps, in Spring Hill and then fought off Forrest's cavalry, who had expected to find an undefended town. Yet although by the afternoon Stanley had his entire division in Spring Hill, it was quickly faced with a corps of Confederates numbering around 10,000 men. A Union defeat seemed inevitable. Most critically, Schofield only began withdrawing all his men from Columbia towards Spring Hill late on 29 November. Hood could still close his trap on the Union troops and prevent them from ever reaching Nashville.

It was at this point that the Confederate achievements began to unravel. Major-General Cheatham launched his corps at Spring Hill into an attack against the hastily prepared Union defences at 4:00 p.m. on 29 November. The fading light made for a bad time to commence battle. Furthermore, the Union troops had managed to emplace good artillery positions, whereas most of the Confederate artillery was either back near Columbia or on the road. Nor did Cheatham commit his forces wisely, but instead threw them into battle in a piecemeal fashion, making it easier for the defenders to deal with each wave in turn. (Cheatham's tactical errors were in part due to a lack of knowledge of the precise layout of the Union defences.)

In a short, violent battle, the Union soldiers held on to Spring Hill, inflicting heavy casualties on their attackers with artillery and musket fire. The failed attack did allow the Confederates to gain a better sense of the location of Union defences, and they repositioned for a second attack that had a much higher likelihood of success.

The attack was not launched before nightfall, and it was during the night that Hood's battle plan truly unwound. Despite his men bivouacking close to the Columbia Turnpike, Schofield managed to sneak his entire force past them in the dark and take them north. How this was even possible is hard to imagine, as the road was literally within visual and auditory distance of the Confederate troops. Nonetheless, under Hood's very nose, Schofield made it to Spring Hill, and then led all his troops on to the town of Franklin. The Army of the Ohio had slipped through Hood's noose.

CONFEDERATE DISASTER

Hood's failure to cut off the Union forces in Tennessee had a crushing impact on Confederate campaigning in the region. Schofield heavily reinforced Franklin's defensive works, and waited for the Confederate attack. Hood, enraged by the Federal escape, ordered a frontal attack on the town – a decision that required Confederate troops to assault across 3.2km (2 miles) of open ground – despite vigorous protestations from his field commanders. Without waiting for his artillery, Hood sent the attack in at 4:00 p.m. on 30 November. The attack nearly succeeded. Confederate troops overran the Union forward lines but became locked in a horrifying close-range

battle against the main lines. The battle only stopped at 9:00 p.m. The Confederates had not taken Franklin, but had lost 6200 men, including six generals. Schofield's men had also suffered terribly, with loses of 2326 soldiers, but their resistance enabled the Army of the Ohio to move on successfully to Nashville.

The Battle of Nashville brought the final collapse of Hood's plans in Tennessee. Hood placed Nashville under a virtual siege from 2 to 15 December, keeping his army back and hoping to draw Thomas' forces out to attack the Confederate defences, whereupon they could be broken apart before a Confederate attack stormed in to take the city. The plan came apart, and over two days of fighting, in which Hood was outmanoeuvred by Thomas' troops, the Confederates took an unsustainable 13,000 casualties, against about 3000 Union dead and injured. Hood's tattered army was forced to retreat, with the Union forces now in the role of pursuers.

Hood resigned from his command on 13 January 1865. By this point the Army of Tennessee was effectively crushed, and no longer capable of having a major effect on the war's overall outcome. The actions around Columbia and Spring Hill may have been comparatively small in terms of fighting, but their implications for the war in the west were great.

A scene from the Battle of Nashville, 15 December 1864. The battle was a final, devastating defeat for the Army of Tennessee, which lost 13,000 men. Hood resigned a month later.

PETERSBURG

2 APRIL 1865

THE UNION VICTORY AT PETERSBURG IN APRIL 1865, ACCOMPLISHED AFTER THE CITY HAD ENDURED MONTHS OF SIEGE CONDITIONS, WAS ONE OF THE LAST CONFEDERATE DOMINOES TO FALL IN THE AMERICAN CIVIL WAR. ONCE THE CITY HAD FALLEN, THE CONFEDERATE CAPITAL AT RICHMOND WAS OPEN FOR THE TAKING, AND THE SOUTH BEGAN ITS FINAL POLITICAL AND MILITARY COLLAPSE.

WHY DID IT HAPPEN?

WHO Five Union corps under Lieutenant-General Ulysses S Grant (1822–85), totalling over 97,000 troops, launched a final attack against General Robert E Lee's (1807–70) thinly spread 45,000 Confederate troops around Petersburg.

WHAT The battle was the culmination of a long Union siege of Petersburg. The Union forces attacked all along the Confederate line, with Sixth Corps making the decisive break south of the city.

WHERE The battle lines ran from east of Petersburg, Virginia, then south of the city and out west to positions around Five Forks.

WHEN 2 April 1865.

WHY The battle was Grant's attempt to conclude the Petersburg siege, and to take advantage of the previous day's victory secured at Five Forks.

OUTCOME The Confederate defences around Petersburg were shattered, and Lee ordered the evacuation of the city.

By the end of March 1865, the city of Petersburg had been under siege for more than eight months. In scenes that many historians have likened to the conditions in Western Europe during World War I (1914–18), the two sides had settled into huge static trench systems, frequently probing the other's lines with raids and other minor actions. The Confederate commander in Virginia, the renowned General Robert E Lee, realized that his strategic options were contracting. The siege was steadily eating into the city's supplies. Supply lines were open, particularly the Southside Railroad running into Petersburg from the west, but it was mainly the winter weather that had prevented the Federal troops under Lieutenant-General Ulysses S Grant from

moving against these. With the improvement of weather in spring, time was running out. Furthermore, the extended length of the Confederate lines – around 60km (37 miles) from Petersburg to Richmond – meant that Lee's troops were, in many places, spread unacceptably thin, with gaps of several metres between each man enforced in places.

Lee did have something of a plan in mind, although it required a healthy dose of optimism to believe in it. If he could break his forces out of Petersburg, Lee felt that he might be able to drive to the south, resupplying on the way, and eventually join forces with the Confederate troops of General Joseph E Johnston (1807–91) in North Carolina. If this could be achieved then, maybe, the combined force could

The Battle of Five Forks was a critical defeat for the Confederates that destabilized their defence of Petersburg. Here Union cavalry charge a line of Confederate riflemen.

defeat Major-General William Tecumseh Sherman's (1820–91) units in the Carolinas, then return north to battle with Grant on a more equal footing.

As it turned out, it was Grant who took the initiative in the Virginia theatre. As spring approached, Grant diligently reinforced his positions, which snaked in a long line from east of Petersburg, ran south around the city, and then ran out well west parallel with the Hatcher's Run River. Significant additions to his aggregate strength were Major-General Philip H Sheridan's (1831–88) Army of the Shenandoah and Major-General Edward OC Ord's (1818–83) Army of the James. With a bolstered force, Grant now launched a new series of offensives aimed at breaking the Confederate hold on Petersburg.

UNION MANOEUVRES

Back in February 1864, Federal troops had carried out several assaults southwest of Petersburg around Hatcher's Run, attempting to consolidate their advantage over the Confederate supply route along the Boydton Plank Road. On 29 March, they renewed their efforts in the area, using Sheridan's cavalry units and Fifth Corps infantry under Major-General Gouverneur K Warren (1830–82) to attack towards Dinwiddie Court House.

Although the Federal troops had a numerical advantage, the Confederates were obdurate in defence. Sheridan's attempts to outflank the Confederates were stopped by defences at White Oak Road, Boydton Road, Dinwiddie Court House, Crow's House and Hatcher's Run. Even so, the Confederate commanding officer in the region – the much-criticized Major-General George Pickett (1825–75) – understood that his defences would eventually crumble, so he pulled his troops back to the Five Forks crossroads.

Pickett actually wanted to retreat further, but Lee insisted that he hold the strategically important crossroads, stating clearly: 'Hold Five Forks at all hazards. Protect road to Ford's Depot and prevent Union forces from striking the Southside Railroad. Regret exceedingly your forces' withdrawal, and your inability to hold the advantage you had gained.'

CONFEDERATE SOLDIER (LATE WAR)

This is a typical Confederate soldier of the late war period. He is already showing signs of the collapse in the Confederate supply chain and economy, indicated by the patching of his jacket and trousers. He wears the standard grey-blue Confederate uniform, with piped trousers and jacket collar and matching kepi. Around his body he has a simple bedding roll, which would also have provided additional warmth in winter. The great length of Civil War rifles is apparent here. Although some breech-loading rifles did appear during the 1860s, most remained muzzle-loaders, as indicated here by the visible ramrod. A well-trained soldier would be able to fire four to five rounds every minute from such a weapon, and the effective combat range would be in the region of 100–200m (110–220 yards).

Pickett ordered his troops to dig in and await the inevitable attack – which came on 1 April. Sheridan and Warren were once again partnered for the operation, Sheridan using cavalry to make a frontal pinning action while Warren's cavalry were sent on a flanking manoeuvre. The Union assault was poorly executed. Union intelligence had marked the Confederate defences as beginning further east than they actually did. This, combined with treacherous wooded terrain, led to slow and confused manoeuvring by the frontal divisions of Warren's Fifth Corps.

In the end, Sheridan's judicious use of Warren's reserve division permitted the

LOCATION

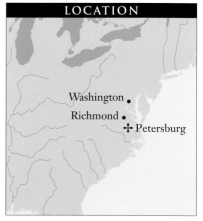

Once Petersburg was taken by the Union, the Confederate defence of Richmond was unsustainable, the city trapped between Union forces in the north and south. Richmond's evacuation was quickly ordered.

PETERSBURG

attack to go in, and the Confederate left flank was quickly punctured. (Pickett was actually 3.2km (2 miles) away having a meal with fellow generals, blissfully unaware that his troops were battling for their lives without central leadership.) In the end, Five Forks was abandoned, with 2950 Southern casualties against 840 Union losses, although the fight had been hard for the Union (Sheridan relieved Warren of his command), and the Confederates re-established and held a new line of defence.

The loss of Five Forks was a critical blow for Lee's defence of Petersburg, as the Federal forces had broken the main Confederate line and were moving inexorably closer to the Southside Railroad. Lee recognized that the Petersburg-Richmond line would eventually crumble, so he telegraphed Richmond advising that the city authorities make preparations to abandon the city. The defence of Petersburg was also acknowledged as unsustainable, a point that the Union forces would prove on 2 April.

ATTACK ON PETERSBURG

Grant understood that the Union victory at Five Forks presented him with the opportunity to take Petersburg with the 50,000 troops he had deployed there. Lee's line had been thinned by losses and redeployments, and the move towards retreat would leave his forces tactically vulnerable. Five corps held the Union lines around Petersburg. The eastern side of the lines was manned by Ninth Corps under Major-General John G Parke (1827–1900), while next to him was a southern front held by Sixth Corps, under the command of Major-General Horatio G Wright (1820–99). Major-General John Gibbon's (1827–96) 24th Corps, Major-General AA Humphreys' (1810–83) Second Corps and Fifth Corps, now under Major-General Charles Griffin (1825–67), ran the Union lines out to positions at Five Forks.

THE OPPOSED FORCES

FEDERAL
Five corps around Petersburg
Total: 90,000

CONFEDERATE
Mixed units dug into defensive earthworks
Total: 45,000

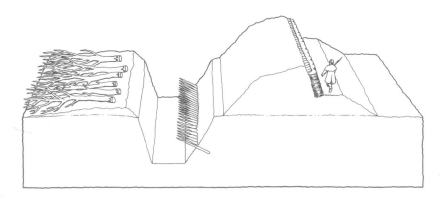

A typical earthwork fortification of the Civil War, such as was found around Petersburg in 1865. These defences were designed to break up the impetus and formations of enemy attacks, while providing superb protection from rifle and cannon fire.

PETERSBURG

Union Zouaves display their muskets, complete with fixed bayonets. The Zouaves' dress, with its North African origins, created a memorable sight on the battlefields of the Civil War, and sometimes included the classic tasseled fez.

Grant planned a major assault along the entire length of the line, with the heaviest weight of attack concentrated in Wright's sector. Start time for the operation was 4:00 a.m. (just before first light at 4:40 a.m.), but at 2:00 a.m., Union artillery conducted a night bombardment of Confederate lines to mask the movement of around 14,000 men into positions in no-man's-land.

At 4:00 a.m., the first Union troops surged towards the Confederate lines. Although the actions basically occurred simultaneously, it is useful to separate them out into their respective events. Looking

A dramatic bird's-eye view of the defences at Fort Steadman, 25 March 1865. A daring Confederate assault had taken the fort, but a massive Union counterattack reclaimed it the same day. The fruitless action cost the Confederate forces 5000 men.

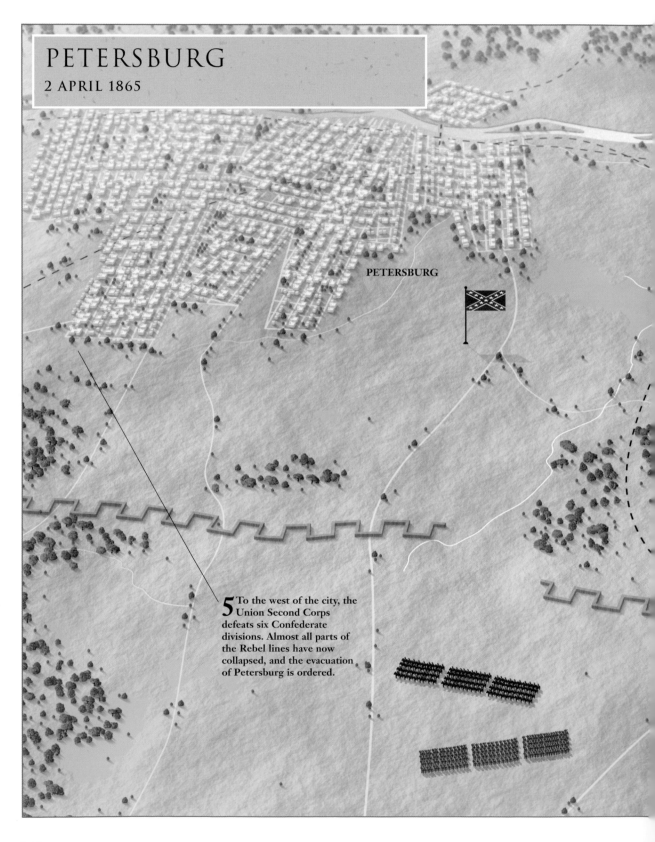

PETERSBURG
2 APRIL 1865

PETERSBURG

5 To the west of the city, the Union Second Corps defeats six Confederate divisions. Almost all parts of the Rebel lines have now collapsed, and the evacuation of Petersburg is ordered.